BEYOND THE HOT SEAT
Gestalt Approaches to Group

Beyond the Hot Seat
Gestalt Approaches to Group

Edited by
BUD FEDER
and
RUTH RONALL

BRUNNER/MAZEL, *Publishers* • **New York**

Library of Congress Cataloging in Publication Data

Main entry under title:

Beyond the hot seat.

  Bibliography: p.
  Includes index.
  1. Gestalt therapy.   2. Group psychotherapy.   I. Feder, Bud, 1930-
II. Ronall, Ruth, 1916-
RC489.G4B49   616.8'915   79-20648
ISBN 0-87630-205-3

Published by
BRUNNER/MAZEL, INC.
19 Union Square
New York, New York 10003

MANUFACTURED IN THE UNITED STATES OF AMERICA

We dedicate this book to the memory of

JOACHIM RONALL

1912-1979

who quietly and patiently, in health

and sickness, gave us much of the

support we needed.

Contents

Introduction ix

Section I
THEORY

1. Gestalt Group Process—*Elaine Kepner* 5
2. The Gestalt Group—*Richard Kitzler* 25
3. An Organismic Formulation of the Gestalt Group
   —*Norman J. Liberman* 37
4. Safety and Danger in the Gestalt Group—*Bud Feder* 41

Section II
CLINICAL APPLICATIONS

5. The Developmental Process of a Gestalt Therapy Group
   —*Joseph C. Zinker* 55
6. Gestalt Family Therapy: A Case Study—*Susan M. Campbell* .. 78
7. Gestalt Art Therapy in Groups—*Elaine Rapp* 86
8. Gestalt Movement Therapy in Groups—*Deldon McNeely Tyler* 105
9. The Gestalt Therapy Marathon—*Elizabeth E. Mintz* 116

Section III
EDUCATIONAL APPLICATIONS

10. Educating for Autonomy: A Gestalt Approach to Higher
    Education—*John David Flynn* 133
11. Contact and Boundary: Creating a Nontraditional College
    Classroom—*Rona Gross Laves* 155
12. Gestalt Therapy Training in Group—*Bud Feder* 167

Contents

Section IV
COMMUNITY APPLICATIONS

13. Intensive Gestalt Workshops: Experiences in Community
    —*Ruth Ronall* 179
14. Exploring Sex Roles in Gestalt Workshops—*Ginger Lapid* 212
15. Identity House: A Gestalt Experiment for Gays—*Patrick Kelley* 219
16. Application of Gestalt Therapy Principles to Organizational
    Consultation—*Joan S. Alevras and Barry J. Wepman* 229

    Postscript 239

    Bibliography 241

    About the Authors 245

    Index 251

Introduction

Within the last few years the literature on Gestalt therapy has been rapidly increasing and yet comparatively little has been written on the significance of the group-as-a-whole in the therapeutic or growth process. This lack of attention to group process continues although much of Gestalt therapy is practiced in groups. Perhaps this is because Fritz and Laura Perls for many years used Gestalt therapy solely for individual treatment, and only considerably later in group settings— each developing his/her own style. Fritz Perls demonstrated Gestalt therapy in groups, large and small, through the "hot seat" method. In this situation, the therapist works with an individual volunteer in front of an audience. The complete group (therapist, person on the "hot seat," and audience) only occasionally emerges as a lively figure. It is as if the audience is seen almost entirely as background for the figure of the encounter between the individual participant* and the leader,* and it—the audience—is taken for granted. Laura Perls, on the other hand, while working primarily with small groups, also tends to work one-to-one much of the time. Within this context, however, the group develops cohesiveness and becomes a social matrix for its members.

These models may be one reason why, until now, most Gestalt therapists have not paid much attention to group process. Simkin, for example, (1974, p. 4) says: "In Gestalt therapy, it is not necessary to emphasize the group dynamics, although some Gestalt therapists do." Yet, as group therapists and group leaders know, the group-as-a-whole—more than and different from the sum of its parts—is a powerful force for better or worse. If recognized and skillfully used by the leader, the

---

* Throughout this volume we shall use the terms "participant" or "group member" on the one hand, and the term "group leader" on the other hand, generically. This is possible because the dynamics between—as well as for—leader and participants are basically the same, regardless of the type of group.

forces inherent in the group become agents for growth and healing; if ignored, misunderstood or misused, these forces can prevent or hamper growth and movement, and their effect can be toxic. A large and increasing literature in the field of group dynamics documents this in detail.

In Gestalt therapy terms, a "good," well-functioning group provides the kind of safe, nurturing environment that will enable its members, the individual organisms, to risk exposure and experimentation. This atmosphere then provides the ground for the "safe emergency," the Gestalt experiment which offers the opportunity to risk new and creative solutions, previously untried. Vital, though, for the maintenance of this atmosphere is the leader's awareness that the group-as-a-whole becomes an organism that needs cultivation and nurturance in order to develop in a healthy manner.

From a Gestalt therapy point of view, the above recognitions are intertwined and lead to numerous questions. Among these are: 1) How do Gestalt group therapists approach the theory of group process? 2) How do they lead groups in practice? 3) What is the Gestalt approach to specialized groups, such as family groups, marathon groups and training groups? 4) Is there a Gestalt approach to co-leading?

The book begins, then, with a section on theory. Elaine Kepner, in the lead chapter of Section I, gives a frame of reference to the whole book by presenting an overview of the development of the group process that emerged at the Gestalt Institute of Cleveland. She sees its roots in the principles of Gestalt therapy, on the one hand, and of group dynamics, on the other. Furthermore, she demonstrates their integration, as she presents a model of the developmental stages of the group. Richard Kitzler, in the next chapter, offers his original and highly personal views on the Gestalt group. Chapter 3, by Norman Liberman, is a poetic and inspiring statement on his experience as a Gestalt group leader. Bud Feder, in the final theoretical chapter, deals with the important aspects of safety and danger as they affect the group process and offers valuable guidelines for the practitioner .

The second section, on clinical applications, starts with Joseph Zinker's chapter on "The Developmental Process of a Gestalt Therapy Group." He vividly describes his approach to, and experience with, ongoing Gestalt therapy groups such as are most commonly conducted in office practice. His conceptualization in Gestalt terms of the development of a group should prove valuable to any clinician. Susan Campbell follows with an interesting case study in Gestalt family therapy. In the next two chapters, Gestalt art therapy and Gestalt movement therapy in groups are illustrated and discussed by Elaine Rapp and Deldon McNeely Tyler, respectively. Both authors offer colorful and practical descriptions of their creative work—stimulating to any group leader with imagination. The clinical section concludes with an exciting chapter on the Gestalt therapy marathon by Elizabeth E. Mintz, well-known authority on this topic.

Section III, on educational applications, contains two chapters, by John D. Flynn and Rona Gross Laves, respectively, which demonstrate the use of Gestalt group therapy concepts in the development of college teaching inducive to contactful and autonomous learning. Although the context—higher education—is the same, each author has her/his own frame of reference and views the field from a different perspective, thereby illuminating various facets of it. Bud Feder concludes this section with a lively presentation of his model of an experiential/didactic training group.

The book ends with a section on uses of Gestalt therapy concepts and principles in the community. Ruth Ronall, drawing on her experiences in leading intensive Gestalt workshops, presents her model, which stresses the development of a sense of community among the participants, and offers a rationale, as well as principles and guidelines, for accomplishing this. In her chapter, "Exploring Sex Roles In Gestalt Workshops," Ginger Lapid portrays her consciousness-raising workshops which she conducts imaginatively and sensitively. Patrick Kelley then recounts —with friends—the emergence on Gestalt principles of a community for gays, an original contribution to community organization. In the final chapter, Joan S. Alevras and Barry Wepman also describe their application of Gestalt concepts within organizations, this time in the business world.

BUD FEDER
RUTH RONALL

* * *

Beyond the Hot Seat

ACKNOWLEDGMENTS

We wish to thank all the authors of the chapters for their patience and support during the time this book was in gestation.

We thank Ruth C. Cohn, who helped us make many connections, including that with the publisher, and who gave invaluable editorial advice.

And thanks to Ruth Marcus, Michael Montgomery, Ma Pren Taruna and Angela Villavecchia for their painstaking work in typing the manuscript.

BEYOND THE HOT SEAT
Gestalt Approaches to Group

Section I

THEORY

1

Gestalt Group Process

ELAINE KEPNER

FOREGROUND

In this chapter I describe what I call "Gestalt group process," which integrates the principles and practices of Gestalt therapy and group dynamics. It is a model in which the leader wears bifocal lenses, paying attention to the development of the individuals in the group *and* to the development of the group as a social system. From this perspective, the group is regarded not just as a collection of individuals, but as a potent psychosocial environment which profoundly affects the feelings, attitudes and behaviors of the individuals in that system, and conversely, is profoundly affected by the feelings, attitudes and behaviors of the individual in that system. The chapter is divided into two sections: The first part deals with some personal and historical antecedents, and the second part with the theory and practice of this bifocal approach to personal development in groups.

PART I. BACKGROUND

This chapter actually began five years ago, when, halfway through a three-day Gestalt personal growth workshop I was leading, a disgruntled member jumped up from his chair, strode in front of me and shouted, "This is not a *real* Gestalt group, and you are not a *real* Gestalt leader!" I took a deep breath, centered myself in my chair, and asked him to specify his complaints. In rapid-fire succession, he catalogued them. He said that I had not used the empty chair—not even once, that I had discouraged him from working on a dream at the opening session until more support for this had developed in the group, that I had allowed individuals to give feedback to one another and to engage in other forms of "bullshit."

5

Needless to say, I had mixed reactions to this confrontation. One part of me felt defensive and wanted to give him a detailed resumé of my credentials as a Gestalt therapist and group leader. Another part, the group leader, welcomed the challenge. His behavior meant that the group, through one of its members, was testing out the boundaries of authority. By taking a stand against me as leader, this person was setting a new norm and perhaps moving the group toward increasing differentiation and autonomy. It was from this perspective that I responded. However, I was left with strong feelings of frustration mixed with despair. The question that formed in my mind was, "How has it come about that so many have mistaken the medium for the message in Gestalt, and have confused the techniques and gimmicks for the essence of the method?" In this chapter, I attempt to answer my own question, and to deliver the lecture on Gestalt group process I wanted to give five years ago to this questioning client.

In retrospect, it seems wise that I chose to repress that lecture. At that time, I was struggling to integrate what I had learned about groups from colleagues at the Gestalt Institute of Cleveland and from staff persons I had worked with at the National Training Laboratories. I was assimilating the powerful experiences in groups and community that had occurred for me as a participant of the Arica Training Institute in San Francisco. When I returned to Cleveland from the West Coast, I intentionally changed my style of leadership from being a Gestalt "therapist" to being a teacher of process on an intrapersonal, interpersonal and group level. I had not abandoned individual work in a group, but was expanding awareness of "what is" to include these other dimensions. Having been socialized as a professional in a variety of types of groups, I was trying to integrate what appeared to be a number of differences, conflicts and polarities in relation to individuals and systems. The more familiar I became with each polarity, the more I began to realize that I did not have to make an either-or choice. Having struggled with these dilemmas for several years, I now believe that I have come to what is a serviceable integration of these polarities for me, which I trust will be of some service to colleagues who are concerned with some of these same issues.

This model is based on two assumptions: first, that the development of the creative potential in individuals is dependent on and related to a well-functioning and healthy social system; and second, that groups, like individuals, go through stages of development in the process of change that can be roughly characterized behaviorally as a move from dependence through counterdependence to independence. This model then requires a change in leader role and activity over time. It differs substantially from the popular notion of Gestalt groups, namely, that of individual therapy done in a group setting, as practiced by Fritz Perls and others in their workshops, and so widely communicated through films and videotapes. Paradoxically, it builds on what Fritz articulated in the theory of Gestalt but did not practice, for reasons which I shall go into later.

What is not generally understood is that both Gestalt therapy and group dynamics developed from common roots in psychology and philosophy. So before describing the way in which this integrated group process model works, I want to fill in some of this important historical background.

Essentially, the concept of contact and contact boundaries, so central in Gestalt theory, is a statement about the individual organism in an environmental field, and the interaction of each with the other. Laura Perls (1976, p. 223) describes contact as a boundary phenomenon between organism and environment: "It is the other acknowledgment of, and the coping with the *other,* the not-me, the different, the strange."

In Gestalt theory we also consider the individual and the environment as a unified field or system, in which all parts are interdependent, so that a change in one part of the total affects all other parts. This relation between the individual and the environment is succinctly stated by Fritz Perls (1973, p. 16) when he speaks of the contact boundary:

> No individual is self-sufficient; the individual can exist only in an environmental field. The individual is inevitably, at every moment, a part of some field, which includes both him and his environment. The nature of the relationship between him and his environment determines the human being's behavior. With this new outlook, the environment and the organism stand in a relationship of mutuality to one another.

This quotation, or a similar one, could as easily have been taken from the writings of Kurt Lewin, the seminal thinker in the field of group dynamics. This is not surprising, considering that both of these men derived their models of personal and social change from two sources: the work of the German psychologists, Koffka, Köhler and Wertheimer (whose experimental studies in perception and learning became the foundation of Gestalt psychology); and the contributions of a German researcher and physician, Kurt Goldstein, who extended these principles to the study of the whole person. While each of these men, Lewin and Perls, were dedicated to changing behavior, they developed their ideas into what may appear to be very different and seemingly polarized fields of application—individuals and systems. Lewin was a social psychologist, and although he did not lose sight of the individual, what became "figural" for him was the social environment. The major goal for him was *social* change. His work as a scholar and research scientist provided the theoretical foundations of the field of applied behavioral science, which includes what is now known as group dynamics, organizational development and large systems change.

Perls was a physician and psychotherapist. For him, the individual was "figural" and *individual* change the major goal of his method. Perls, like Lewin, saw the individual from a systems perspective, but he focused in on the phenomenology of the intrapersonal system. Indeed, the major goal in Gestalt therapy is to "heal the splits" within the personal sub-systems—mind, body and soul—and integration is defined as all parts being unified and available for contact with the environment.

Given the fact that Lewin and Perls focused on different aspects of the total person-environment configuration, it is no wonder that the followers of each have tended to ignore or neglect the work of the other. Although Gestalt therapy and group dynamics developed simultaneously in the United States, they ran parallel rather than intersecting courses. Perls acknowledged the contribution of Lewin to Gestalt psychology, but remained an individualist and an individual therapist throughout his career. He never claimed to be doing group therapy. In a talk delivered to the American Psychological Association in September, 1966, he spelled out the ways in which he differed from group therapists and encounter group leaders:

> In contrast to the usual type of group meeting, I carry the load of the session, by either doing individual therapy or conducting mass experiments. I often interfere if the group plays opinion and interpretation games or has similar purely verbal encounters. . . . In the Gestalt workshop, anyone who feels the urge can work with me. I am *available,* but never pushing. A dyad is temporarily developed between myself and the patient; but the rest of the group is fully involved, though seldom as active participants. Mostly they act as an audience which is stimulated to do quite a bit of silent self-therapy (Perls, 1967, p. 309).

However, although Perls expressed his preference for individual therapy in a group setting, in that same paper he said that he considered individual therapy to be out of date, and that it should be replaced by group workshops. Through his many years of experience, he had discovered the power of a group in the process of individual change, but he did not, or could not, exploit this learning. For Perls, the participants in a workshop were a collection of individuals. He used them as an audience, regarding them as an important presence or social environment that could be used in the service of the needs of the individual; the participants were discouraged from becoming a group.

This particular model of one-to-one therapy had another *raison d'être*, beyond that of personal preference. The original and explicitly understood goal of Gestalt workshops in the 1950s and early '60s was to train mental health professionals in the theory and methods of Gestalt as it applied to individual therapy. Fritz and Laura Perls invented this strategy of experiential learning, believing that a method which stressed the phenomenology of the "here and now" needed to be experienced in the here-and-now. This turned out to be a very creative strategy for communicating and teaching Gestalt as a new theory and method of practice, especially in view of the professional scene that Laura and Fritz Perls stepped into when they arrived in New York City in 1947 to establish their practice.

At that time, the psychoanalytic approach was firmly entrenched in the mental health training institutions, supported by a vast literature and a host of journals and professional societies devoted exclusively to the analytic approach. By contrast, only two books in Gestalt therapy had been published by 1952, when the New York Gestalt Institute was established: *Ego, Hunger and Aggression* by F. Perls (1947) and *Gestalt Therapy* by Perls, Hefferline and Goodman (1951). The workshop method, developed by the Perls and later used by, among others, Isador From, Paul Goodman, and Paul Weisz, proved to be a dramatic and effective teaching model and a powerful way of recruiting mental health professionals for training. It was an appropriate model for the needs and learning goals of the trainees. At that time, the participants in these workshops were either practicing therapists or advanced graduate students in one of the mental health disciplines. Many of them had some previous experience as a client in therapy. Most of them knew a good deal about psychotherapeutic theories and clinical practice, but little about what to do with a living client. Gestalt therapy, with its emphasis on what to do and how to do it, provided some sorely needed tools, and the workshop setting made it possible to see and experience the effects of the methods.

Given this history, we can view group dynamics and Gestalt therapy as two species from the same lineage. From the phenotypes, or superficial characteristics, they do not seem to belong to the same category. They do not look alike; they dress differently, talk differently, and often do not think alike. Nevertheless, they have the potential for mating with each other, and creating a new breed, a new synthesis.

The Emerging Gestalt

This new form, Gestalt group process, was evolved by the teaching faculty of the Gestalt Institute of Cleveland. It represents an integration of the experiences of that community as well as the conceptualizations of a number of individuals in that community.* I will be reporting about my view and particular integration, but it is essential to acknowledge the joint creation of these formulations.

Since 1958, when the faculty of the Gestalt Institute of Cleveland began offering Gestalt groups to the general public, three distinct forms of group processes have been used: the individually-oriented psychotherapeutic model; the personal growth model, sometimes describes as "therapy for normals"; and the group-process-oriented model, which I shall describe in greater detail in this chapter. These models have some things in common: namely, the theoretical perspectives of Gestalt therapy, as well as certain methods and techniques that have emerged from the practice of Gestalt therapy. However, the goals or tasks of each of these groups are substantially different, and the leader interventions are directed to different levels of phenomenological process in each case.

A schema has been developed that can be useful in understanding the differences between these three types of groups. David Singer et al. (1975) have characterized small groups in terms of two basic parameters: (a) the

---

* We have had a community process at the Gestalt Institute of Cleveland which makes it difficult to ascribe a formulation to any one individual. Since we began offering workshops and training programs to the public in 1958, the majority of programs have been planned, designed and led by staff teams in varying combinations. Because of this there has been a continuous and reciprocal faculty learning process, so that the formulations and practices of any one person tend to be that person's unique synthesis rather than that person's unique contribution. However, there are several persons whose inputs and perspectives on group dynamics and system processes have been highly important and influential. They are Edwin Nevis, Carolyn Hirsch Lukensmeier, Leonard Hirsch, and Richard Wallen (deceased).

major goal or task of the group; and (b) the psychological levels involved in the task. Group tasks are placed on a continuum that has *learning* (in the sense of cognitive/perceptual change) at one end and psychological change (in the sense of altered coping capacity, personality structure, or response repertoire) at the other end. In between is the region of dual task systems, with co-equal learning and change tasks located at the midpoint. By "levels," these authors are referring to the three kinds of processes that are occurring simultaneously in every group: intrapersonal process, interpersonal processes, and group processes.

The original teaching members of the Gestalt Institute of Cleveland were trained by the faculty of the New York Institute for Gestalt Therapy—Fritz Perls, Laura Perls, Isador From, Paul Goodman and Paul Weisz. In terms of Singer et al.'s schema, all of our teachers operated from the model of the individually-oriented psychotherapeutic group. Psychological change was the major task or purpose of this group experience, and the leader interventions were primarily on the intrapersonal level of functioning. For the most part, interpersonal transactions were limited to those that occurred between the leader and a group member. This was the model which we naturally followed as we began to lead our own groups in Cleveland. However, over time, we began to realize that this type of group process was not appropriate for the needs or characteristics of the people who were coming to our workshops. For one thing, a number of group members found this intensive intrapersonal experience a stressful one that required more than a weekend to assimilate and integrate. Furthermore, most of our participants wanted something other than being cured of their neuroses; they wanted to learn something about themselves and about the Gestalt perspective, philosophy and values. Many of them did *not* want to become therapists; they wanted to find some better ways of relating to themselves and to each other, and perhaps to see whether Gestalt could be meaningfully applied to their "outside" lives as teachers, businessmen, family members, etc.

Gradually, the staff began to shift to a personal growth model, and to design these experiences with dual and co-equal learning and change tasks. In other words, we added the task of understanding Gestalt on a perceptual/cognitive level to the task of personal change. The major focus of the learning remained on the intrapersonal level of awareness, but the leaders stimulated and used the interpersonal reactions among the group members to facilitate the dual learning and change tasks. Our roles as leaders became more varied and complex. We became teachers and significant others to the group members as well as therapists. We gave short lectures on Gestalt theory and the process of change. We modeled what we were teaching by sharing our feelings and perceptions in the here-and-now; we used a variety of exercises so that all members of the group would have some common experiences from which to learn about their intrapersonal and interpersonal functioning.

The thrust to develop an expanded model that would include members' learning about group processes came about because some of us experienced dissonance between our values and what people actually received reinforcement for during a personal growth group. As a faculty we had moved away from the individually-oriented psychotherapeutic model, partly to avoid some of the paradoxes and imbalances of this type of group process, which, among other things, reinforces the "cult of the individual" and creates a leader-dependent relationship between members and leaders.*

However, while the personal growth group model does facilitate learnings about oneself in relation to others, and about the necessity of transcending the self-boundaries in order to enter into and maintain interpersonal relationships, the leader still maintains a central role throughout the group process, and the members tend to come away from these experiences with the belief that it is sufficient to express oneself and be responsible for oneself in order to create a better personal life, or family, or work team, or community. This belief is not only naive but dysfunctional, since it neglects the reality of the social environment in which we are all embedded. Given the persistent dilemmas and difficulties which we all face in becoming conscious human beings in this lifetime, and living as we do within the context of a new world order that is struggling to be born, it no longer seems sufficient to free the individual to become more differentiated and individuated without bringing in the polarities of being related and committed to that which transcends the self. Walter Kempler (1974, pp. 64-65), a Gestalt family therapist, has written eloquently on this point:

---

* As Yalom (1970, p. 450) pointed out with reference to the leadership style of Fritz Perls: ". . . Perls was so acutely aware of the necessity for each individual to assume responsibility for himself and his therapy. Much of Perls' *modus operandi* was, in fact, explicitly directed toward that end. Yet, beneath the technique, beneath the imperative to assume responsibility, the Gestalt therapist creates a bewildering paradox: on the one hand, he exhorts the patient to be, to act for himself, while, on the other hand, he says, through his leadership style: 'I will take charge, I will lead you. Depend on me to provide energy and ingenious techniques.' "

Relatedness is often considered optional. It isn't. We are related. The question is not if, but how. The extremes of relatedness are separateness and unity. Separateness is a dimension of relatedness, not a disruption of it. . . . From the neighborhood squabbles of children to the challenging task of diplomats at the United Nations, all endeavor is characterized by the endlessly undulating desire for separateness and unity. . . . Although the best preparation for union is the successful separation, it is not enough for the therapist to stop work at this point. Neither separateness nor union is the goal of the therapeutic process, but rather the exhortation of the endless and often painful undulation between them.

Gestalt group process, then, is an attempt to create conditions for learning about what it means to be a member of a group (whether that group be a personal growth group, a work team, a family, or a community), so that the polarities and dilemmas of separateness and unity can be experienced in the context of personal growth.

PART II. GESTALT GROUP PROCESS

In a Gestalt group-process-oriented experience, the leader is committed to working with both the individual and the group for the enhancement of both. This stance is not unique. It has been developed and described by a number of theoretically diverse practitioners, including Bion (1961), the originator of the Tavistock model in England, Berne (1966), in his early work on group transactional analysis, Whitaker and Lieberman (1964), Yalom (1970) and Astrachan (1970). What I am presenting is an integration of this group-as-a-system perspective with Gestalt group practice.

In some sense, a Gestalt therapist always works from a systems perspective (whether the client is an individual, a family or a group) and considers therapy as a process that takes place within the boundaries of a social system. Like all social systems, the therapeutic system consists of people, a common task and a method for accomplishing this task. In Gestalt therapy terms, personal growth can be described as a boundary phenomenon, the result of contact between self and environment. The therapist functions as a teacher of phenomenological process, and assists the client to identify how and in what ways awareness and energy are being blocked and excitement and contact with the environment are being avoided. The therapist provides the client with some learning tools, namely Gestalt methods and techniques, and establishes a particular kind of learning environment, not only by the way she/he uses these tools, but also by and through the emotional relationship that is established with the client.

Within the boundaries of that social system, phenomenological processes are occurring simultaneously on all three system levels: the intrapersonal level, the interpersonal level and the systems level. What I mean by systems level process are the dynamic patterns of interaction that develop among people over time and create a way of being together. These system processes create a social milieu which affects the way people in that system feel about themselves and each other, as well as the way they behave in that environment. These system processes account for the whole being greater than the sum of the parts. Some examples of system processes are the beliefs and assumptions that people hold, the way they go about accomplishing their tasks and making decisions, the roles they play, and the informal and formal rules and norms that operate in the relationship.

Given the nature of the contract in individual therapy, which is to help the client change personally, most of the therapist's interventions direct the client's attention to processes that are occurring on the intrapersonal or interpersonal level of awareness. The output—that is, what gets learned by the client—is a great deal about what goes on inside the boundary of her/his skin, often a considerable amount about what takes place in the process of making interpersonal contact, but not much about what occurs on the dyadic or system level. This is understandable, since the therapist is a part of the system, and this makes it difficult for the therapist to be an objective observer of the system processes. Furthermore, the therapist's role as a teacher and guide through the labyrinths of individual phenomenological processes necessitates certain priorities. In working with individuals, the major questions for the therapist are: "How can I tap the resources available to me so that I will expand the learning potentials of this client?" and "How can I create a relationship that will promote optimal conditions for learning for this client?"

Let us now shift to the group situation. In groups, there are many clients present, and the interactional possibilities increase exponentially, particularly if conditions are such that the members can interact with each other as well as with the therapist. The therapist now has the opportunity of being a *manager* of a learning process, one in which the critical questions become: "How can I create the conditions that will enable these people to tap into each other as resources here?" "How can I help them create the kind of relationships that will provide the richest learning environment for all?" and "How can I help them develop awareness of the polarities and choices between taking care of individuals and taking care of the group?"

In terms of the schema of Singer et al. previously discussed, the Gestalt group process leader adds the learning task of awareness of group processes to the task of intrapersonal and interpersonal awareness. This new task requires a change in the role and skills of the leader. The leader who relates to the group-as-a-system as well as to the intrapersonal and the interpersonal processes going on is like a juggler who has a variety of balls, each of a different size and shape, that must be kept moving and balanced. The leader has three types of role choices available that determine the level at which the intervention will take place. She/he can function as a therapist for an individual, as a facilitator of interpersonal processes or as a consultant to the group-as-a-system. Obviously, the leader can intervene on only one level at a time, and her/his implicit or explicit priorities determine which level of learning will be pursued at the expense of the others.

To illustrate, let us consider the following example:

> This is the second meeting of a personal growth group in which all the members are also involved in an intensive, month-long residential Gestalt training program. This group consists of six female members and four males.
>
> One of the women begins the session by saying, "Wow! This is going to be fun—there are so many strong women here!" Sam replies, "Your statement makes me feel angry. I feel excluded here just because I'm a man."
>
> Another woman, Alice, seated across the room from him, says in a trembling voice, "I *want* to exclude you. I want to exclude *all* men from my life now." When Sam asks her, "But why me?" Alice goes into a long list of complaints about his behavior with her (or, more accurately, about the meaning she is making out of what he said to her and how he has behaved with her in their encounters both in and outside the group). She ends her tirade with, "I'm angry with *you* because you are not being forceful enough with me, and I end up doing all the work of relationship building, and I'm goddamned sick and tired of doing that!"
>
> As Alice finishes, a third woman bursts out, "And I'm angry now because you and some of the other women here are making demands that men be a particular way here and I don't like that."

This short sequence can be viewed and responded to on any one of the three system levels. If the therapist decides to intervene on the intrapersonal level, Alice would work on her anger toward men in general and, perhaps, toward Sam in particular. If the intervention is directed to the interpersonal level, both parties would be encouraged to explore their perceptions of one another, their communication patterns, and their differences. At the group level, the leader would call attention to this interactional sequence as one in which the members are talking about criteria for acceptance to membership in this group. Each of these interventions gives a different message about the major learning task of the group and about what types of interactions will be attended to and made a priority in this experience.

Given the multiple group learning tasks and the multiple leader roles which become operationalized through the choice of level of intervention, what are some guidelines that can help the leader in making these choices? What I have found useful is a framework that conceptualizes the group in terms of stages of development. This framework is based on that developed by Schutz (1966) to understand the behavior of individuals in groups and the dynamics of group process. He suggests that there are three categories of needs people bring into groups, and these needs, while interrelated, tend to emerge in a hierarchical order: the need to affiliate or to belong; the need for autonomy; and the need for affection. On an emotional level, these needs are experienced as issues around identity, power and influence, and intimacy. Certain types of behaviors are associated with each of these needs and emotional issues: The need to affiliate and belong and to establish one's identity produces dependent behavior; the need for autonomy mobilizes the individual to test out the limits of authority and control, and produces counterdependent behavior; the need for affection and intimacy motivates people to relate effectively with one another and to behave interdependently. These basic needs, emotional issues and behaviors appear over and over again in the life of any group, but in looking at the development of the group over time, they tend to occur in sequence and can be used to characterize the stages of group development.

I will now discuss each of these stages more fully and the implications of these stages for the leader role.

Stage One: Identity and Dependence

The identity of each member of the group is dependent, to some degree, on the way in which she/he is perceived and responded to by every other member of the group, including the leader. On some level of awareness, each individual coming into a group has three sets of questions. The first set are questions about *me* and *my* identity here:

"How should I present myself here?"
"What do I want and what do I have to do to get it?"
"Can I be who I am here and belong to this group?"
"What's safe to express or disclose about myself here?"
"Will I be seen as the unique and special person I am?"
"Will I be so different that I will feel alone?"

Another set of questions relate to the identity of the others present:

"Is there anyone else here like me?"
"Will I get understanding or support from anyone here?"
"How are they going to feel about me and what are they going to think about me?"

The third set of questions relates to the leader and the process:

"What are we going to be doing here?"
"What are the rules or expectations here?"
"What are they going to find out about me, and what am I going to find out about myself that I don't know or don't want others to know about me?"
"How will I be treated—judged? rejected? bullied?—or accepted and cared for?"

During this phase, the primary task of the leader is to set up relationships with the members and among the members as quickly as possible, and to get some data generated around the three sets of questions the members are silently asking. Some of the activities that facilitate this task are:

1) *Contracting and setting boundaries.* This includes letting the members know what the tasks of the group are as she/he understands them, and defining the leader role in relation to these tasks. I, and/or I and my co-leader, usually begin a group by making some statements about our ideas and values about personal growth and describing our role in the group, which is as facilitators of awareness on the intrapersonal, interpersonal and group process level. Given the issues of identity that are in the foreground, we structure some process through which the members can share relevant information about themselves on the intrapersonal

level. There are several ways to do this: One way is to break them into subgroups and give them some information-sharing task; another is to use some group exercise. A third choice is to go through the somewhat tedious process of having each person introduce her/himself in some way to the total group. At this phase, the leader is invested with so much power that everything she/he does and says is much more important and impactful than what anyone else in the group says and does. The dilemma for the leader at this point is: "How much or how little do I do, and when?" My experience has shown me that when I structure some lively activity for the group, this introductory phase goes faster and is more interesting; the price we pay is that the members become more dependent on the leader to draw something out of a bag of tricks to keep the process going, rather than reaching into themselves or into each other for energy. My present preference is to go with the tedium rather than the excitement during this early phase, so that the members begin to rely on themselves and each other, rather than on the leader(s).

2) *Encouraging interpersonal contact.* This is a means of exploring the interpersonal environment and of discovering resources present in the group. I can do this very simply by noticing when eye contact or verbal statements are directed at me, and by suggesting that people look around and find someone else in the group to whom they can make these comments. This is not to say that I do not respond or interact with individuals at all, but only that I choose when and for how long I respond, since what I do as a leader begins to establish some rules and norms in the group.

3) *Giving some messages about the approach we will be using.* As leader, I do this through verbal and nonverbal modeling. For example, I share my own internal process—the feelings I am having, the observations I am making and the inferences I am drawing from these data. If I am attentive and listen rather than jumping in with "therapeutic" interventions, I am giving the message that we are making space here to be what we are.

4) *Legitimizing work on all systems levels.* At this stage, group members are most concerned about determining how safe it is going to be for them in this group and what is acceptable to bring up. I want to legitimize individual work on the intrapersonal level, but not until a number of people have shared their feelings. At this stage, rather than intervening on an intrapersonal level, I work on the assumption that each person is a spokesperson for others and is verbalizing what may be an

important issue or theme for some, if not all, of the members of the group. I inquire whether anyone else can relate to the issue this particular person is sharing. In this way, the individual issue is seen and treated as a more universal theme and an issue of the system as a whole.

To summarize, the leader activities in this first phase are directed toward providing a climate of trust that will support some risk-taking, and toward making some connections with individuals' inner experience, among individuals, and with the group-as-a-whole. Usually the way people make contact with each other during this first phase is through the discovery of commonalities and similarities. This leads to a norm of politeness and oversolicitousness, the energy in the group falls off, and this signals that the work of differentiation must begin.

Stage Two: Influence and Counterdependence

The major issues the individuals and the group must grapple with in this stage are those of influence, authority and control. At this stage, each member of the group is aware that she/he is being influenced by what is happening in the group and that certain implicit or explicit norms are operating which make it difficult to behave differently from what appears to be acceptable. Norms, of course, are ways of describing what is permissible or valued in a group, or what is not acceptable and devalued. Norms are inferred from behavior and reflect the assumptions people make about themselves, one another, and how things "ought to be."

Members may begin to challenge whatever norms are operating by interrupting, by expressing negative reactions to each other or to what is happening, or by directly taking on the leader and questioning her/his authority and competence. The priority tasks for the leader in this phase is to work for increasing differentiation, divergence and role flexibility among members. Leader activities that facilitate this task are as follows:

1) *Heightening awareness of the norms that are operating in the group.* Since norms are based on untested assumptions members are making about what is or is not acceptable, the leader can heighten awareness of norms by turning the assumptions people are making into questions. For example, the leader can observe that there seems to be a norm operating that it is not OK to differ or disagree in this group, and asks, "Is it OK to differ or be disagreeable here?" In this way, group

members learn to identify the norms that are operating, as well as their consequences, and make decisions to change them by monitoring their own behavior.

2) *Encouraging challenge and open expression of difference and dissatisfaction.* Whatever is happening or not happening in a group, the conflicts occurring on a personal, interpersonal and group level must be allowed to become explicit. Dealing with divergence at any level generates strong emotional reactions and is experienced as very risky for the individual and for the integrity of the group. How much conflict an individual can tolerate is a function of that person and the situation she/he is in. How much divergence a group can tolerate and still operate as a system is a function of the cohesiveness of that group. At this stage the leader is faced with some critical choices around the level of intervention: "Do I pay attention to the person who is obviously in pain because the conflicts in the group have triggered off an old piece of unfinished business?" or "Do I consult with the group about the way it is working and dealing with conflict and difference?" Here, as elsewhere, I am not proposing any answers—only posing the dilemmas that arise around level of intervention.

3) *Differentiating roles from persons.* In a group, members often play out roles that are a function of the needs of a group rather than simply a function of the personality or character of that person. A group, like an individual, requires that certain functions be performed to enable it to go through the cycle of experience of awareness, energy, contact, and withdrawal or completion. Depending on how people behave in the early stages of a group, one person is more likely to carry, or be identified with, one of these functions. For example, the person who initially provides the energy to get things moving in a group gets "assigned" to this role, and the other members, and perhaps the leader, rely on, or provoke, this person to energize them. Some people carry the awareness function because they are particularly good observers and reporters of their own experience, or of what they see, hear, or sense going on in others. Some people who are outgoing and caring tend to carry the contact or caretaker function; those who are assertive or more spontaneous provide the impulsivity and creativity in the group. All of these functions are positive ones and help the group to accomplish its work. However, when these functions are identified with one person rather than being seen as functions which everyone has the capacity of expressing, everyone's behavior becomes stereotyped. Once roles become somewhat fixed,

group members are likely to resist the attempts of any one person to deviate from the assigned position, since a change in any one person in a system affects the functioning of everyone else in that system.

The leader can bring this role-taking behavior into awareness by commenting on the stereotypes when she/he sees them operating and thereby helping the group to recognize the consequences of this for the group as a system and for the individual members.

Often the roles which get played out in a group are projections of the disowned part of the other members' personality. Scapegoating is an example of this. When any one person in a group carries the role of "victim," the leader can make a group level intervention to get the members to consider what is being avoided by having someone in the group act out that part of themselves.

Stage Three: Intimacy and Interdependence

This is the stage at which real contact occurs within and among members of a group, as contrasted with the pseudo-intimacy which develops in the first stage when group members are discovering that they all belong to the human race and are feeling warm and cozy with one another. Real contact requires the experience of being nose-to-nose against that which is different and other than the self. Real intimacy, which I define as those relationships which nurture and sustain us over time and through separation, usually need to be forged in the crucible of divergence and conflict. Fighting often precedes real loving, and so it is in groups. Working through the issues of influence, power and authority that characterize the second phase and living through this experience provide the support for taking high risks on an intrapersonal and interpersonal level.

At this stage, members behave interdependently in the sense that they can depend on each other for understanding, support and challenge; also the relationships are reciprocal. Members are significant to each other, and the group as a system becomes a significant other, providing the nourishment and the resources for growth. The leader is no longer regarded as the ultimate authority, but as an experienced resource. If the leader has focused previously on the group level interventions, the members learn to monitor and maintain their own functioning as a system. They serve as resources to each other, asking for and accepting help from the leader when her/his skills or perspective are required.

When a group is functioning at this level, the processing goes at a quick pace, the energy level is synergistic and mellow rather than frantic, and the level of self-disclosure very high. Even when the issues being dealt with are those of loss, separation, grief and remorse, the group can accept, support and absorb some of the terror and pain.

It takes being together for a long time for a group to be able to sustain functioning at this third stage, and my experience has been that a group's capacity to maintain themselves at this stage requires at least a year or two years. Groups that meet for a shorter time sometimes reach this stage, but only temporarily. Therefore, the remarks I am making about the functions of a leader at this stage primarily apply to groups that have a long history so that members can depend on each other and on the way their system as a whole functions over time.

The functions of the leader at this stage are as follows:

1) *Maintain a consultant role to the group, and stay out of the way.* Interventions that are required from the leader at this stage are few and far between.

2) *Help the group to arrive at some closure.* Groups, whatever their duration, are temporary systems, and must go through a closure process that includes a reentry into the "real" world. Members must say "goodbye" to those with whom they have shared this group experience, and plan for the transfer and support of these learnings to their lives outside of the group. This usually requires some simple structures that focus members on these issues. In a weekend group I can ask them to share the most important learning for them from this experience and to think about ways in which they can support this process for themselves when they return home. In groups of longer duration, for example, training groups, this planning becomes the closure experience.

3) *Acknowledge the unfinished business that could not be dealt with in this group.* Given the cyclical nature of these stages of development, all groups do not end when the group is at the stage of intimacy and interdependence. In this case, the closure process needs to acknowledge the negative as well as the positive aspects of the experience—the needs that did not get satisfied and the expectations that were not fulfilled. Some assessment must be made about the discrepancy between what was hoped for and what actually happened. It is from this assessment process that the polarities and dilemmas of change are learned.

I would like to think that all of the groups I lead go into the closure phase from the intimacy-interdependence stage, but I would be lying if I claimed that to be the case. The fact is that I have learned the most meaningful lessons when the closure is not one of full satisfaction for all. If nothing else, I rediscover the virtue of humility and the awesomeness, complexity and mystery of individuals and systems.

EPILOGUE

The whole is greater than the sum of its parts.

This statement is not only the foundation of Gestalt psychology and Gestalt therapy, but also the essence of all systems of thought which attempt to make meaning out of the apparent distinctions, contradictions and discontinuities in the natural and human universe. To describe a process that is based on this holistic perspective, as I have been doing in this paper, is a contradiction. A group is more than the sum of its parts, and Gestalt group process is more than the sum of the principles and elements which I have reviewed. However, as E. F. Schumacher (1977, p. 87) has said:

> One way of looking at the world as a whole is by means of a map, that is to say, some sort of plan or outline that shows where various things are to be found—not all things, of course, for that would make the map as big as the world, but the things that are most important for orientation: outstanding landmarks, as it were, which you cannot miss or which, if you do miss them, leave you in total perplexity.

What I have done in this paper is to sketch out a map of the territory. Anyone who has traveled knows that a map is not the territory: It is a two-dimensional abstraction of a three-dimensional reality.

Obviously, how useful you, the reader, find this map will depend on your goal as therapist or group leader, or what you regard as the primary mission of psychotherapy and personal growth. The mission, as I see it, is to raise consciousness, and that is different from the aims usually associated with psychotherapy. The overriding aim of therapy as I see it is *not* simply to cure people (whatever "cure" may mean), nor is it to teach clients how to become more adept at manipulating the environment rather than themselves. Nor is the goal to enable each individual to develop a more differentiated and integrated self. It may be all of the above, but the essential aim is to assist in the evolution of a self which can ultimately transcend the self. This means that at the core of personal development there is this central polarity: freedom and liberation on the one hand, and discipline and social responsibility on the other. It is the tension between these opposites which permeates everything we do.

This basic paradox was succinctly captured almost one thousand years ago by the Jewish sage, Rabbi Hillel, when he asked:

If I am not for myself, who will be for me?
If I am for myself only, what am I?
If not now, when?

2

The Gestalt Group

RICHARD KITZLER

Primarily, the theory, development and practice of Gestalt therapy groups come not out of the traditional psychotherapies but rather from the background of Gestalt psychology and, principally, from the group dynamics insights of Kurt Lewin, as well as from work in education and group development. These insights, as applied among myriad groups in education and group development, for example, through so-called "sensitivity training"' (Yalom, 1975), provided further points of departure for Gestalt therapy. With this core of theory about individuals tending to move toward that equilibrium known as "group," these concepts from the theory of Gestalt therapy were integrated: concentration on the present actuality and attending to its whole/part structure; elasticity of figure/ground formation in the organism/environment field; contact, assimilation and, ultimately, growth on the work of the self. The awareness of meaningful wholes is critical—"meaningful in the sense that the whole explains the parts" (Perls, Hefferline, & Goodman, 1957, p. 258); another important concept is that of purposiveness "in the parts to complete the wholes" (Perls, Hefferline, & Goodman, 1957, p. 258).

The anarchism of Paul Goodman, who stressed the tendency of citizens to regulate themselves freely and to promote groups that provided ground for the individual's best effort and happiness had profound impact on the theory of Gestalt therapy, individual as well as group. For example, as he turns to the tyranny of the majority:

> The minority is always a repressed part of the majority. . . . Thus the minority is always right in its demands for it is moral and psychological wisdom for the majority to accept the repressed part of itself . . . (Goodman, 1966, p. 181).

Paul Goodman's insights here set the egalitarian norm of a good Gestalt group where the leader is at best *primus inter pares* as the group learns to free its members to their best growth.

This theory is severely eclectic and implies corollaries with compelling direction: If one's concern is for elasticity in the *process* of forming meaningful wholes or clear figures against homogeneous (undisturbed) grounds, then the self is not discovered in the figure it creates but in the *creating* of that figure. The figure is importantly irrelevant. Again, if the clarity of the figure as against *its* ground is crucial—*is* contact— then *"an autonomous criterion of the depth and reality* of the experience" is immediately given (Perls, Hefferline, & Goodman, 1957, p. 234). "It is not necessary to have theories of 'normal behavior' or 'adjustment to reality' *except in order to explore"* (Perls, 1957, p. 232). At this stroke the vast fortress of psychotherapy—interpretations, symbols, symptoms, diagnoses, psychohistories, protocols—is laid siege. It is in the shoals between, on the one side, the freedom and ambiguity mandated in the autonomous criterion of self-as-creating and, on the other, the security reposing in the specious certainty of a sure human nature manifestly reduced and interpreted in its figures that much psychotherapy and all jejune Gestalt therapy founder.

What is more, if self and growth are to be found not in the figures but in the creating, then teaching individuals about themselves (interpreting their figures based on yours, the therapist's) is useless, indeed counterproductive. So the "contextual method of argument" was developed: The individual creates figures from his/her conditions of experience and those conditions must be analyzed contextually as the ground for those figures. Within group therapy each individual can become figure against the group as ground or conditions-of-experience in the here-and-now of the group development.

A Gestalt approach to group therapy is essentially no different, therefore, from any Gestalt therapy approach. The bother is that by the very nature of a group there is an *apparent* plethora of interaction, a welter of material that threatens to overwhelm the situation (and the therapist) so that to feel effective at all some therapists may be tempted to retreat to a more comfortable (primitive) position, based on their capacity to tolerate the (intolerable) experienced uncertainties and ambiguities (or as yet unknown potential) of the group. Other reasons for creating a leader-bound group may lie in the therapist's theory, training and style.

A prime example of such a therapist is Frederick S. Perls. With a background that included theater and medicine, as well as psychoanalysis, he began experimenting with group psychotherapy. He soon found individual psychotherapy intolerable and stressed group work as more therapeutic and parsimonious of his labor and time (Perls, 1967). In the eclectic Gestalt spirit he adapted the "hot seat" from psychodrama and preferred to work one-to-one ("Ja, who wants to work?"), therapist with volunteer. He further adapted role-playing, dream work, dialoguing polarities, etc. Thus Perls brought to bear his 50 years of experience on the volunteer's figure/ground experiences in the context of the group, which he used as projection screen when needed. In this way his later style, now so familiar, emerged.

Disavowals notwithstanding, that style, successful as it was in Perls' hands, is still leader-bound and leader-oriented; it is directly transferential (the superego/leader smiles on the ego/volunteer). The group process is denigrated. Therapists lacking the vast experience, sharp intuition and insight, delicate touch and barbed—often vicious—sarcasm that Dr. Perls made so public imitate him in peril and darkness.*

When I began training in group development a quarter of a century ago, I was struck by my ease in transferring to that training my work with Perls and the New York Institute for Gestalt Therapy during its early days. It was as though the work I had done in individual and group therapy and supervision had been specifically tailored for group work.

There were in the universities, of course, many models ranging from the here-and-now Freudian interpretations of the Tavistock school, to the group role and identification formulations of group dynamics, and to the group cultures of Bion (1959). But it always seemed to me that

---

* The criticism of our technique and the charge of gimmickry are, indeed, frequently well-founded. The writer holds that they confront squarely—precisely—some therapists' lack of awareness of our theory, except insofar as they have introjected and supinely imitated skilled and powerful practitioners, such as Fritz Perls, whose influence has not been chewed (destroyed), assimilated and made one's own—"the Word made flesh," so to speak. Of these therapists and their reactions it may be said:

But such reactions are a failure to accept the present actuality of our achieved pasts as if we were given to ourselves in the present as anything but what we have become or will go on to be. Clearly in such cases the contact was never complete, the situation was not finished; some inhibiting force was introjected as part of the experience and is now part of the ego-concept against which we are measuring ourselves (Perls, 1957, p. 432).

One does not *use* but *is* his ever-experimental techniques.

the models led to codifications and the codifications led to facile, cook-book techniques that somehow missed the mark—both of the group and of the leader. The material of the clinician must be part of him/herself and not a set of formulae applied on demand. The group leader is not an introjector but one who has suffered the conflicts of opposing material and forged his tools in the smithy of his soul. Therefore, the Gestalt therapy training had the required "fit" in my view.

Since Gestalt therapy stresses contacting the novel in the here-and-now at the boundary, as well as experiment, assimilation, and growth toward an as yet unkown potentiality, I had not far to go to see more clearly how capital for group work were the theory and insights of Gestalt therapy. Specifically, the group is a here-and-now phenomenon that has no existence except when it meets. I intend this radically. The group has a presentness and force of identity, scattered or astonishingly cohesive, that is its form and motor. If we believe, as we must, that each person in the group will work to his best potential, and has within him all the informa-tion there is or that ever can be necessary to the group in its presentness, then *all* members at *all* times are participating and *must* have available to them modes for the expression of this information of themselves. This belief reflects nothing more than paying the closest attention to interruptions in the process of experiment that are so familiar in in-dividual Gestalt therapy: One would stress experiencing the blocks in the perceptual, motor, sensory/awareness and emotional fields, as the individual concentrates on the experiment.

Of course, in groups one is immediately aware of the interruptions, false starts, futility, facile solutions overriding real issues, and superego resolutions as the group carries flowers to the leader's altar. This parallels the transference phenomenon in individual therapy. But it is precisely the great gift of the group that, if its uniqueness is respected, the so-called transference is diluted to the extent of its membership, and distortions are corrigible—usually, however, following the cue of the leader. In Gestalt terms, the transference is undifferentiated confluence, its hall-mark lack of awareness and differentiation.

So we maintain that, in order to shed light in this confluential dark-ness, we have always to cleave to the faith that the members, given the opportunity, will correct themselves to their own best functioning. The experiment for this correction is the "go-around" without prejudice, including the refusal to comment. This includes the "How did you feel when you said (did) that?" and "What are you aware of now?" questions that are, almost embarrassingly, the Scout's oath of Gestalt therapy.

By "without prejudice," we mean that every contribution is valued as *the* contribution of the individual; it is not prejudged. For example, a group member says, "I don't want to participate in this stupid going around as you call it and I resent being asked." "Okay," replies the leader, or "Thank you, next." The person's presentness is respected, not interpreted. The tone is democratic, egalitarian and faithful—faith in each and all members doing their present best, in this process of cumulating and adding to the fund of trust and cohesion that makes communication possible. "There are no liars in Hell." For then Hell could not exist.

To present a notion opposite in reasoning:

> Thus, through the technique of "going around," the therapist as permissive *parent* assures the *patient-child* that the patient's perceptions are valuable, meaningful, and are not to be ignored (Mullan & Rosenbaum, 1962, p. 164).

No. This is the model of the Oedipal group in which the interactions are viewed ultimately in the terms of classical psychoanalysis. My question is, "How is it that this group is so structured that precisely thus-and-so (parent-child, sibling, etc.) interactions seem to be happening?" That is, subject the group to a contextual analysis. The answer must be that the leader has allowed himself to be cast in the role of the parent and the inevitable, routine Oedipal interactions follow—all-familiar, all-knowing and all-embracing in their repetition. These interactions are to be expected in the early stages of the group's development as reflections of the routine family development of mankind. They are so in individual therapy. But if the ground of the group is begun and maintained with an earnest democratic faith, then the figures that emerge will be increasingly strengthened by and enhancing of the group-as-culture. It is on this ground that the individual can stand and personally make the creative adjustments that are won with so much suffering and conflict as the group clears away its underbrush and reaches toward light. It is finally civilization *versus* its discontents.

So, for example, if we view the group as the field of the individual, or more properly, view the whole as the group/individual field in which each is part of the other indispensably and the whole is more than the parts—if we view this whole so, then we do not see parent-child interactions—permissive, rebellious or otherwise—but we see movements towards growth of the whole complex. In dynamic terms, we witness the group maturing to its unique cohesion as *the* ground on which to stand for *all* its members. This is irreducible and, of course, not subject to interpretation. It is *group* contact.

Gestalt Therapy (Perls, Hefferline, & Goodman, 1957, p. 303) points toward this formulation in the chapter "Maturing, and the Recollection of Childhood," as it criticizes the pyschoanalytic developmental theory: "In Freud's scheme, this (maturing) would occur after a normal evolution of object choices from the auto-erotic through the narcissistic homosexual (ego-ideal and gang) to the heterosexual. He conceives of a healthy early introjection of (identification with) the father; and then maturity is to accept this introject as oneself and assume the parental role." And then, later, maturity is seen by "para-Freudians" as the interactions with others who have so assumed their roles in "a kind of contractual relation with other adults" (p. 303). I'm OK *and* you're OK.

In contrast, Perls et al. (pp. 303-304) state a field theory as I apply it to group therapy:

> We can interpret this growth to responsibility again as organismic self-regulation in a changing field. A child's irresponsibility follows from his dependency; to the extent that he is closely part of the parental field, he is not answerable to himself for his behavior. Given more *mobility, meaningful speech, personal relationships, and choices* (italics mine: is this not a group?), he begins to require of himself, to *mean,* a closer accounting between promise and performance, intention and commitment, choice and consequences. And the relationship of contract is not so much taken on as duty, as a development of the feeling for symmetry that is very strong in the youngest.

So much for the individual side of the group/individual field. What could be a better statement of a group and its functioning? And how are the group functions of "mobility, meaningful speech, personal relationships, and choices" enhanced? Let us look to the field of the "leader":

> With the stage of becoming an authority, a teacher, a parent, the field has altered again. For the independent person is now less on his own, since others spontaneously attach themselves to or depend on him simply because he has ability, and they give him in turn occasions for new out-going acts. It is a rare person who grows as mature as this: to advise, guide, and care for without embarrass-

ment, domination, etc., but simply *noblesse oblige,* giving up his "independent" interest as really less interesting (Perls, Hefferline, & Goodman, 1957, p. 304).

The group members, *by example,* develop at the hands of the leader; they feel more and more included—and the group becomes cohesive, a viable whole—as the leader makes available the tools of the group process until they can do it themselves. They are trainees in group psycho-therapy. The leader is exemplar or nothing.

Writers should also be exemplar, in this case by giving an example from a group in its earliest stages:*

Leader: We're working our own theory here and we'll see what happens. How we're going to do that is going to be the problem. Does anybody have any ideas?
Member I: Just do it.
Leader: Okay. You mean I said, "Stop the bullshit and get on with it."
Member I: Right.
Member II: We could each make an animal sound.
Leader: Make an animal sound.
Member II: I don't feel like it right now.
Leader: Good members always make good suggestions for other good members.
Group: (Large laughter.)

Notice the simultaneous push and pull as the leader—only because it is the initial phase of the group—takes *seriously* and *humorously* the member interactions, as he fights off the leadership *role* offered by the members and invites leadership from them. This is leadership. Again, notice the large release of feeling in the laughter of the whole group, precisely *not at the member's expense* (which would have been competitive—sibling rivalry, and repressive—Dear Old Dad), but in the collective, open recognition that we're all in the same boat—and what a relief! Of course, it could be interpreted: The leader is skillfully making fools of the members to demonstrate his prowess; they will shortly succumb; the laughter is relief that the other got shafted while they got off free.

---

* The examples, though real, are quite edited. One can always think of other views. That is in the nature of human potentiality. I remember to my dismay my youthful irritation with Sigmund Freud for having missed the really important in "Dora."

There is *some* of that, too. However, more and more is offered and given up as the group goes-around. If this were not the case, we could not then explain the subsequent group cohesion and emotion and should have expected pairing, fight/flight and denouement.

Leader: Did you want something from me?
Member II: To understand the nature of power.
Leader: Let's assume you've got it; what are you going to do with it?
Member II: (*Pause*) Why should I have to understand the nature of power? I can just do my powerful thing okay for me.
Member III: While you're doing it, how do you feel?
Member II: I didn't know I was having it.
Member III: What do you think you've got right now? (*Pause*) You've got the whole group.
Member II: (*Enormous laughter from group and Member II*) I've got the whole group. There you go!
Member III: You do know after all?
Member II: Yes.

The foregoing may be simply summed: How one clears the background —in this case the group—so a safe emergency can be experienced by the individual, new material brought to the conflict, the individual allowed to suffer it and arrive at a new integration. The emergency is safe because of the immense power of the group to hold, focus and support its members—provided, however, that the group has experienced itself as itself, not as congeries of ill-formed and unaware, though perhaps eager, citizens.

For example, at a particularly tense point:

Member I: I'm scared, terrified. I feel immobilized.
Leader: How is it you're not interested by your excitement?
Member II: I often experience being immobilized because of fear. And if I can conquer the fear, I can conquer the task.
Leader: Do you know what she is saying?
Member I: She said the opposite.
Leader: She said *fear* is of *fear* and has nothing to do with tasks. But you prefer to be immobilized and to immobilize us with your plight. Could you try an experiment and try to frighten us?
Member I: I don't like to have that power to get someone else scared.

(*Group laughter.*) (*Pause, to leader*) You're right, it *is* interesting. Why can't I be simply scared?

To avoid the terror of the present, the shock and anxiety of pressing on to the next resistance, the individuals of the group may retreat to a favorite neurotic dichotomy mind/body split. Any here-and-now experience can be displaced to hyper-mentation or pseudo-analysis. For example, in a group whose central theme is sexual identity:

Jerry: (*A 20-year old college student*) I'm feeling uptight and confused these days. (*Looks shy; hopefully scans the group.*)
Group: (*Asks him to tell more.*)
Jerry: Well, I'd like a definition of bisexual.
Group: (*Much conceptualizing and theorizing from the other members, frequently with an air of expert testimony.*)
Leader: Jerry, what *is* going on with you?
Jerry: Nothing. I was interested.
Leader: Really? I thought I could almost see the movie you were watching.
Jerry: (*Taking the plunge.*) Well. I went through so much agony coming out as a homosexual and I thought that was that.
Leader: But right now?
Jerry: Well. (*Excruciating shyness and heavy and eager group silence.*) Well, now I'm finding stirrings for the opposite sex, and . . .
Leader: You mean, "women"?
Jerry: Yes, thanks, women, that I don't know what to do. It's like I came out of one closet and then I find there's another one I've got to come out of.
Leader: You have guts, Jerry. How can we help you, practically, here and now?
Jerry: I really don't know. (*Said hopefully*)
Leader: Well, there are one-two-three-four women here.
Jerry: (*Enthusiastically*) Right! Tell me what to do next. Barbara, how do I take the next step?
Group: (*Spirited, practical suggestions and offers of introductions*)
Leader: There are big words to describe what you'll face, Jerry—despair, disgust, terror, excitement—but they'll all dissolve with each little step. Can you have faith?
Jerry: I remember coming from the first closet. Yes.

I have said that the leader is an exemplar, is perhaps initially the repository of values that he hopes the group will integrate. These are democratic, egalitarian, purposively conflictful, experimental values that are intrinsic to the group, those which move the group toward its goal, as opposed to imposed standards extrinsic to the group's development on its own. In a therapy group one of my goals is to provide those conditions in which the individuals can develop and integrate more and more awareness—to grow and mature through self-regulation. Therefore, every intervention by the leader will make these considerations explicitly as to the present content and implicitly by example and style. Alfred North Whitehead's definition of style as the way in which one delivers one's power is meant here. Tone, syntax, presence, stance, and one's being are all included. And the intervention must be *meant*. This is clearly an existential position and carries the awareness that the group, like life, is a phenomenon that could cease at any moment. This awareness of ephemerality brings us instantly to the despair over impermanence; appropriately stated by the leader/exemplarity drains the group's need to force a premature cohesion against a feared dissolution.

Co-leader I: What I present is what I don't know, what I'm not sure of. I see no reason to present what I do know. The questions that I ask relate to what I don't know, what I'm not sure of.

Member I: You mean bearing knowledge is somehow invalid?

Member II: There's no reason for you to be completely non-knowing.

Co-leader II: I want to tell you something I'm sure I know right now . . . (I would use your word "share" but I don't know what it means.) I'm feeling a sense of defeat and oppression and dread. The group is bored and is boring; people are going to leave. I felt that despair coming on and wanted to *do* something, dynamite, shake people. I wasn't sure what to do. But that despair—that was sure so I've stayed with that.

Group: (Heavy silence, then uproar.)

Member III: I can really see what you are saying and that's how I feel. Another thing I see how well you (*two leaders*) are *really* doing your part and it's so well that at first I thought you were play-acting. But I don't think so anymore. You're in a place where I hardly *ever* find myself. It's terrifying.

Another word may be said on style in reference to the totally humorless group: It is not only boring, but it also indicates the heavy hand of self-righteous oppression. Humor combines the elements of love, wit, and pathos—a sympathetic view of the human condition. The leader can foster this very human expression as he demonstrates his own capacity to tolerate the infinite human stupidity—and brilliance—by which people repress themselves.

The dialectic of polarities gives a golden opportunity to demonstrate the absurdity of half-baked notions; the humor implied softens the shock of learning and lubricates the whole process. Group members can watch as they whip themselves into their absurdities: Try to prove you exist or have a sense of humor. Sorry people with unfinished sadnesses so engraved in their faces that they could hold a three-day rain will literally chirp with jollity. How—softly—to get at the sadness:

Member I: (A particularly lachrymose visage.) I have a great sense of humor.
Leader: (Increduously) You? *(Obstreporous laughter from all including Member I as the contradiction between the woeful countenance and cheerful boast is felt.)* Mischief perhaps?
Member I: (Relieved) Oh, yes.

Another example I remember from a group with Fritz Perls:

Member I: (Particularly loquacious and anxious)
Fritz Perls: (Sighing and twinkling) Ja, Dick, you remind me of the old German proverb "after you are dead they will have to kill your voice ten times."
Group and Member I: (Laughter)

Comic sense, irony, wit, droll comparison and exaggeration—all are the tools of humor to bring the group to its fundamental humanity and humility.

Finally, there is the opportunity to draw on our capacity for contact through imagery. I frequently ask all group members to hold hands, close their eyes and withdraw to a spontaneous fantasy; to let the fantasy develop until it completes itself; to return to the group and await others' return until all the fantasies are completed. As we hold hands, I hear soft sighs go around with mine. The profound gathering silence of group contact literally fills all the space. We are together and separate at peace with the hint of paradise that is the essence of religious hope. From the group naturally emerges the great Golden Rule as a function of trust and community. In my ear swells the great anthem: "Nearer My God To Thee, Nearer To Thee."

3

An Organismic Formulation of the Gestalt Group

NORMAN J. LIBERMAN

The very first awareness in me as I sit silently and almost motionless, about to begin writing, is: Gestalt is a word and "the Gestalt approach" is to invite moment-to-moment feelings rather than verbal dialogue. Having gone through the motions of writing this sentence, I am at the threshold of a new moment: In the background of this moment is the obvious paradox of verbalizing an approach to group therapy which specializes in the ever-changing flux of bodily experiences that in principle often defy my attempts to put them into words. In the foreground now emerges a determination to say, as exactly as ever I can, how I use "Gestalt" in groups as a means of living-learning.

Now, I pause and write this next sentence almost without conscious effort. I feel I am clearly focused on my task and the difficulties and possibilities are in balance. For the moment, I do nothing . . . feel restful —and my behind weighing down this chair comes to my attention. I flatten my feet hard against the carpeted floor and notice that I sit back further and my left hand presses down firmly on my work-table. What Fritz Perls calls "the computer" says to me: "You are ready to work." So speaks my computer, using a typical verbalism. What I am actually aware of in my body (undoubtedly due to the context of this tiny work moment) is that I am braced for combat: One voice in me says "You can do it! See—you've already begun . . . more than a page completed . . . and your writing even has a certain clever flair." Another voice begins even before I can shape the words of the last utterance: "Bullshit, you're just mimicking the style of Fritz in *In And Out of the Garbage Pail* . . . It was something when he did it; this is just the stunt of an upstart putting his immature feet in the shoes of a genius and pretending that makes him a dancer too."

Now, I stop again. Stop writing, stop talking to myself even. I'm restful ... I'm not forced to write. I really stop.

I go into myself and no longer feel pushed to exhibit my ability to write. I will not write in a mood of being judged. The quiet inactive time I took has brought me to a very still center which is mine to enjoy whenever I wish. And very gradually, with no sense of hurry or of being pushed by I don't know whom, comes this voice: "I, Norman, want to write what I think about Gestalt based on my work up to now as a group therapist and teacher of those who lead and want to learn to lead groups. I want people I have never seen face-to-face to know what I think now. My responsibility is to be as direct and clear as I can, and theirs, meaning yours—you who have read this far—is to take what you can from my words and change them back to *experience*. Possibly, some new and useful nuances of theory will emerge from the contiguities of what I believe and what you know to be true.

With no further ado about my fleeting flux of awareness in getting going, I will adopt the customary manner of expository writing. I will put before you my conscious thoughts, considered in the most logical sequence.

*   *   *

What I have just shared with you, the reader, illustrates the four cornerstones of Gestalt as process. These are: 1) now, 2) here, 3) aware, 4) contact with bodily experience. Here this leads to your getting to know something about me, the me who leads groups as well as writes about them. In group therapy, this leads to an almost uncompromising emphasis on interaction—actual interaction of every possible kind: between persons, between words and deeds, between the leader and each and every group member.

What happens from moment to moment induces certain kinds of emotions and certain ways of moving, and holds back or lames other styles of action. The feeling in you or in me changes when I name it, when I utter it. And what one member of the group does in one moment has bearing on what another does. So the very word "moment" (Perls' *Now*) contains discrete elements of movement and awareness which must be separately uttered so that the multifaceted wholeness of any given *now* can be arrived at in the group. Whereas Freudians speak of regression in service of "the ego," we Perlsians need speak of specific detailing of now—awareness in the service of arriving at less-partial, "more whole" group moments.

I think of the group as "a body"—even though it is biologically untrue. This is convenient but because I believe there is organismic reality in the aware, self-moving, self-fulfilling and self-healing group. Perls, following Wertheimer and Köhler, thought that wholeness of perceptual field and task entity also applies to the wholeness of personal experience in general. Perls saw one body—one experience at a time, a necessary contacting between the individual and his surroundings (or "Umwelt")—as the sine qua non tendency of healthy men and women. And I choose to take this "Weltanschauung" one sensible step further and see that the "whole group" needs to be as much an organismic unit as an individual, if each and every *member* is to experience his own wholeness. I see group integrity and personal integrity as endemically connected and interdependent.

It is possible that, with the proper group approach, the group can function better than most of the participants usually do in their everyday living. This is because each person can lend his special talents and is freed to give of his surplus. It is possible that one person has eyes to see more than he needs for his own good. And another has enough heart that he can supply warmth and empathy to those in the group whose life has robbed them. Another person has hands to reach out to someone who is locked in his torso. This, of course, is heuristic for the self-actualization of those the group includes and resocializes. Conventional face-to-face therapy accepts the pivotal function of leader as model. Also, advanced or better integrated, more socially sensitive group members have always been recognized as indispensable in their function of raising the level of group interaction in group therapy. They likewise help to deepen the level of psychic understanding, dream interpretation and old-time human sympathy which their therapeutic sophistication helps to tailor to the occasion. So, the model of an integrated, ongoing group which functions like the physically and mentally healthy person, where the left hand does know what the right hand is doing, is catalytic for the Perls model of Man: Man who is aware, experientially potent, able to do what he actually needs and wants to do, and lives predominantly in the now. Such as individual discovers the most fitting and fulfilling way to connect with the other and the situation, inviting the aliveness of each protagonist.

Ideally, a group, as it develops and as its therapeutic history unfolds, is the most real familial upbringing that ill-formed or relatively inadequate individual members can possibly have. *This* Gestalt concept, a logical next step from Wertheimer, to Köhler, to Perls, is what I stress in my approach to group therapy. In a Reichian sense, I foster an energy-field which engenders and enhances Or-energy. In a G. H. Meadian sense, I build a clearly relating small-world in which I-We-It can be better defined and more normatively established. I am influenced also by Mowrer's concept that a group is an entity which stands for the real social world and that confession to and within the whole group leads to an especially health-giving catharsis which he terms "implosive therapy." Mowrer's concept relates to the Aristotelian idea of Tragedy which happens in one place, during one day, to one hero, leading to dual-catharsis: true pity for the protagonist, and fear and trembling that it could also surely happen to me. In this way I am trying to include in therapy the esthetic sense which makes drama moving and beautiful, thereby making therapy a pathway to more dramatic self-actualization.

In simplest possible statement, I would say the group is a single complex energy field or it is not. To satisfy the followers of Kurt Lewin, who thought as I do, I would say we can certainly observe and describe smaller energy fields emerging, clashing and resolving in the group. The group dynamicists have set forth the workings of such interactions in terms that are convenient for teaching and research purposes. By dint of the fact that we experience or chronicle any complex sequence of human interactions as a "group," we are lending credence to the postulate that it is one field.

The detailed approach to group therapy and group leadership that follows from the Gestalt concepts that I have set forth is exceedingly practical. In well-trained hands it is dramatically effective and can become an inspiration to those involved. It has much in common with old-fashioned socio-religious attitudes and, at the same time, it brings into common-sense language and everyday behavioral repertory the best findings of humanistic empiricism and contemporary experientialism regarding individual work in groups. It also illuminates how groups, including families and schools, shape babies and children into the adults they become. And, most important, it suggests that we can *consciously design* groups that are more joyful, more cooperative and more able to endure pain in the now, in order to achieve more meaningful nows to come for each and all involved.

4

Safety and Danger in the
Gestalt Group

BUD FEDER

Positive growth through psychotherapy can occur only if certain
conditions prevail, among which is the establishment of a climate of
relative safety. This is equally true of individual and group psychotherapy, although the technical problems in creating such a climate in
these settings are different. The organism grows via its exchanges at the
contact-boundary; clients in psychotherapy grow via their work at the
contact-boundary in the form of experiments, often perceived as risky,
with the novel. The challenge to the therapist is to significantly contribute to the client's perception of the therapeutic situation as safe
enough to permit risk-taking, even though it may seem dangerous for
the experiment. In other words, the therapist helps to promote the
"safe atmosphere" within the individual or group therapeutic situation.
This chapter focuses on this particular facet of Gestalt therapy in the
group context.

HISTORY

Gestalt therapists have certainly not always believed that the group
situation needs nurturing in order for the safe-enough atmosphere to
develop. This is obvious when we look at the work of both Fritz Perls
and of Laura Perls, as well as the more recent work of Jim Simkin. In
1966 Fritz delivered a paper on "Group vs. Individual Therapy" at the
American Psychological Association's annual meeting. In this paper,
which was published in 1967, Fritz casually states that one of the advantages of group therapy over individual therapy is that in a group
the client, for some unspecified reason, is more trusting than in individual
therapy:

41

Now, in the group situation something happens that is not possible in the private interview. To the whole group it is obvious that the person in distress does not see the obvious, does not see the way out of the impasse, does not see (for instance) that most of his misery is a purely imagined one. In the face of this collective conviction of the group, he cannot use his usual phobic way of disowning the therapist when he cannot manipulate him. *Somehow* [italics mine], trust in the group seems to be greater than trust in the therapist— in spite of all so-called transference confidences (Perls, 1967, p. 311).

In reading some of Perls' work, however, we note that the protagonists often express mistrust of the group. In one excerpt, for instance (Perls, 1969), Perls is working with a dream seminar participant in the group setting. The participant, Bill, is conflicted between his need to cry and his block to crying. When pushed by Perls, he says that his objection to crying is his mistrust of the audience's reaction: the fear of condemnation of some kind from the group. Perls aids Bill to overcome his block by guiding him to say good-bye to an old and deceased friend. After sobbing, Bill is questioned and reports he had become unaware of the group's presence. Apparently, the intensity of Bill's work resulted in crying emerging as figure, as the group became a murky background. At that point, trust of the group was no longer an issue.

On another occasion (Perls, 1969, p. 129), Perls very quickly assists a participant, Beverly, to dissolve her stage fright by paying careful attention to the group. Initial fear of the group gives way to trust when Beverly becomes aware of the group as it is rather than as she had imagined it to be. Both of these vignettes, with Bill and with Beverly, illustrate that the *somehow* of Perls' statement, "Somehow, trust in the group seems to be greater than trust in the therapist . . . ," actually means paying attention to the immobilizing anxiety from too great a sense of danger, and then creating ways to lower that level of anxiety until the "safe climate" level is reached.

Laura Perls has not published any articles about group process, but my own experience in her training groups indicates a different approach from Fritz's. Unlike Fritz, Laura did a lot of ongoing, regular weekly group training. The groups were small, compared to Fritz' workshops, with a maximum of about 15 people. The group members were drawn almost exclusively from the metropolitan New York City area. As a result, members often formed subgroups and had common interests and connections, such as membership in the New York Institute for Gestalt

Therapy. All of these factors, as well as Laura's graciousness and respect-fulness and the homey atmosphere in her living room where she worked, contributed to the creation of a safe-enough environment and to at least tenuous group cohesiveness. So, although she did not emphasize certain other aspects of group process, which I shall mention below and which I believe greatly assist in promoting the safe climate, Laura nevertheless intuitively and fortuitously fostered this development.

Simkin (1974, p. 4) states that "in Gestalt therapy it is not necessary to emphasize the group dynamics. . . ." Interestingly, although he alludes to paying at least some attention to the interactive process between some group members, he never mentions the *group-as-a-whole*. This is particu-larly fascinating in light of Gestalt therapy's persistent and self-defining focus on wholes. It is not at all clear to me why Simkin takes this posi-tion. Despite this lack of support for and modeling of attention to group process in Gestalt therapy, there is evidence that many current Gestalt group therapists do not employ the "pure" hot-seat work which uses the group-as-a-whole in a very limited fashion.*

RECENT CONTRIBUTIONS

In recent years several of the second generation of Gestalt therapists, including Derman, Greenwald, Zinker and Rosenblatt, have begun to publish articles and books about Gestalt therapy in groups. Of particular interest with reference to the emphasis of this chapter are Derman's and Greenwald's contributions. Derman (1976) briefly reviews the history of Gestalt groups and then describes his approach, which he calls "Gestalt-thematic." This approach stresses an integration of group process with individual work, but it does not pay any attention to the theory and details of creating a safe climate.

Greenwald (1976), in a chapter entitled "The Art of Emotional Nour-ishment: Nourishing and Toxic Encounter Groups," describes toxicity in groups as resulting from an overemphasis on catharsis, on "turning everybody on," and on pressuring the participant; it also results, says Greenwald, from a lack of warmth on the part of the therapist. Nourish-ment, on the other hand, is seen as resulting from a caring, respectful,

---

* In a survey done in 1974 (Feder, 1974), for example, approximately two out of three respondents indicated that they favored some forms of group process flow over Fritz' hot-seat method (147 of 196). Speculatively, without any systematic data, I suggest this is due to influences coming from outside of Gestalt therapy, such as the National Training Laboratories.

accepting leader. In Gestalt terms, Greenwald sees the nourishing group as promoting self-support, awareness, experimentation, risk-taking and excitement. His chapter does not, however, explicate the numerous obstacles to developing and maintaining a safe climate in a group or detail the various key maneuvers on the part of the group therapist which are necessary for the promotion, maintenance and reinstatement of the safe climate during the life of a group.

Zinker (1977) discusses the needs for and indications of group cohesiveness. His chapter on groups is a fine contribution to the issue of integrating Gestalt therapy with group process. Rosenblatt (1975) addresses the need for safety in groups, although he does not use the specific term. For instance, if he believes a group member is being overloaded, Rosenblatt does "not hesitate to interrupt and slow down the action" (p. 102). He also promotes a nourishing atmosphere by greeting members individually at the beginning of a session and, quite concretely, by providing some food and beverage (p. 73). Nevertheless, Rosenblatt does not discuss, in any systematic way, the development and maintenance of a safe climate, nor does he stress safety for the group-as-a-whole as much as he does for its individual members.

GROUP CLIMATE AS FIGURE

For myself, the atmosphere within the group-as-a-whole has assumed increasing importance over the years. I have become convinced that allowing, promoting and creating a nurturing environment within the group is the therapist's first task, and one that often needs attention repeatedly throughout the group process. Unless the overall group environment is perceived as relatively safe, therapeutic work will be significantly limited. Members will maintain secrets from the group and keep important aspects of themselves hidden. These hidden parts, facets and conflicts will never emerge and members will never make full contact with each other. As a result, growth which might have occurred from work in these unmentioned areas cannot occur. Furthermore, there is a progressive effect—secrets breed toxicity, which in turn breeds further secrets, and so on.

Gestalt therapy places particular emphasis on exploring the novel and experimenting with new behaviors. In my experience, perceived safety is even more necsesary for active experiments than for strictly verbal experiments. For instance, I believe greater safety is generally needed for the action of reaching out with one's hand than for the parallel experiment of verbally reaching out—provided, of course, that the participant in question has difficulty in this area. This makes it even more important that the Gestalt group, which features active experiments, have the necessary degree of safety.

A nurturing, safe-enough group environment is, then, a vital background for meaningful therapeutic work. Within the context of this atmosphere, members will more readily expose secrets, risk expression, and enter into experiments. For me as therapist, any signs or indication that the group-as-a-whole is not a safe place for any or all members result in the climate reemerging as figure, demanding my attention and efforts to reestablish the necessary level of safety.

After a brief discussion of how frustration fits into this formulation, the remainder of this chapter will be devoted to the establishment of the group as a safe place—and the reestablishment of safety when necessary.

THE USES OF FRUSTRATION

Laura Perls has said, "Give as much support as necessary and as little as possible."* Although she was not referring to the group-as-a-whole, this rule-of-thumb is as applicable to group as it is to individuals. In individual therapy, I strive for the client to develop as much self-support as possible; likewise, in group therapy, I strive for the group to develop its own supportive climate. Consequently, I try to do no more than is necessary in the group to promote the safe climate. With this in mind, I also feel comfortable about frustrating the group. Obviously, this is a matter of walking some fine lines. Fritz Perls said (1976, p. 51) ". . . therapy *starts out* with a certain balance of frustration and satisfaction" (italics mine). I think this statement can be extended to say that therapy also *continues* and *ends* with such a balance. These two emphases and polarities—frustration-support or safety-danger—are complementary. Within a relatively safe climate, frustration can be introduced and used productively; the greater the sense of safety, the more frustration the therapist can permit. The greater the sense of danger, the more support is required, whether to an individual or to the group-as-a-whole.

* Personal communication.

CREATING THERAPEUTIC SAFETY

Whenever I begin a new group—whether it is to be an ongoing weekly group which may last for many years (though the membership will certainly change) or a one-shot workshop lasting no more than two hours—my foreground is preempted by my concern that the environment be safe enough for meaningful work, for risk-taking, and for the safe-emergency experience.

No doubt the single most important variable affecting the group's sense of safety is the person of the therapist. If the therapist comes across in a positive manner (i.e., caring, respectful, flexible, warm), the likelihood of a safe-enough climate is greatly enhanced. In this respect I agree with Greenwald (1976), as well as Carl Rogers (1957). Assuming that the leader is warm and caring, the further challenge still remains: to build upon this base in order to ensure that the group climate is a safe-enough one. Toward this end I often make contact with group members prior to the formal start of the group. When feasible, I meet with each group member individually. For instance, prior to admitting a new client, previously unknown to me, into an ongoing group, I see the person individually at least once. Although this is done in part for screening purposes, it also gives the member some sense of me and some initial feeling of trust and confidence in me. Although the bulk of this trust and confidence may have to be earned over a long period of time, I recognize that, as leader, I am a disproportionately important person for the group, at least initially.

At workshops or marathons where I have not met the participants before, I try to have a brief direct contact with each person prior to the group's formal beginning. As people enter the meeting room I introduce myself and shake hands. The verbal, eye and hand contact establishes a sense of mutuality and interest that sets the tone for a respectful relationship. I also try to do this for classroom situations (in those instances where my role as group leader is in the form of instructor).

Initially, my focus is global, on the group-as-a-whole. Individuals are somewhat blurry in comparison. I address and connect myself to the whole group and try to get a feel of how the group-as-a-whole is doing. What is the atmosphere in the room? In general, how is the group feeling as far as safety? How do *I* feel with *this* group. What's different and special about this group that I need to pay attention to in order to promote a safe-enough environment?

As this process develops, the individuals emerge as separate units. So the overall group is one unit and each person in a separate unit. The group-as-a-whole has a safety level and each individual experiences his/her own sense of safety-danger. As individuals share and work through their fears, not only do their safety levels rise, but the safety level of the group-as-a-whole also rises. It is tenuous and delicate, this safety level. It requires sensing and pulse-taking, directly and indirectly, but it's there. For example, in a two-day training group for professionals, I felt at first an overall moderate sense of safety but some sharp individual fluctuations. Exploring this, it developed that those people who were meeting me for the first time felt pretty safe; however, two who had been in attendance at a panel meeting I'd chaired a few months earlier felt very vulnerable, resulting from some acerbic comment on my part as chairperson. Before an operable safety level could be attained it was necessary to explore these feelings with those two and to work on and identify both my shortcomings at the panel and their own histories with acerbic parents.

A simple device that I use which helps gauge the safety level is called the "safety index." This involves a round in which each member assigns a number between 0 and 10 to the level of safety the individual is currently feeling within the group, with 10 the highest level. I find this particularly useful in training groups to sensitize participants to this variable. Often I ask for a review of the current safety level. Interesting and useful information and work evolve out of these reports, both for individuals and for the group-as-a-whole. For example, when a long-standing group of several years approached its agreed-upon final session, members were not dealing openly with this ending. A safety index check revealed a low safety level for the group-as-a-whole. When this was explored, strong and varied feelings regarding the group's dissolution emerged, resulting in important work overall and individually.

It is important to be aware, of course, that every group at every point in time has its safety limit and that this limit varies for each member. Productive work cannot be achieved when this limit has been reached with a given person. For instance, in the first of a two-session series of supervising experiences for a college counseling staff, one counselor presented a difficult case. He talked at some length about his resistant, slippery client. As he did so, I noted a repetitive foot-and-leg movement. When I called his attention to this and asked him to exaggerate it, he complied willingly. He felt safe enough to that point. He then got in touch with anger toward the client and an impulse to kick him. So far, still safe enough. Next he made an angry statement to the client in absentia. After he did so, the group interjected some reactions. When this subsided, I noticed that the counselor had drifted away from us and asked where he was. He said that he had experienced some very strong feelings and memories about a family member but didn't feel comfortable sharing them with the group. Safety limit reached; work ended, with this person at this time. If this had been an ongoing group, a wider safety limit might have been developed later and the counselor would have been able to openly share his memories and work on them in the group.

Getting back, though, to initially creating the safe-enough environment, there are several other things the leader(s) can do at the outset. One is to provide some food and drink. Usually I have available the makings for tea and coffee and I often provide food like cheese, crackers, and fruit. In ongoing groups, it is rare that a special effort on my part goes unnoticed and unappreciated. I believe that there are generalized benefits in terms of incremental gains in feelings of safety.

When the group actually begins, the first thing I do is suggest a round, in which members identify themselves, their feelings, their goals, etc. I usually employ this initial round at the beginning of any group session, whether it be an ongoing group, a one-shot meeting or a module in a marathon. This immediately emphasizes the primacy of the whole group and often brings to the fore any disturbances existing already within the group. In this connection, one method I've learned from Ruth Ronall* is to request each member to indicate any prior relationship to any other member. This is useful at the very start of a new group, particularly marathons or long training workshops. Often unfinished business between participants is uncovered, such as residuals from old love affairs, or a sense of danger may arise from current outside connections, such as two participants' being neighbors. Whatever the source of perceived danger, it is necessary to work it through as much as possible in order for the affected participants to feel safe enough for some exposure; the other participants also have a stake in this, for a sense of danger among some affects the group-as-a-whole.

Other disturbances predating the formal beginning of the group are those which have occurred while the group has been gathering. Aloofness

---

* Personal communication.

in the waiting room, jostling at the coffee pot, physical similarity to a feared brother, etc.—these can be elicited, dealt with and put to rest, resulting in a safer feeling and a greater willingness to risk. In fact, often these interchanges lead directly and immediately to productive work.

Sometimes preexisting relationships present enormous obstacles to developing a safe-enough environment within the group. For example, in one weekend workshop, a married couple, Gerald and Susan, were present, as was Lillian, who at one time had been Gerald's lover. The couple had begun their relationship secretly while Gerald was still living with Lillian. Lillian had never met her successful rival. She hated her passionately and this hatred erupted immediately on the first round. There were recurrences of bitterness, recriminations and anguish over this unfinished situation for the next 24 hours. Each time, the group was shaken and divided. Although meaningful work evolved out of this feud, it was not until the two women engaged in a vicious wrestling match, from which they ended up in hilarity and unity against men, that a real sense of group wholeness emerged; following it, some important vital work was possible. A safe-enough atmosphere had finally been achieved. Had I known beforehand of this preexisting relationship, I would have discussed it with the people involved, to give them a chance to avoid this situation. In an ongoing group I clear such an issue with an active group member before admitting anyone I know has some connection with her/ him.

In the initial stages of a group and at the beginning of each group session, I am especially alert to indications that members are fearful of expressing themselves or are mistrustful of each other or me. For instance, Laurie, a new member attending her second session had been quiet and observant. When one of the other participants finished working on a subject known to the leader to be relevant to Laurie, namely, problems with a loud bullying father, he asked her for her reaction. She responded in a soft, throaty voice. The leader asked how she was feeling; she owned to feeling tense and scared. When asked to listen to the sound of her voice, she was able to identify it as soft and stuck in her throat. The leader suggested that Laurie find a loud, strong voice and address each member in turn. When she was able to do this, she felt better and safer; she had opened the way for her more active participation in later sessions. At this early stage, she had needed a lot of support and direction to break into the group and get some sense of the safe-enough atmosphere.

On the other hand, when the same kind of quiet behavior was noted in Carl, a long-standing member of the group, a different tactic was employed. Not only was Carl not participating, but he was also in the initial round at each session reporting trivia and stating everything in his life was fine. This rang hollow. In this instance, the leader, at the end of a session, announced to the group that next time he, the leader, was going to perform a miracle, namely, get Carl to work. With this, he clapped Carl on the leg (they were sitting side by side) and closed the session. The leader had judged that Carl was feeling so safe in his unchallenged silence that it might be months before he would deal with his avoidance and lack of communication. It was necessary in this instance to create some tension in Carl over his unproductive behavior. Sure enough, at the next session Carl owned up to his hiding role and acknowledged stewing about it all week. He was then helped to explore the sense of danger he felt about working in the group, a much more productive (though hardly "miraculous") tack.

Once a safe-enough atmosphere has been established within a group, the leader can let his/her concern about this aspect of the group slip into the background for a while. The group, though, most certainly will not remain static and variations in the sense of safety will constantly occur. Whenever the feeling of safety drops below a certain point, it reemerges into my foreground and I attend to reestablishing the necessary safe-enough feeling. (Actually, there is no *single* sense of safety, for different matters require different degrees of safety.)

LATER CONSIDERATIONS

Some of the ensuing factors which threaten the group safety sense are departures of old members (especially premature dropouts), arrival of new members, fluctuations in the leader's moods or health, relations between co-leaders, mistakes by the leader, misuse of confidential information by members, vacations, etc. Each of these requires airing and working through and it is very important that all members be surveyed and involved in these dealings.

Here is one example of the effect of the leader's mood on the group's sense of safety. Recently I taught an experiential course on Gestalt therapy to doctoral candidates. The course ran for one semester. For the first two-thirds I was in a moderately depressed mood. My divorce was impending, and I was feeling upset about it. As fate would have it, my court hearing for the divorce was scheduled just before the group met. Actually, I arrived from court to the group a few minutes late. With the help of the group I explored my experience in court and expressed my sadness and relief. For the rest of the semester I was in a good mood. In evaluating the course at the end, all agreed they felt much safer after the divorce, enabling them to deal more openly with heavier issues. This example of how the leader's mood affects the sense of safety of the group also illustrates that this matter is not always controllable by the leader. If the divorce had occurred after the end of the semester, I suppose the greater sense of safety would never have been reached in this group.

Sometimes the issue of the safety level becomes predominant in a group. For example, a new member named Saul joined a long-standing group which had attained a remarkable level of trust and support, allowing extremely sensitive work to take place. Saul was abrasively outspoken, opinionated, intellectualizing, and disruptive. Tension mounted, particularly in Sam, an extremely sensitive person. Sam felt increasingly unsafe and vulnerable with Saul in the group. Sam stored up these feelings until one day he exploded, challenging Saul to a fight and threatening to quit the group. An epidemic of mistrust swept the group. The next three or four sessions were devoted almost exclusively to the trust and safety issues, with related issues like confidentiality emerging as well. At times during this period, individuals worked on connections between trust in the group and trust in other relationships in their lives, past and present. Mostly, though, the emphasis was here-and-now. Only when this issue had been thoroughly aired and worked on did the group reestablish a workable level of safety. At this point, intensive work on other issues could once again proceed.

Another aspect of the sense of safety is that different degrees of safety are required for work on different issues. Margaret, for example, was an active member of the group immediately on joining. She exposed and worked on various issues, such as dependency and sexuality. But only a year after joining the group did she announce that she had kept some secrets from the group that she now felt safe enough to share. Dramatically and poignantly she revealed a history of a convulsive disorder, and her intense conflict concerning it. This illustrates that the safety factor is a dynamic variable, always in process and always delicate.

As mentioned, the relationship between co-leaders certainly can affect the group's sense of safety—in both directions. When co-leaders are in harmony with each other emotionally and technically, the group responds favorably and moves toward openness. If the leaders get into a negative place with each other through disaffection brought into the group or through nasty competition in the group, the safety level drops sharply. After numerous experiences in co-leading marathons, I have concluded that I have a great responsibility to participants to choose and consider co-leaders carefully. If possible, I work with a co-leader I truly love (although this degree of harmony is not essential to good work); in that circumstance (real deep love between co-leaders), beautiful moments of intense risking can result, reflecting a high sense of safety—and perhaps reflecting the group members' feeling like children safe in the hands of loving, harmonious parents. This is not an immediate feeling at the beginning of the marathon, but emerges gradually—usually after testing and stressful moments—and reaches a peak to be cherished. On the other hand, if poorly-paired leaders work together, disastrous results can accrue and it is very difficult to salvage much out of the shambles. Choose carefully!

Despite the difficulty in assessing the group-as-a-whole or individual members on this matter of sense of safety, the attention appears more and more to me to be highly productive. My hope is that through a combination of attention to this detail and the spontaneous caring and respect which I bring to my work, the group experience emerges ultimately as safe enough for the necessary risks to be taken. If so, the possibility for an important and useful experience is greatly enhanced.

Section II

CLINICAL APPLICATIONS

5

The Developmental Process of a
Gestalt Therapy Group

JOSEPH C. ZINKER

I have always experienced Gestalt therapy as an integrative force in the field of psychotherapy. It is fitting: The word "Gestalt" implies whole configurations. We integrate phenomenology and behaviorism when we attend to the group's own experience and, at the same time, provoke the group to act. We also integrate two levels of work in groups; the powerful and compelling "one-to-one" therapy is integrated with group process, group liveliness, group energy.

The group is a living, organic entity. It is larger than the sum of individuals in it. That large figure, that organism, is in process, constantly changing. Aside from its initial scattered quality and subsequent cohesiveness, the group transforms itself: Its color, its playfulness, its mourning, its sense of family, its serene or nervous silences, its intensity of contact, as well as its deflections, may stand out at any given moment in its life.

Individual members are constantly transformed. They move through time as the color frames of a motion picture, changing their internal frames of reference and external personae. They are in constant process. The Gestalt of their self-concept becomes more varied, enriched, fattened.* One's inner construct of "self" is transformed or modified or colored with every novel interaction with another person. The ongoing group becomes a gallery of shifting portraits: portraits which, having lost their static quality, step out of their frames, become more lively, and

I want to express my appreciation to my colleagues and friends at The Gestalt Institute of Cleveland, without whom this chapter would have been impoverished.
* A favorite metaphor borrowed from Sonia Nevis.

move rhythmically in relation to each other. This is where community comes in—the sense that I open myself to be touched by another in allowing her or his impact on my vulnerabilities.

Because there is no end to growth, the ongoing group behaves as if it has no end—it flows like life itself, unaware that individual organisms within it are terminal. Flow and process are of essence in every aspect of life. Gestalt groups are no exception. It is the liquid quality of process that fascinates me. Constantly expanding analogues of self and other deepen in meaning and awareness and are lived out in the life of the group.

It is this acting, this movement from enriched awareness toward contact, which makes Gestalt groups unique. Acting with responsibility toward another—out of compassion, anger or some other feeling—is of essence in gestalt groups. In acting, one modifies the very fibers and interstices of one's being and the being of others. Enriched awareness itself is not enough if we don't touch others, give to others, take from others with our senses, our muscles. Gestalt groups are contrasts to the cognitive flooding of competing analytic minds in academic seminars. They are more like Picasso's "Guernica" transformed to life, and Robin's "The Kiss" in the flesh. The emphasis is on process, energy, movement, contact, honesty and authenticity of presence.

THE GESTALT GROUP CYCLE

Each event within a Gestalt group can be characterized as a cycle: Beginning at the level of sensation, the group develops its own sense of awareness, its peculiar altitude of energy, its special dialectical action system, its climactic completions and its sense of groundedness and silence (see Diagram 1).

In the group's sensation phase, individuals see and hear, smell and touch each other. Words are used only to communicate the content of sensation: "You look tense," or "Your face is tight," or "You are all slumped over and caved in at the chest," or "Your eyes seem ready to spill over with tears," or "Your hands are cold," or "Our chatter sounds like the cackling of chickens." When a group attends to its sensations, it is in touch with its most concrete and fundamental experience. A group that leaps prematurely into individual awarenesses and ruminations jumps over the obvious, that which has immediacy and concrete urgency.

Group awareness develops out of that which is sensed in the here-and-

Diagram I

THE GESTALT GROUP CYCLE*

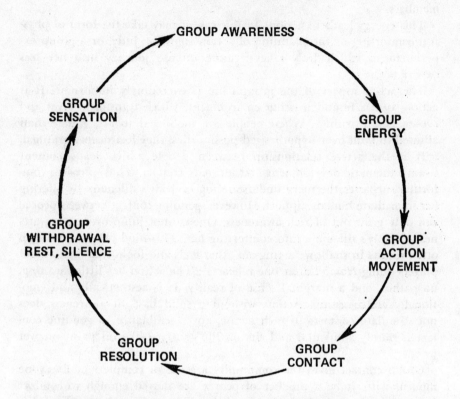

*The notion of a gestalt awareness cycle, as it was originally referred to, was formulated by Bill Warner and Miriam Polster, of The Gestalt Institute of Cleveland.

now: "Your face is tight . . . you seem ready to scream at John . . . is that what you are feeling?" Or, "You are all slumped over and caved in at the chest, Judy." Judy: "Yes, I feel really sad and sunken, as if life is seeping out of me. . . ." In order to act meaningfully, people need adequate information about and understanding of each other's lives. Then a theme emerges and can be developed. Attention to sensations stimulates a search for meaning, and rich, urgent meanings excite further interest and awareness. Group energy is mobilized. Thus, Judy's sadness over the sudden loss of a friend stimulates people to ask for more information and to express their own loss experiences. The group is energized by shared awareness of the constant losses and gains in the lives of its individual members.

This energy leads to action: In this case it may take the form of physical comforting or the planning of action steps for Judy, or a group experiment in which Judy takes a more intense journey into her loss experience.

The active aspect of the group's life is exceedingly important. It is action, in a safe and trusting environment, which transforms lives and evokes new learnings. When people are mobilized to act, rather than allowed to mull over hypothesized possibilities, they feel deeply gratified.

It is the active relationship between people which leads content toward thematic development and ultimate contact. Thus, physical comforting surpasses the mere understanding of Judy's dilemma by offering her immediate human support. However, genuine contact between people can only grow out of rich awareness. One cannot jump over the awareness of Judy's dilemma into comforting her. This kind of quantum leap often results in shallow "acting-out" that feels and looks like high school players doing *Hamlet* after one rehearsal: The action has little meaning, no pathos, and a marginal sense of reality. It is aesthetically and emotionally embarrassing. Action without a solid base in awareness does not stimulate contact. In such a case, any resemblance to genuine contact is purely accidental and sits on life's surface like oil paint on wet wood.

Group contact gives the community a sense of completion. Everyone mourns with Judy; a number of people are moved enough to comfort her; some may even shed a tear with her. The community comes to life and lives out its mobilized energy. Now everyone is ready for a respite, withdrawal and silence. Silence provides the background against which the group experiences its levels of anxiety, the depth of astounding itself with its own drama, as well as its sense of serenity.

If there is time left, a new theme may emerge, so that the group cycle may develop once again from sensation to awareness to energy to action, contact, completion and rest. Each of these modalities enters the group's phenomenological space and then recedes—sometimes in order, in linear fashion, and, sometimes, like the instruments of an orchestra, collaborating simultaneously on the same theme. In the beginning stages of a group, transitions from one phase to another may be disjointed and awkward; the group may get stuck in its awareness, unable to mobilize itself into action, or unable to resolve the action and withdraw. In the course of time, the group does not fixate on any one modality but moves smoothly from one cycle to the next, in an ascending spiral (see Zinker, 1977).

GOALS, VALUES AND ROLE DEFINITIONS

I want to review some basic propositions about Gestalt process groups. What are the goals of a Gestalt group? First, we can examine the goals of individual group members. The range of goals encompasses the full scope of human needs, from the need to rid oneself of debilitating symptoms at a maintenance level to higher level needs related to aspirations for fuller functioning and self-actualization. In Gestalt terms, individuals struggle to:

> integrate conflicting intrapsychic polarities;
>
> become more aware of their sensory life;
>
> enrich and expand awareness;
>
> stretch awareness into excitement and action;
>
> achieve contact with themselves and others;
>
> learn a comfortable way of withdrawing, of nourishing and renewing themselves;
>
> learn to support themselves with their whole beings;
>
> learn to flow smoothly through the awareness-excitement-contact cycle without serious blockage.

At the group level, members learn how to ask each other for what they want or need—and to deal with both the yes's and no's which come back to them. They learn how to deal effectively and creatively with interpersonal conflicts—for example, how they disown their own feelings, prejudices or actions by projecting them onto other group members. They also learn how to energize each other and how to use the group to achieve a sense of community, mutual support and respect. They discover how to learn about their own identities from one another and the group leader, as well as how to be inventive and experimental in solving problems as a community. They find out how to achieve a sense of trust, loyalty, and intimacy and, at the same time, to respect each other's needs for distance, personal taste, and values. They learn how to give each other feedback without interpreting away what they see and feel.

They learn to work with and help each without relying constantly on the group leader, and how to use the therapist not as a projected daddy-mommy guru but as a skilled professional fellow-adult who can facilitate their work with each other.

The Gestalt group carries certain values which are communicated (implicitly or explicitly) to group members by the leadership. These values are usually related to contact with oneself and others. Emphasis on certain behaviors varies from one practitioner to another as well as between Gestalt institutes in different parts of the world. Generally, behaviors which enhance here-and-now contact are encouraged. At The Gestalt Institute of Cleveland, we value the following group behaviors:

> Address yourself to a specific person (try not to speak into an empty space in the middle of the room).
>
> If you speak to someone, look at him/her and try to use the person's name.
>
> Attend to and express what you experienced here-and-now.
>
> Attend to your physical experience of the situation and learn to observe and respond to other people's body language.
>
> Make an effort to be direct with others (i.e., don't speak *about* Jack to Mary; address yourself directly to Jack).
>
> Respect each other's needs, individual boundaries, space, privacy; at the same time, learn how to nudge each other into growthful action.
>
> When other people are in the middle of their work, do not intrude; bracket off your feelings and/or actions for the time being. (After all, this is what we often need to do in the real world; it does not mean, of course, that you should be a passive, compliant observer).
>
> Use your observations, responses and feelings to enhance the process of the group;
>
> Speak in the first person: First person statements enhance ownership of your feelings and observations.
>
> Convert your questions into statements; often questions are safe ways of not owning feelings: "Mary, did you feel that was fair to do to Bill?" may mean, "Mary, I feel you are a cruel bitch!"
>
> Avoid giving advice; it is easily ignored and often mobilizes resistance ("You're mind-fucking"); get the person to become his or her own advisor;

Achieve a balance between your words and actions: Act instead of over-philosophizing, especially if you tend to bullshit a lot; on the other hand, learn to verbalize and explain yourself if you tend to constantly act out.

What are some desirable qualities of a Gestalt group leader? What is the leader's role? It is, of course, important that the leader be capable of understanding his/her observations and interventions not only at a gut level but also at a theoretical, clinical and methodological level. He/she is able to work intensely at the individual level and to expand individual work into the group arena.

The leader is able to see the group as a system rather than a mere conglomerate of persons. Individuals are seen not only for their personal uniqueness, but also for the unique manner in which they cooperate or collude with others in building a community. The leader's sharing of his/her understanding of a group system changes its process from fragmentary individual encounters to group awareness of the group-as-a-whole. This is a precondition to cooperative action and an enhancement of a sense of community. The Gestalt group leader is able to convert observations of the group system into experimental situations in which the group may fully appreciate its own nature and at the same time transcend it. The leader is a person in whose presence the community becomes respectful of its own integrity and can move more seriously and decisively toward its mission of self-discovery and community enrichment. The leader allows the group its own organic development without stifling it by leaning too heavily on his/her authority. He/she observes the group process and reflects that process back to the group.

Ideally, the Gestalt group leader should have a broad experiential and emotional range :from being a rock and an uncompromising bastard, to being an ever-so-gentle and loving grandparent. He/she should be capable of self-revelation and generosity as well as self-protectiveness and stinginess. The male group leader needs a well-developed female archetype (anima) and the female leader a well-developed animus. He/she should have an adequate background—an apperceptive mass—in many areas of life besides the behavioral and social sciences, so that his/her interventions emerge from this fullness of being, this compassion for the human condition and not simply from technical skill as a "Gestaltist."

I realize that I set high goals for myself and my colleagues; these qualities are not necessarily learned in training programs: They can only be pointed out. They are achieved by living a full life, struggling, making errors and learning—often in very small steps—to be a human being.

DEVELOPMENT STAGES AND THE USE OF EXPERIMENT

Gestalt groups, be they weekend workshops or ongoing groups, follow a developmental pattern similar to that of other therapy groups. Our groups begin with initial social superficiality and exploration and the cautious testing of trust levels; they then move into identity conflicts and power struggles. Resolution of this phase is often followed by entrenchment in stereotypic roles; ". . . much later the fully developed group work emerges . . . characterized by high cohesiveness, considerable inter- and intrapersonal investigation and full commitment to the primary task" (Yalom, 1970, p. 232).

Superficial Contact and Exploration

In the beginning the group experiences disjointedness and awkwardness. One hears choked voices, pitched high with anxiety. Anything resembling humor breaks the tension and fills the room with laughter. People tend to project their comments into the spaces between them, not gazing into each other's faces. There is no building: group members don't respond to the content of each other's inquiries. Rather, each drops his/her verbal pebble into the existential void of an unformed community:

> *Person 1*: So when are we going to start the work?
> *Person 2*: (*Responding*) What's your name anyway?
> *Person 3*: Why can't you two stay with the silence?
> *Person 4*: I didn't pay 100 bucks for silence!

Later, a more active exploration of the rules (explicit and implicit) of the game takes place. What is allowed here? Can I trust the leader(s)? Can I trust the group or individuals not to ridicule or attack me? Some people remain self-consciously silent until they feel the atmosphere is comfortable enough to express themselves. Others feel guarded about revealing important feelings which may put them in a vulnerable position. Much attention is directed at the leader or leaders. Group members look to them both for what subject matter is valid to reveal in the group and for the style of expression which is modeled and rewarded.

Gradually, group participants realize that no matter what is modeled or explicitly verbalized as valued behavior, they must carve out a life in the group for themselves. The group must organize its own unique existence, its own sense of authenticity, confrontation, timing, playfulness and groundedness. Individuals test the "system" by saying or doing what is most urgent for them in the here-and-now. They discover how others respond to them and what behavior is sanctioned, frowned upon or valued, not only from the leaders but from each other.

Conflict and Identity

Individual identity often evolves in the form of people's testing and probing each other's statements. The individual's identity in the community is shaped by conflicts with others. As people confront each other, leaders encourage independent action from a variety of sectors in the group. The process is lubricated by the leader's assumption that whatever displeases us in others is grist for the mill in our own intrapsychic and interpersonal existences.

As an example, let's consider the sixth session in a time-limited therapy group which will last for nine months. The group meets for two hours weekly, generally in the evening. There are 12 of us.

Barbara, a pretty, 28-year-old social worker, speaks about her confusion and loneliness and how men tend to "reject me because . . . well, I don't know why really." Her strange voice dominates the content. She is almost whining and seems to be trying to impress the group with her individual specialness and her need for support. Her monologue seems endless.

Everyone in the group, except Roger, seems to listen sympathetically. Greta is shaking her head, yes. The therapist benignly watches the other faces. Barbara's eyes seem to check him out periodically, as if to make sure there is approval to keep talking.

Roger, generally a quiet and passively observant man, erupts suddenly: "You know, Barb, I don't believe anything you're saying! Nothing!"

Barbara looks stunned. Her face turns a dark pink.

"For one thing," Roger continues, "half the time you talk, you seem to be like an actress. You're half smiling while talking about seemingly painful things . . ."

The dialogue continues

Stella: Now wait a minute, Roger, Barb . . .
Roger: Let me finish, Stella! You're smiling and you say you're lonely.

What kind of bullshit is that? And another thing, you say something and you check people out for the effect, like an actress trying to impress an audience.

Therapist: Roger, I've never seen you act so excited. My God, you're really pissed.

Barbara: (*to group*) I was just trying to express my feelings.

Stella: I was going to say that I really understand, Barb, what it feels like to be lonely.

Margaret: Yeah, but you are smiling while talking about these painful things. That distracts me. I have a hard time taking you seriously even when I believe your words.

Barbara's eyes fill with tears. She sits quietly and listens.

Roger: I don't believe you, Barb.

Therapist: I wonder what the two of you have in common.

Roger: What? Barbara and me?

Therapist: You heard me.

Dick: You, Roger, create distance from me with your silent vigilance, while Barb distances me with her acting.

Barb: I don't *mean* to distance anybody.

Roberta: Maybe that's how you distance your friends—with your smile and your looking for effect . . .

Roger: The thing is, Barb, I'm *attracted* to you until you start acting this way . . .

Therapist: How about starting all over again, Barb. Tell your feelings to Roger, but without the smile and the checking-out, without looking around.

Barb moves over toward Roger and sits silently, gazing at him. She takes time to settle herself. Her face is still full of color, but the smile is gone. The muscles in her face are relaxed, making it look longer, older. She tells him of her loneliness and pain. Her voice has lost its high pitch. It is quiet, yet audible. There is a richness in it—the full timbre one experiences with some old people. Her words seem to reach Roger in his eyes and his chest. His anger is gone. His breathing is full and deep. There is a respectful silence in the group. Stella is leaning forward. Dick has moved closer to Barb, as if to make sure he can see her full face. Then Barb stops. No one speaks for a while, waiting for Roger's reply. Roger adjusts his rimless spectacles. His face is expressionless. "Barbara, I can hear you now. I can feel your pain a little bit."

They speak to each other for a while. Their voices soften. Now Roger's eyes are filled with tears.

Roger: I know what it's like not to be heard. As a kid I was never heard in my family and I protected myself with my silence. (*Roger goes on to tell his story of childhood loneliness.*)

Therapist: (*to Roger*) Mostly, Roger, you have been quiet with us . . . living in a kind of self-imposed solitude.

Roger: Yes, and so it pains me, Barb, when I see you alienating yourself from me and many others with your lousy act; at least you might be more successful.

Barbara: I want to know how you experience me *now.* Now!

Roger: I hear you and I like you. I guess we both tried to cope with the same problem in different ways.

The therapist proposes an experiment based on the notion that what Roger dislikes in Barbara is what he needs to own in himself: "Roger, could you be an actor, a better actor than Barbara—dramatizing your thoughts and feelings?" The idea strikes Roger with such impact that he suddenly stands up and paces around in the center of the group.

The therapist continues: "Go head, show us how much of an exhibitionist you can be. You might even enjoy it." (Some hesitating laughter emerges from Stella and Margaret—as if relieved by the change of atmosphere in the room.)

Roger proceeds to imitate, often sarcastically, the voices and gestures of a number of group members, including the therapist. At times he is hilariously funny, captivating all of us with his performance. The room is filled with laughter. This is Roger's first real entry into the group after weeks of meeting. He is getting from *this* family, *this* community, what he always wanted at home: attentiveness and appreciation.

After about a half hour of his "performance," Roger throws himself back on some pillows on the floor. There is a brief silence. His gaze finally fixes on Barbara: "You know, Barb, I want to thank you. If I want people's attention, I may need to be a bit more expressive like you!" A volley of laughter fills the room.

Barb responds slowly: "And I learned that I might get more from people if I let myself express my feelings without having to dress them up with smiles and blushes. . . ."

In this instance, the group had overcome its initial "testing the system" phase. Members were able to use their senses, understand an issue, and come up with a theme which needs attention in their lives. An implicit value emerged: the importance of congruence between a person's words and nonverbal behavior. Non-congruence was discouraged because it distracted from the seriousness of Barbara's concern and from her contactfulness with Roger and other group members.

In contrast to one-to-one work, a number of people participated in the exchange with Barbara. Although the therapist's influence was there, it was not distracting. In this case, he let the group take care of the problem of Barbara's incongruence. He had no need to protect or defend her. She needed to discover who she was in this place for herself. Once a resolution was achieved between Barbara and Roger, the therapist used Roger's distaste for Barb's acting to get Roger in touch with his own withdrawal and lack of active behavior in the group. He designed an experiment in which Roger imitated Barb's acting and thereby came into active contact with a repressed part of himself. In the process, Roger established a lively identity in the group.

The therapist saw and treated Barbara and Roger as a system, rather than taking sides or getting trapped by Roger's righteousness. The system was split in such a way that one person was a "poor actress" and the other was a "righteous judge" who held back his exhibitionism. She needed to learn to be more congruent, to use her judgment better, while he needed to be more expressive. Other members of the larger system, the total group, witnessed the fact that no one was slaughtered in the action, that both individuals had something to learn from each other, and that there was freedom to speak up and say what one experiences. The group began to learn that all of us have something to teach each other and that learning is most effective and powerful when we try out new behavior and experiment with what would initially seem phony, forced or personally distasteful.

Confluence and Isolation

Once a group stays together long enough, it develops group confluence and isolation through fixed Gestalten. This is most often manifested by the freezing of each person's characterization in the community. The dye is cast: Each person is stuck in a role, even though he or she has changed significantly in his or her private life. Another form of this is either non-discriminating support accompanied by playfulness and physical contact, or non-discriminating hostile attacks and challenges which lack warmth and commitment. The following is an example of this group stage where people become fixed by old assumptions about each other.

A group I worked with recently was split into several factions. There was a small nucleus of senior members who, within their own ranks, disagreed and chronically bickered about a variety of issues. Another subgroup, consisting of newer and chronologically younger people, had become a docile audience to the central and older power group. With time, the total group began to lose its sense of mission, due in part to its numerous internal deflections and conflicts.

I came to this group as a visiting consultant for several consecutive sessions. I found that each decision took an enormous amount of time. Even minor things became a cause for discussion and senseless, stubborn arguing. As I sat with them I became aware that the participants behaved differently in the outside world from the way they did in the group. Inside the community each person became a caricature of him/herself. Somehow the whole community colluded with each member to support this caricature. The distorted construction of each person contributed to the splits in the group. Several new members took on extraordinarily complacent, passive roles, thereby allowing the bullies and complainers to take over. Aggressive, powerful members were supported by their tenure in the group, the power they were given by those who did not take initiative, and the reluctance of other tenured members to confront their old friends.

I shared my image of these caricatures with the group and together we created the following experiment:* Each member sits in the middle of the group, and describes his/her caricature and how he/she has helped the group to create it. The purpose of the experiment was to: 1) identify the caricature; 2) investigate ways in which it was supported in the group; 3) open new avenues for expanding individual identities within the group; and 4) help the group become more integrated and cohesive.

Richard, a tall, handsome man, the life of the group, moves to the center and sits down. After a short pause, he speaks. "I am the creative

---

* Readers who are interested in the mechanics of constructing individual and group experiments will find it useful to read two chapters devoted to this in Zinker (1977).

superman here. Also, I make all the arrangements every time I think of something lively to do. I support this caricature of myself by not attending to other people's ideas as fully as I can. I get easily impatient and bored with others."

The group decides that each member should have a polarity or alter ego sitting back-to-back with him or her, so as to reveal a part of his/her personality which does not emerge (and is not supported) in the group. Marcia volunteers and sits back-to-back with Richard. She speaks for his alter ego: "You folks don't realize how often I feel scared here, even terrified. I need your support and strokes at those times." There are voices of affirmation in the background. Richard looks surprised by Marcia's insight, surprised and almost pleased to be known that way.

To be sure that Richard and Marcia are heard, one or two members of the group volunteer to feedback what they heard them say. After this initial affirmation of Richard's caricature, each member tells Richard how he/she has colluded in creating this caricature.

Betty: Dick, I support your caricature by moving away from you when you express your vulnerability.

Joseph: Betty, would you be more concrete, give an example, an incident?

Betty: Dick, the other day we were talking and you told me about the anginal pain you have and how it frightens you. And do you remember what I did? I moved away from you by taking the subject away and telling about my Uncle Max's anginal pains. You continued listening politely . . .

Ben: Dick, I have supported your caricature by not sharing my own inventiveness with you for fear that you would find my ideas rather barren and commonplace. In the process I deprived myself of the pleasure of showing off to you, and also of getting your reactions to my images and thoughts.

Richard: I feel badly about that, Ben. I don't always find you very colorful. And whatever color you have inside, you hoard for yourself and don't give to me. In that way you support my caricature by making a caricature of yourself.

Everyone bursts out laughing. It is a laughter of relief. The experiment continues, with each member sharing how he or she colludes in Richard's group caricature. At the end of this segment, Dick tells the group how he wants to grow in the group, how he wants to change his behavior in the future. He follows this by requesting specific support for this new behavior from several group members who said they would help him get out of his superman box.

Richard: You know, I am shaking inside. I got goose pimples. I feel so full and moved.
Marcia (his alter ego): I could feel those vibrations in your back as I was leaning against you.

All members took turns in the center of the room, sharing their caricatures—as they experienced them—getting affirmations and statements of collusion.

At the end of the weekend I saw the group at a new level of cooperation and cohesiveness. The cohesiveness was created, perhaps only temporarily, by breaking down the group's stale characterizations of its members and mobilizing energy toward greater exploration and fresher perceptions of one another. Those who felt stereotyped by the group took responsibility for the manner in which they helped the group box them. At the end, the boxed person felt freed to pursue alternate aspects of himself/herself within a more honest and supportive community.

High Cohesiveness: The Metaphor of Family

There is no such thing as a final stage of anything, for process does not know its own end. It flows on as long as a group functions and serves as a forum for its members' continuous development. High cohesiveness in a Gestalt process group is characterized by interpersonal trust, capacity for caring and confrontation, and a respect for each other's level of developmental individuation. No one person is more valued than another. Each has something special to give and to take away from the group. Giving and taking are merged into functional unity. There is a continuous interest in exploring one another with seriousness and with patience. The process takes as long as necessary for each person (within the limits of the time assigned). People are able, with relative ease, to share their emotional reactions to each other's behavior, rather than advising or preaching. The group's work takes on more clarity, thematic pointedness and elegance in resolution. The leader tracks the themes of the ongoing action effectively and suggests original ways of resolving group dilemmas. The leader reveals himself or herself as a group member with a special task rather than an insulated, role-bound guru.* The leader shares his or her own life themes and feelings and does not feel discomfort when group members challenge or offer aid in clarifying his/her thinking or behavior.

My experience has been that as a group progresses, more traumatic (or happy) childhood material is brought to the group for clarification or working-through. The material is brought into the present when group members participate in reenactments of unfinished events, or in bold, new constructions of experiences wished for in the lifetime of an individual member. Here is one example of an enacted wish.

Miriam, a 34-year-old woman, seemed interested in other people's emergence, coming out. She had been an adopted child who had searched for her biological mother and had been successful in finding her. Miriam spoke to us of her search. At lunch, Steve told Miriam that he could identify with her having looked for her biological mother because he had met his biological father only recently in his life, at the age of 25. We spoke of the ideal ways of being wanted as a baby.

Back in the group, while I was working with Jack, Miriam noticed how Bob, while lying down, rubbed his head against the pillows next to him. She thought he was "straining to be born." What emerged was Miriam's image of abandonment after birth, her fear of being left all alone, stranded and frightened and helpless. When Miriam found her biological mother, she was somewhat relieved to let the ghost out of the closet—to dispel the mystery of this idealized figure. But she was disappointed, too, because her mother didn't have much to give other than to ask her daughter for forgiveness for having given her away. Steve had a similar experience: He, too, was disappointed to discover that his "real" father was weak, and "always gave in" to his mother. Steve found his stepfather to be a much more attractive figure. Both Miriam and Steve were pleased with the *notion* of having met their original lost parents.

Miriam: (*to Steve*) I wish I could have another chance to be born and to be wanted this time around, and to have an older brother, like you Steve, who was looking forward to having a little sister . . .

---

* Sonia Nevis (personal communication) points out that a guru charms but does not explain his work. By not teaching the reasons for his actions, he remains mysterious, powerful and in a position of being admired, adulated. Group members attend to his artistry more than their own learning experiences, their own insights. I have often felt that the aim of a good teacher is to explain what he does so well that in the future former students supersede him.

Joseph: (*to group*) We have been together for a day-and-a-half and I feel close to all of you. I would like it if we could offer you, Miriam, a special present: the opportunity for a brand new birth experience . . . an ideal birth.

Miriam is asked to pick an ideal mother and father for this ideal birth, one in which she is truly wanted. She can't find a female in the group who fits the mother she has in mind. Besides, her present therapist is a female and she doesn't want to get herself confused. She picks Gregory for her mother because of his softness and caring, and Mike for her father because they seemed to have worked lovingly with each other in the group.

She proceeds to pick a doctor—Jack, a nurse—Loretta, her mother's mother—Gretchen, an uncle—David, a family friend—Julian, someone representing her own thrust, her power to be born—Jackie. And she asks Steve to be the nine-year-old brother of the baby girl about to be born. (Steve had been an unwanted and neglected second child with an older sister.)

Miriam tells of the bed on which she will be conceived, and how her birth will take place. She helps the group construct the environment in which she would like to be born.

The father and mother (Mike and Greg) lie on the bed talking about having a baby girl, how nice it would be, how much they love each other, what the child would be like:

Mother: You know, dear, our son is already eight years old, and I think it would be nice to have another baby before he gets any older. It would be wonderful to have a daughter.

Father: Well, I've resisted for a long time, but I think you're right. I would love to have a beautiful little girl. (*Gregory looks at Miriam.*) Imagine having a daughter! A girl as beautiful as her mother. A daughter of our very own!

(*At this point, Miriam begins to cry softly.*)

Mother: Do you think our daughter will have red hair like I do, or do you think she'll have dark hair like yours?

Father: I don't really care, as long as she's healthy, but if I had a choice I'd want a girl who looks as beautiful as you do. You know, I really

like the thought of having a little girl. I have a lot of fun with our
son, but I could sit and cuddle more with a daughter.

Mother: What if we have another boy?

Father: I would love any child we have together, but I have a strange
feeling that we'll have a girl. I'm feeling so soft and warm inside, I
just think we'll have a daughter this time.

Mother: I have the same feeling.

As they speak, the two people have their arms around each other and
look very involved in the process. There is a respectful silence in the
group; you can hear Miriam's soft crying in the background.

Group Member: I think you'd better prepare the baby's brother for this
experience.

Another Group Member: Why the rush? They've got nine months or
more.

Father: I think we should tell Steve that he's going to be a big brother.
We want him to look forward to that, and to love the baby when she
arrives.

Mother: Come here, Steve. Come sit on the bed with Dad and me. (*She
puts her arm around him, while Father pats his shoulder.*)

Father: You're really a big guy for your age. You know, your Mother
and I are very proud of you. We're lucky to have a son like you.

Mother: We're all lucky to have each other. And you know, Steve, because
we all love each other so much, we think it would be nice to have
another person in our family to love too, and who would love us
in return. Wouldn't it be nice to have a little sister to play with and
to teach things to? You could tell her so many things, and she would
think her big brother was so smart and so wonderful.

Steve: I think that would be terrific. Most of my friends have brothers
or sisters, and I would really like that. (*They all smile at one another
and embrace.*)

The group sits on the floor in a tight circle surrounding the three of
them. The two men who play the parents enact a relationship that seems
loving and physically affectionate. There is a deeply warm sense of caring
between two people. One woman in the group whispers to another,
"Wouldn't it be nice if all men were like this?"

The mother and father continue talking and caressing each other.
They caress and stroke each other's hair and hold each other tightly,

propped up against some pillows. They are sitting close to each other on the floor in a thick atmosphere of supportive caring emanating from the circle of people around them. Symbolic body movements indicate that they are engaged in sexual intercourse.

The mother whispers into the father's ear, "We're going to have a beautiful little girl." The father answers, "I love you."

Someone suggests that Miriam curl up and wedge herself between the mother and the father, and that the birth consist of Miriam expanding herself more and more. Miriam crouches between Greg and Mike. Jack, the doctor, and Loretta, the nurse, move closer. The mother holds the father's hand on her tummy: "Do you feel the baby moving?"

Father: That baby is really kicking! Maybe it's going to be a boy after all.
Mother: Today's girls are strong—they can kick as well as boys!
　(There is laughter in the group.)
Miriam: *(from between the parents)* I have been strong all my life, and
　　I've got a good chance of surviving. *(She then begins to stretch and*
　　move. Jackie, her "power," moves closer to help her stretch.)
Nurse: Doctor, it looks like the contractions are getting stronger.
Joseph: *(to group)* Let's lower the lights and make this as serene as we
　　can.

One of the women begins to sing softly. A humming melody emerges from the group: an accompaniment to a birth. The mother groans with pain and actually begins to sweat, while the father comforts her and strokes her forehead. The group is in awe of the fact that this is happening between two men, that two men can be so gentle and caring with each other. After several minutes of sounds and movements that seem to be coming from a delivery room, Miriam begins to move out from within the tight folds of the couple. Loretta and Jack gently pull on her head as Greg groans louder.

Mother: Our baby is coming!

With the help of the various assistants, Miriam explodes out of the duo with a powerful thrust.

Nurse: You have a beautiful redheaded girl!
Mother: Let me see her.
Father: Yes.

The doctor (Jack) puts his arms around Miriam and presents her to the parents (Greg and Mike), who stroke her head, examine her fingers one by one, and glance lovingly at each other. Miriam is aglow. Her face is soft and wet with perspiration. Her eyes are shining. She is totally immersed in the process. She looks pure, cleansed, childlike, beautiful.

Mother: Isn't she lovely? Look, she has all her fingers and toes—and look at that long red hair!
Father: She's exactly what I'd hoped for. I'm so happy.

The other members of the family move closer to the parents and the baby.

Mother: Steve, dear, this is your little sister. I hope you like her . . . here, you can touch her . . . feel her hair.
Steve: She's so tiny and cute! I'll take good care of her. It's going to be fun to be a big brother. (*He gently holds one of Miriam's hands.*)
Grandmother: (*looks at the baby and the baby's mother*) She's so sweet. She looks just like you did when you were born—just beautiful!

In hushed voices the other family members and friends express their gladness.
Now Mike and the others move away. The mother and child are alone together. Miriam looks as if she had just come out of a bath. Her face is soft and pink. She is breathing gently. Her eyes are moist.

Miriam: My God, I feel as if I'm a new person. I love you all for letting me have this special birthday. I . . . I . . . I don't feel alone anymore.

Mike begins to sing: "Happy birthday to you, happy birthday to you." (*All of us join in.*)
Several people in the group are sniffing. People are holding each other and the group seems even more tightly woven, as if it had become one physical organism. There is a long silence.
A group can recreate itself by enacting a metaphor. It can be a circus, a zoo, wolves in lambs' clothing, an audience at a concert, architectural structures, or pictures in an exhibition . . . every metaphor provides the potential for a creation with which the group can transform itself and modify its process.

In the above example, a family developed out of the drama of one member's birth. The ritual was a spontaneous creation of the leader and members, and the action grew out of a profound sense of trust and an attitude of mutual generosity and graciousness. That an important event took place for Miriam is without question. I believe that it allowed her to change her self-concept from that of an unwanted child to a wanted adult. In addition, each individual could work on some specific area for him/herself. For example, Gregory, who acted as Miriam's ideal mother was able to get in touch with his female archetype. He was also able, perhaps for the first time in his life, to feel intimate with another man without experiencing homosexual panic. Mike, the father, was also pleased about his newly discovered tenderness with another man. Both men also spoke about the pleasure of parenting a baby as a non-sex-linked phenomenon. Steve was able, at least in part, to work through his angry feelings toward his own sister and parents. Every person in the group nourished him/herself in that experience. Such experimentation could take place only in a group of high caliber contact and high cohesiveness.

A FINAL NOTE

I have described how for every event in a Gestalt group process there is a cycle: sensation → awareness → mobilization of energy → action → contact → resolution → rest and silence. Then I illustrated Yalom's premise that a group moves through stages: Beginning with superficial contact, it moves to conflict and formation of identity; next it moves on to solve the problems stemming from the formation of confluent and fixed roles; finally, it develops high cohesiveness, as exemplified in the metaphor of birth in a family.

In the superficial contact phase we encounter a group which has low sensory and cognitive levels of input and a high level of energy, energy which is usually experienced as anxiety. Contact is shallow and, as a result, there is little sense of resolution.

In the conflict and identity phase, members begin to attend to what they hear and see and start to notice different levels of incongruence in each other's behavior. As a result, awareness of group members become modified, expanded, enriched. Group energy is used to pursue a given theme. The theme is developed and the use of experiment intensifies intrapsychic and interpersonal contact. Resolution and rest generally follow as the group's energy is used up in the process.

When a group moves into modifying confluent, caricature-like roles of its members, it has a high level of awareness and a willingness to challenge its own creations. The energy level must be high for such a task and, generally, the group is rewarded with a renewed sense of closeness and contact. Resolution follows and everyone falls back both exhilarated and exhausted from the work.

In the high cohesiveness stage, awareness is rich and varied and the group is willing to take high risks for the sake of new learning. Here, as well as in the preceding stage, group members utilize the experiment as a tool to clarify a given theme and make significant discoveries. Experimentation is not possible without a high level of energy as well as a willingness to tolerate contactful conflict or contactful loving. Experiment modifies the group members' perception of their own inner lives as well as the lives of others. When awareness is high and energy is utilized contactfully, group issues are resolved and people are able to sit back and let go of having to work. At these special moments, group silences are peaceful and serene—as if the group-as-a-whole was in a stage of meditation.

Yalom's stages of group development are, therefore, integrated with the Gestalt group process as shown in Diagram II. From the beginning

Diagram II
GESTALT GROUP PROCESS

GREATER COHESIVENESS

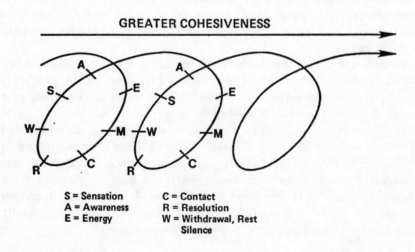

S = Sensation   C = Contact
A = Awareness   R = Resolution
E = Energy   W = Withdrawal, Rest
                 Silence

when people are chatting as if at a cocktail party, to the more advanced stages of cohesiveness, the group process has an internal structure, an integrity, a validity of movement. The trajectory and quality of this movement are always determined by the special configuration, the unique Gestalt which a community of persons is able to carve out for itself. The creative potential of a Gestalt group emerges from the range of special talents, limitations and resistances to contact of its members and its leaders.

6

Gestalt Family Therapy: A Case Study

SUSAN M. CAMPBELL

Being part of a family system provides a context for individuals to experience their separateness and their connectedness. Each family member is both "a part" of and "apart" from the family. Managing this tension between the parts and the whole is the essential task of every family. And when a family needs assistance, it is at this individual-group interface that Gestalt family therapist can be helpful.

Individuals experience various disturbances at the contact-boundary (such as projection and deflection) which interrupt the flow of information or energy within and without the individual's body-mind system. Similarly, families use such processes to alienate some of their parts from the whole, thereby creating blocks to contact. The most common example of such alienation is the "family scapegoat" process, whereby one family member is identified as the "patient," the "sick one," the one for whom the family seeks therapy. This person is often the one who is most different or *apart* from family norms or "rules." In Gestalt terms, this individual may be seen as the "disowned" or "projected" part of the family system.

The task of the therapist, then, is to foster dialogue between the disowned part and the whole so that contact can be established or reestablished. Contact between the identified patient and the other members of the family can involve both the experience of separateness and the experience of unity (i.e., the sense that "we're all in this together" and in some sense mutually responsible for our common experience).

Fostering dialogue is akin, therefore, to the facilitation of an I-Thou relationship (Buber, 1970; Naranjo, 1968). This does not necessarily

78

imply, however, that the family must stay intact in its present form at all cost; at times an individual's integrity may be so threatened by membership in the family the therapist may need to support the strengthening of the individual's boundaries in ways that make him or her less susceptible to influence by the group (i.e., family). This is often the case when the family system is characterized by a high degree of interpersonal confluence (also called "enmeshment" in the family systems language).

Gestalt family therapy, therefore, is a method for encouraging dialogue within the group so that each individual's needs can be heard, felt and, if possible, responded to. If such adequate response is not possible, then the system boundaries need to expand to allow for greater responseability within the family or to allow for greater self-differentiation on the part of individuals (or a particular individual).

When a family scapegoating process is occurring, this is a sign that the system lacks response-ability—or the ability to respond appropriately —to the needs of its members. Perhaps, for example, there is a "rule" in the family (similar to a norm in a group or a taboo in a society) against expressing anger. In such a case, most family members will conform to this rule, thereby keeping their anger out of their awareness; one family member may be "elected" to live out the blocked feeling or receive the projections of the others.

In order to heal the internal split or alienation caused by this scapegoating process, each individual must come to terms with the alienated part within him/herself before true dialogue can occur with the alienated part "out there," i.e. with the family scapegoat. As every experienced therapist knows, however, we cannot rush this process of unfolding awareness and responsibility for one's disowned, alienated, or projected parts. We must start where the client (the scapegoated family member) is—with the known—moving with the client's ebb and flow of contact and withdrawal more and more into the unknown. Thus, when a family seeks therapy for itself because one of its members exhibits problems, we trust that as the dialogue (and, therefore, the clarity of interpersonal contact) increases, this problem assigned to a single part will eventually come to be owned by the whole family. Attaining such awareness usually requires a considerable amount of work on the part of the family, both as individuals and as parts of a larger whole.

In order to demonstrate some of the aspects of such work, guided by a Gestalt family therapist, I will describe in some detail my work with the

Platt family. Although I worked with the Platts for approximately six months, I will give only the highlights as they explicate the Gestalt dialogue process in fostering a clearer part-whole relationship.

Verona Platt, a social worker in her early forties, called me to arrange a visit for her 15-year old daughter, Joya. In our phone conversation Verona was articulate, calm, and rational as she described Joya's "acting-out behavior" (her words) in school and with peers. Her other two daughters, she volunteered, were model students and a delight to her and her husband, Carl. She could not understand, therefore, why this one child, her oldest, was so different. Although she seemed unaware of it at the time, Verona actually presented her daughter's problem as a family problem: For instance, she mentioned how Joya's behavior was upsetting everyone in the family, made several comparisons between Joya and her other two children, and continued this comparison by puzzling over the question of why Joya was "different" from others in the family. For these reasons (rather than any preconception that family therapy is better than individual therapy), I asked if she had considered the whole family's seeing me conjointly. When she acknowledged that she had, we discussed her reservations, and she decided to present the idea of family therapy to the others.

A week later the Platt family was assembled in my office for the initial consultation. The mood was tense and restrained, but cordial. Each individual family member seemed to be behaving according to the same set of "rules." Even Joya, the "problem child," was conforming to the model of restraint and politeness. I began to make contact with them from a position of relaxed interest (my genuine reaction to the situation), asking each person in turn to tell me how it felt right now to be a part of this family, assuring them that I, too, would disclose how the situation felt to me.

Verona responded almost immediately with the words, "eager . . . I feel eager . . . and hopeful, too." She was followed by Carl, who said he was tired, and that he'd had a long, hard day at the retail shoe store where he was manager and supervisor of six employees. Next to enter the conversation was Kate, the youngest, nine years old, who commented on her father's response before giving her own, "Oh, he's always tired . . . and I'm, well, I'm not sure how a feel . . . good, I guess." The middle child, Freda, age 13, was next with, "I'm anxious to see what's going to happen . . . and a little afraid . . . but not very." Joya took her place as last to speak with a challenge to me, "I want to see what you're going to do with us." I experienced this as an attempt to make a connection with me rather than as a distancing attempt.

I responded with my own feelings about being with them in this context, beginning with an overall reaction, which was followed by "playback" to each family member as an individual: "I feel energized at the prospect of getting to know you . . . already you've given me a lot of information about who you are as a family—information that I'd like to reflect back to you so you can see how you look from the outside. You, Verona, spoke first, saying you felt eager and hopeful . . . and you, Carl, spoke next about your tiredness. You, Kate, at first you weren't sure, and then you said, 'good, ¹ guess' . . . and Freda, you spoke of being anxious to see what would happen and a little afraid, but not very. And the last one in the family to speak was you, Joya, and you were wondering what I was going to do with you all. I'd be wondering that, too, if I were you."

This non-interpretive "playing back of the tape" is a way of promoting self-awareness while communicating my feelings of acceptance of "what is." I am careful not to program them to change any of what they have presented to me. The important thing at this stage of our relationship is *contact* and *awareness*, not *change*. As a Gestalt family therapist, I have learned that change is the only constant in life, and that my job is not to induce it but to identify and work with blocks to awareness of the changes that are continually occurring in peoples' lives.

My goal during this "awareness phase" of therapy is to provide a structure in which each family member can experience being a part of the family as well as apart from the family. This aids all members in becoming aware of the family's influence on them and their unique impact on or roles in the family. One of the best ways to accomplish these objectives is the Gestalt dialogue process. In a family context this dialogue is often among several parts rather than between the polar opposites on a continuum. It is often a *multi-larity* rather than a *polarity* that we are working with. Thus, instead of simply a top-dog and under-dog battling it out or reaching toward one another, we might have a top-dog, an under-dog, and a middle-dog mediating between the two.

The dialogue process in families usually starts with two protagonists as in Gestalt polarity work (cf. Perls, 1969, p. 73ff.). Thus, at first (after the total family has become engaged in the therapeutic process), the dialogue may occur between mother and father or between mother and identified patient (IP). Before long, however, others come into the act.

Father may enter as a buffer between mother and IP, or the IP may act
to defuse conflict between the parents, etc. Thus, a whole system of interdependent forces comes into play, demonstrating that the whole is, indeed, greater than the sum of its parts.

One of the structures that I found useful in promoting such intra-
family dialogue during the early part of my work with the Platt family
was a modification of the family sculpting technique. This process affords the opportunity to portray in a family drama the dynamic relationship of the several parts that are interacting at one time. The process
looks like a kind of nonverbal psychodrama with one member at a time
playing the role of protagonist.

In introducing this approach to the Platts, I asked each family member in turn to engage with me in an "experimental enactment" (a combination of the Gestalt "experiment" and the process of "enactment").
The experiment arises out of the context of whatever has been happening in the session. It may occur as a reflection of a theme which has
been identified, or it may occur out of an effort to identify what theme
or themes may be present but not yet apparent. In the situation to be
described, the theme of "listening" had emerged as a central issue, illustrated by such comments as, "no one in this family ever listens to anyone else," and "mom listens to everyone, but nobody listens to her."
Around the theme of "listening" there were obviously differences in perception. In order to help clear away the confusion surrounding this
issue, I suggested the following:

> I'd like us all to try an experiment. It's an experiment designed
> to show all the different ways people in the same family might feel
> about a question like the one we've just been asking, the question
> about listening. Now, of course, no one *has* to do anything. But if
> you think you'd like to try this experiment, I'm going to ask one
> of you to be the "sculptor" while the others cooperate with the
> sculptor by allowing yourselves to take whatever positions or pos-
> tures the sculptor places you in. I'll act as a guide in this process, so
> that when we're finished, we'll have a piece of sculpture composed
> of all five people in the family, depicting how people do or don't
> listen to each other in this family. The steps in this procedure will
> become clearer as we go along. I'll help whoever volunteers to be
> the sculptor. Who wants to volunteer first?

Joya spoke up almost immediately. I asked her to stand up with me,
while the rest of the family formed an audience around us. I then asked

her to imagine a scene in which all members of the family were present. Next, I asked her to describe her scene for us: "Where does it take place? What is the mood or feeling tone? Where are the various family members sitting or standing in relation to one another?" When her image was clear to all of us, I asked her to recreate her image with the people here, placing them as they appeared in her imagination, and molding them into the postures, shapes and facial expressions of her image.

As Joya began to recreate her image, she was visibly tense and tentative in her movements. She started with her two sisters, placing them in a far corner of the room, sitting side by side with their hands folded neatly in their laps. She placed her father behind an imaginary newspaper in the center of the room, placing herself on the floor to his left. When she got to her mother, she paused for a very long time, as if she were about to take a dangerous plunge into very deep water. When she finally drew her mother into the center of the room, she still appeared undecided as to how to portray her image: First, she placed her mother sitting in a chair, head in hands, weeping; then, she had her standing up waving her arms and hands in silent frustration; then, after a very long pause, she moved her mother toward her father, waving her arms, and finally knocking the newspaper out of his hands with a violent gesture.

At this point, all family members were experiencing increased excitement, as evidenced by their deep and rapid breathing. In order to allow for resolution of the tension, I continued guiding Joya in her enactment. I now asked her to "be" her mother in the sculpture (i.e., to play the projection), using words or sounds to flesh out the picture. Then, I asked her to "be" her father; then, each of her sisters; and finally, herself in the five-part sculpture.

In "contacting" (or "being") each of the others, she made a real attempt to see the world through their eyes. For example, as her mother, she looked and appeared to feel genuine anger; as her father, surprise and annoyance; as her sister Kate, muffled glee; and as Freda, fear.

Joya had broken the ice with her dynamic family sculpture, giving a kind of nutshell diagnosis of the state of the family's communication process.* Now Verona indicated that she would like to be the next to

---

* It is often found that the IP tends to "see" (experience) the family's dysfunction more completely (albeit often unawares) than other family members who tend to more completely identify with their family roles and are thus less apt to see themselves "objectively."

work with the sculpture. In her work, she focused immediately on her anger at Carl who, she felt, had been ignoring her by hiding behind his newspaper. In Verona's work, too, I asked her to be each person in the family, experiencing or witnessing this confrontation between Verona and Carl. As Verona, in the sculpting process, she was fully present with anger. As the others, however, she could hardly believe what she was seeing. In portraying her daughters' reactions to her outburst, she actually appeared to be horrified. It seemed, therefore, that Verona was having difficulty being seen by others as angry, that she feared her anger mainly because of a belief that it didn't "look good for the children to see." Recognizing this, and putting it together with the fact that, indeed, her children did see and to some degree did accept her anger at Carl, she was able to reevaluate her position with regard to the imagined dangerousness of expressing it.

In subsequent sculpting sessions, by Carl and the other two children, the degree of threat posed by Verona's anger was seen to be less and less—due partly to the familiarity that comes with repeated exposure and partly to some very helpful interventions from Joya. For example, during one angry interchange between her parents, Joya suggested that the two reverse positions and continue their angry contact—a suggestion that not only proved helpful, but, more importantly, showed Joya's capacity for clear, rational and responsible behavior.

Thus, it seemed that as other members of the family became more conscious of and responsible for their "negative" emotions, Joya was no longer "elected" to act these out. Once Verona and the others had contacted their less rational parts, Joya was freer to contact her more rational side. She no longer needed to confront her mother with what she (Verona) had been denying in herself.

Thus, the Gestalt experiment involving family sculpture facilitated awareness in the family members regarding a part of themselves they had been disowning: Joya became more aware of her rational, helpful capacities; the others, especially Verona, experienced and owned responsibility for some "negative" feelings which had been thought to be against the family "rules."

Responsibility and choice flow naturally from awareness if the process is allowed to complete itself, as was the case here. Verona owned or took responsibility for her anger at Carl; at the same time, she owned her responsibility to the family as a *system,* as a whole, in that she saw how her blocked awareness with regard to negative emotions had placed a block not only in her own psyche but also in the *system*, as embodied in Joya's acting-out behavior. When she took responsibility for herself in this regard, energy was freed up in the system, allowing opportunities for others to break out of their rigidly held rules.

Joya's owning responsibility for her more rational aspects also had an impact on the system as a whole. For example, the family now became less compulsively rational. Thus, as each person allowed her/himself to contact the natural, changing feeling-states *within*, she/he became more response-able to each other. Raising this principle to consciousness, following the experiential enactment, gave each family member a clear sense of the interdependence of self- and system actualization: As each individual comes to own and accept more fully all aspects of him/herself, fuller self- and relationship actualization is possible for everyone.

7

Gestalt Art Therapy in Groups

ELAINE RAPP

Art as an ongoing process of experiencing one's experiences —not peripherally, but right there in the thick of it? And it's not only those glorious moments, if by glorious one were to mean moments of ecstasy: . . . But what about the times of despair, when all seems lost and meaningless? Isn't celebrating these times in acts art too?

PAULUS BEHRENSON (1972, p. 150)

The focus of Gestalt art therapy is the search for self, not the search for art talent. In this process, achievement and productivity are of no concern. Past art training and technical ability are irrelevant; in fact, many of the participants have never used or even seen some of the art supplies or sculpture tools provided. There have been in the same workshop professional artists as well as people who thought of themselves as being without any creative ability whatsoever: The experience has been meaningful to both groups. When instruction is necessary—and it is surprising how little is needed—it is provided as a natural part of the group experience.

Because of the setting, people easily slip into using material they might otherwise approach with hesitancy and fear. The group itself provides an environment that is supportive, reducing the anxiety of taking a risk in an art medium, whether it is unknown or familiar. Judging or comparing one's works becomes irrelevant. By avoiding these two traps the individual is then freer to begin creating something unique to her/himself.

For example, in a recent group a young woman who had been having difficulty in painting became aware that she started off free and capable of communicating directly with her work; then after a while she would become blocked. With the help of the group she was able to recognize that, at a particular point in creating, she began to be influenced by imaginary "outside opinions," her introjected parental voices, which questioned what she was doing and why she was doing it. These "outside opinions," she ascribed to her husband and boss, constant critics of her performance. They were a reflection of the introjected voice of her father, whose perpetual message was "be perfect." After she spoke of these opinions, the group expressed them, enabling her to reaffirm, first to each member and then to herself, her need, her right and her ability to produce what she wanted to produce. Once she experienced this, she was able to feel her own energy without the drain of outside opinions and was then capable of getting back into her work, with a new awareness of how she interrupts herself.

The uses of art in therapy involve the relationship between the person (organism) and her/his environment (materials) in a variety of experiments. These experiments are used in the following situations: 1) large group intensive workshops for personal growth and creative development; 2) in-depth individual or group therapy; 3) training sessions for graduate students and professional therapists. The goal of these experiments in any of the above situations is to reach that level of psychological exploration which has been previously agreed on by both client and therapist or student or leader. For example, in a training session, the experiments will instruct in the use of a therapeutic tool and will stop short of therapy. On the other hand, in a therapeutic situation, individual or group, in which the contract is clearly one of therapeutic intent, these experiments are invaluable in ferreting out the client's psychological position at that moment and in moving to deeper levels of integration of unassimilated material in Gestalt therapy terms, that is, attending to the disturbance at the contact-boundary.

It is clearly important that the level and goal of the workshop or session, including the use of these experiments, be defined beforehand. The art therapist/teacher must be aware of how easily individuals attempt to engage at a deeper level than the one previously agreed upon; therefore, the leader has the responsibility of maintaining the integrity of the original contract.

My focus in art therapy workshops is on the participants' sensitivity to inner and outer environment. With these as the parameters, group members are taken on a guided tour of self-discovery. Along the way they become involved with a multiplicity of art materials that become the environment in ways that I design. Instead of talking about their environment, participants come face to face with how they interact with it. In essence, the materials are the tools of the experiments just as the pillow or the empty chair are the tools in other types of Gestalt groups.* There are watercolor markers and oil pastels for drawing, tissue paper for collage, metamorphic rocks for carving, plastelene and terra cotta clay for modeling, tinfoil and armature wire for free-form sculpture. These external objects become the means for exploring internal sensations and feelings. Participants can begin to make changes by experiencing this contact with the environment in the aliveness of the moment, taking in what is needed while rejecting what is not. There is group support for *not* having to interact with all the materials.

There is enough clay, paper, paints, etc., so that a wide range of choice is provided by the environment. This is contrary to the experience most of us have had in the past. In our formative years, both the bottle and the food are given to us and we do not participate in the selection; we are presented with people to relate to whether they are our kind of people or not; we are told how to behave and are rarely asked how we want to behave. As the group value for uniqueness of expression takes hold, participants feel increasingly secure in selecting by their own sense of touch, taste and smell, and connect to the fact that their senses and judgment are the only measures of what is right in the experience.

Since many people have trouble conjuring up fantasies, the objects and the art produced become the objectified fantasies and thereby become the means for exploring internal sensations and feelings. Group members can then begin to explore their own inner landscape. Through Gestalt therapy, with the group as part of the process, each person can begin to experiment and take into him/herself those parts he/she heretofore has not been aware of. For example, in describing the sculpture he/she is working on, someone might become the sculpture and thereby get involved with whatever it is he/she is projecting into the stone. Or fear of hacking away at a stone may lead to fear of cracking it. Upon exploration, this may turn out to be fear of one's own vulnerability to cracking—or of one's own ability or desire to destroy. Exploring one's distaste for

---

* In designing experiments with stone, wire, clay and a variety of other art materials, I have relied upon my own experience over the years as a professional artist. My training as a sculptor coupled with my training as a Gestalt therapist has enabled me to design experiments which would have been impossible to invent without the foundation given by both disciplines.

the coldness of a stone may lead to a discovery of one's own denied coldness. Evolving a beautiful shape out of something that had previously lacked beauty can bring an awareness of the beauty within oneself or within others. Using these materials and Gestalt therapy techniques enables participants to begin a dialogue with those parts of themselves that they have projected. This then creates the possibility of integrating those parts into the participant's personality.

In carefully structured exercises, each person comes to grips with his own behavior as a member of the group, as well as with what emerges graphically from within, as evidenced in the artwork produced. Like other Gestalt therapists, art workshop leaders focus upon what is being expressed here-and-now. Fritz Perls (1976, p. 63) in the *Gestalt Approach and Eye Witness to Therapy* says:

> The goal of therapy, then, must be to give him [in this case, the group member] the means with which he can solve his present problems and any that may arise tomorrow or next year. That tool is dealing with himself and his problems with all the means presently at his command, right now. If he can become *truly aware* at every instant of himself and his actions on whatever level—fantasy, verbal, or physical—he can see how he is producing his difficulties, he can see what his present difficulties are, and he can help himself to solve them in the present, in the here-and-now. Each one he solves makes easier the solution of the next, for every solution increases his self-support.

In Gestalt art therapy groups this is done graphically, since the art materials provide a visible message that can't be wiped out. The instant of perceptual awareness leads to a most meaningful form of insight; at that moment, the group member makes his/her own discovery with clarity and impact.

The group leader does not analyze, but encourages exploration. There is no secret code known only to the leader that assigns specific analytic meaning to shapes or colors or forms. Rather, the explications of these graphic expressions must come from the group member. The question is always: "What does the work mean to you?" This is no different from the way Gestalt therapists work with dreams. James Simkin (1974, p. 87), in discussing dreams, states:

> According to the Gestalt therapy framework, everything in your dreams is some aspect of yourself, and in effect when you are dream-

ing, you are writing your own script. You're saying things about yourself . . . Most therapists see the dream as a disguised message. In Gestalt therapy, the message is an existential message, a message of how you exist, the nature of your existence.

The message of the art produced is also an existential message. Each of the participants in the workshop is different and her/his spontaneous artwork will be as individual as her/his thumbprint.

Workshop leaders must constantly be on the alert so that they can keep the group from going on comparison trips. As soon as participants start comparing their creations, they lose out on what is, they lose out on the intrinsic value of the products they have fashioned, and they can be diminished by juxtaposing themselves to others viewed as either greater or lesser. The moment group members begin to compare their work with one another, somebody is sure to be not imaginative enough or not talented enough. Krishnamurti (1967, p. 8) wrote:

> Most pepole think that learning is encouraged through comparison, whereas the contrary is the fact. Comparison brings about frustration and merely encourages envy, which is called competition. Like other forms of persuasion, comparison prevents learning and breeds fear.

In the workshop environment, differences are treasured. This releases a torrent of creative energy which is so powerful that the leaders may have difficulty in getting the group to stop for a break. There are no shoulds or should nots in the workshops—no good work or bad work— no judgments of any kind. There is only what each person creates *out of* themselves *for* themselves.

* * *

Attendance at a workshop in which one is expected to use art materials can be a frightening prospect. A voice from the past may be comparing the participant to a talented brother or sister or to the class genius; the voice tells him/her that he/she will not do well with the clay or the stone tools or the collage materials. Because of this, many people come to an art experience workshop with at least two sets, one of which is a readiness to fulfill their own worst prophecies about being uncreative and unable to work with their hands.

One way to reduce this anxiety about doing well is not to request the group to make anything. Instead, each new art experience is introduced as a happening. The group becomes involved with the material in a non-threatening situation that leads naturally into the creative process.

For example, the group leader can start a session by tossing into the air hundreds of sheets of tissue paper while appropriate background music adds to the playful mood. The tissues are irresistible and before long the group members join the leader in keeping as many of the light-weight sheets in the air as possible. With the room flooded with color, joyful pandemonium takes over. Tissues are rolled into balls and flung at the nearest convenient human target. The excitement of the moment can free people to fashion bizarre costumes and headdresses. People may disappear under colorful mounds of tissue paper or simply lie on the floor looking up at the sheets drifting down upon them. The group is literally inside the material. This "encounter" with tissue paper becomes a lively experience for each participant.

The interaction with material may go on for 30 or 40 minutes. Finally, the group leader places large sheets of white drawing paper on the floor in the midst of the tissue debris. Alongside each sheet of drawing paper (one for each group member), a paint brush and a container holding a diluted mixture of acrylic polymer gel are placed. The leader then demonstrates how easily the tissues can be ripped into odd-shaped pieces and affixed to the sheets when the translucent gel is applied. Nobody is told how to *make* a collage. The simple demonstration speaks for itself and the group members who have been intimately involved with the tissue paper move naturally into creating their own individual collages.

Another example of how to involve the group with the art material is in the introduction of the plastelene clay experience. Plastelene is used because it requires human warmth and energy to be changed from a rigid block to a consistency that is easily molded into any shape desired.

The experiment begins with the leader asking the participants to select a block of plastelene in a color of their choice. There is no mention of creating anything. The only instruction is to soften the block in any way they can—by twisting, pounding, stomping, or simply by squeezing it in their hands and allowing body heat to do the job. As they do so they create energy in their hands similar to the way one does in massage. Next they are asked to find a partner with whom they will sit face to face with palms extended toward the partner's palms (but not touching). They can now sense the field of energy between them; this is a powerful way of making them aware of their own energy. Finally, they place their palms above their own skin and contact this energy. People who are depressed or out of touch with their vitality are people who cannot contact their own energy. This exercise gives them a beginning awareness of how to do so.

The group is then invited to let loose with any sounds they care to make while dealing with the clay. They can imagine the block is a brother, a sister, a teacher, a parent, or any other convenient target for their feelings. Screams, shouts, and curses fill the room as each participant works with the resistant plastelene. Gradually the noise level subsides as the clay responds to the warmth of the hands and the vigorous pummeling.

When the plastelene is pliant, the leader suggests that each group member let a form emerge. In essence, they are asked to place their trust in their own hands or in their own organism that something will happen without any sense of having to do anything. The participant is fully available to himself without draining off his energies in the usual concern about how well something is going to turn out.

Whether the medium is tissue paper, plastelene, stone, wire or any other substance, the experiment begins by getting people involved with the material. Once this has happened, the group is encouraged to use the material in response to a challenge presented by the leader.

Much of the process outlined in the following experiments is the same as in other forms of Gestalt therapy. The techniques are different, but the philosophy, the goals, and the results are the same. Creative process often evokes fears, such as those of not knowing, of risking, of the taking of new spaces, of the unexpected accident—in short, all the introjects that prevent us from further growth and from contacting our excitement. The group process enables the members to experience their introjected voices, with the possibility of working them through.

I. EXPERIENCE WITH STONE

The sculptor's idea must meet the stone's will, for stone cannot be forced; if it is forced, it will get even with the sculptor by fracturing into many pieces.

The Challenge: Carve your own stone sculpture.

Materials Used: An assortment of stones, safety glasses, bush hammers, rasps, silicone, sandpapers and mineral oil (Rapp, 1969, p. 30).

Stone-carving offers the most here-and-now experience of all art media. If we violate the stone by not listening to what it is saying, then we get the same result as when we "push the river" rather than go with where we are in our own life.

With stone we are always pulled back into the present. If we don't take a risk, the stone doesn't move. As the piece of sculpture takes shape, new possibilities constantly reveal themselves. And there is always the chance that the next stroke of the chisel will hit a flaw in the stone and shatter the piece. When integrated into the workshop setting, a personal experience with stone-carving provides an opportunity for a person to be seen and to see himself in the process of meeting an unfamiliar challenge. There can be no automatically programmed response because the potentialities of the stone and the risks to be taken in carving are constantly changing.

The following experiment with stone is designed for people with no previous art background. The leader starts by forming the group (usually 10 to 12 members) in a circle. In the center are placed a collection of metamorphic rocks.* Ideally, they are from various parts of the world with as many minerals as possible represented. Each rock is small enough to fit in the palm of one hand. These miniature stones are not for carving but rather serve to provide the group with an introduction to the natural variety of forms in which stones are found. Each rock is a mini-landscape unique in its shape, texture and color.

The leader next explains to the group that they are going to play a game with the stones. First, all group members will have an opportunity to examine the different pieces, to feel them, taste them, smell them, get acquainted with them in any way they like. Then each person is invited to choose the stone which most closely represents where he/she is in his/her life right now.

Some people make an immediate choice while others find it hard to make a decision. Frequently, people are drawn simultaneously to two stones that are very different. When this occurs, the leader may work toward enabling these persons to deal with the polarities represented in each stone and what they evoke in them.

When all group members are satisfied that they have the rock they want, the leader moves to the next step. He/she invites the group to take

---

* During the formation of metamorphic rocks the minerals in the earlier sedimentary or igneous rocks may undergo recrystallization, growing into larger crystals having a different chemical composition. Heat, pressure, and movement cause the chemical action.

turns being the piece of mineral selected. This is done by describing the stone, using the words "I am" at the start of each sentence. The participants then go around the circle, with each person talking in turn.

Group members share themselves more readily when given an opportunity to project onto an object outside of themselves. For example, a young man in one group gave this description of his stone: "I am a desert stone. I am rusty, dry, porous, lifeless. I have a spot on me that shines somewhere in the middle, but it is hard to find. I am irregular and I don't stand up too well. I keep coming back to the spot. I like it. I am sad (*tears come*) that I have so little shining from me."

Each time someone slips into talking *about* the stone, the leader brings him/her back to him/herself. The others are asked to hold their reactions to what is being said until they have gone completely around the circle. Then there are 20 to 30 minutes of sharing in which group members talk about how they felt in selecting their stones and how they perceived one another being the stones.

In this way, the participants begin to get to know each other and become involved with the mineral collection, experiencing how alive and fascinating stones can be. The leader now asks them to move to the other side of the room where a selection of the stones to be carved have been placed on a table. These are usually small boulders in a variety of shapes, sizes and colors, weighing six to eight pounds, not unlike the weight of a newborn baby. There might be Italian alabaster, Pakistani steatite, African Wonderstone, pink alabaster from Colorado, and other metamorphic rocks with the special qualities which make them suitable for carving.

Group members are then asked to consider the commitments they are prepared to make before deciding what size stone they want to carve. They are encouraged to go with their feelings in choosing a stone, rather than getting involved in what they may or may not know about its geological makeup. When a person who selects a resistant stone with sharp edges is visually confronted with someone else selecting a softer, more easily carved stone, attitudes about the need to do things the hard way or the easy way can be explored. And by having to choose one stone and see the process through, members are able to explore feelings about commitment.

The leader next introduces the group to the fun of immersing the stones in a bucket of water and seeing how the color and natural markings within the stone are intensified. What they are seeing is the life within the stone that their energy will soon release. The coloring of the stone when wet serves as a preview of what will happen after sanding and oiling of the finished piece on completion. Participants are then invited to tell other pepole the secrets that have emerged when the stone got wet. The projection of these secrets onto the stone are an integral part of the process of self-exploration.

Once group members have selected the stones they want, the leader sets them up with a working platform (usually a pile of telephone books), a pair of safety glasses and a stone-carving tool called a bush hammer. The bush hammer serves two purposes. One side of it can be used as a pulverizer to shape the stone and the other side acts as a pick to cut into the stone. (Later in the session, additional tools are provided, as needed.)

Next, the leader provides instruction in the use of a bush hammer and states the safety rule requiring that glasses be worn at all times. He/she shows how the pick side of the bush hammer can be used to create negative space and how the pulverizing side rounds out rough edges and creates hollow areas. The relationship between positive and negative space, which is the basis of all sculpture, is explained. "To make a mountain, you create a valley." This can also be used in enabling participants to become aware of their own polarities of positives and negatives.

Almost immediately, the metallic clickety-clack of a dozen bush hammers biting into stone will be heard. The stone-carving experience has begun. Over the next six to eight hours most group members will have an experience unlike anything they have had in their lifetime. And, at the conclusion, they will have a piece of stone carved with their own hands as a visible record of their experience.

As the carvers work silently, the energy from the group begins to be communicated to them. This phenomenon of people working together, sensing the sounds, rhythms, and aliveness of the group-as-a-whole, has inspired participants to break out in song—or perhaps to weep. As the community energy touches the participants, they experience a novel contact with the environment and a sense of support for their creative endeavors emerges.

This can be compared to a very early developmental stage of a child who, sensing his/her mother's energy nearby, is comforted by her presence and therefore feels safe to create, explore, and learn. For some members this is the first time they have become aware that an important developmental process was left unfinished. For them creating has meant isolation; the group is often a springboard toward exploring a new aspect of creativity.

The leader next circulates among the carvers, serving both as a resource for instruction and as a facilitator available to group members who want to work on what is emerging in themselves and in the stone. Although each person goes on his/her own journey, the following five aspects of the experience seem to be most meaningful to most people.

1) The Experience of Being in a Situation That Can't Be Programmed

As layer upon layer of the stone is peeled away, there is the revelation of what the stone is like inside. Because these are metamorphic rocks in a living stage of transition, there is no way to know what one will find. There may be a vein of marble within the alabaster, a deposit of iron oxide imbedded in the steatite, a swirling pattern resembling the knob of a tree inside the jet black African Wonderstone. And there is always the possibility of hitting an unsuspected fracture that hadn't shown itself in the stone before.

Carvers learn to appreciate the good and the bad of what their stone reveals about itself and they find that forcing the stone to be what it is not simply will not work. They find that the stone can't be programmed and that if they go with the surprises as they come along, they can make the most of the potential offered by the stone they selected. This is easily equated with the carver's own personality and life.

2) The Experience of Being Part of a Nourishing Community

The group sits on the ground in a circle much the way people in a primitive community do while working. There is no sense of competition among the participants. Rather, there is a great deal of support as individuals stop from time to time to share with the others where they are with their stone and what has been happening to them. The intense feeling of kinship and spontaneous sharing provides all the nourishment needed to sustain the high energy level of the group. The group process at the closure of such intimate experience often borders on the religious. Passing around each other's stones and following with one's hands another's journey is a new way to make contact. Only through working with a group can a participant experience this.

3) *The Experience of Recognizing Male-Female Qualities*

Pounding the stone with the bush hammer offers wide latitude for expressing aggressive and hostile feelings. In contrast, the sanding and polishing stage gives the group a chance to make contact with tender and sensual feelings. This can be used for direct communication with their androgynous feelings as well as with the polarities within them of love and hate. Men and women sit for hours applying successively finer grades of silicone sandpaper to the stone. Finally, with loving care, the mineral oil is rubbed into the stone with the fingers massaging, anointing, to attain the desired degree of polish.

4) *The Experience of Being Creative in a Way Never Thought Possible*

Members of a group frequently say how pleasurable it was to be given all the tools and instruction they needed without the condition that they had to do something right. Within the workshop setting, the leader is an authority figure who is saying: "Go ahead and try it. I think you're capable of what you have undertaken, and I care enough about you to take the trouble to be there with the guidance and support you need. *And I have no expectations that you have to fulfill.*"

What happens in this safe and supportive atmosphere can border on the miraculous. Although the goal of the workshop is not related in any way to aesthetic excellence, the work produced is on a level one would expect to see from professional artists with years of experience. Viewed as the first stones carved by men and women who have never had an art lesson before, the quality of work often is astonishing in its imaginative expression and technical competence.

This may be the only stone that a participant will ever carve, but he/ she has seen what is possible when one's creative energies are not blocked by fears and inhibitions. It is a discovery of self with implications far beyond the limited workshop experience.

5) *The Experience of Being Able to Create Something One Can See, Touch and Take Home*

Participants leave the workshop with their own sculpture—the personal statement they have carved in stone. Often participants say that the work has taken on new meaning in the months that followed. Placed on a mantle or upon a bedside table, the stone is viewed over and over again and the dialogue which started in the workshop continues.

For some people, the fact of completion is in itself therapeutic. "There it is—shaped by my own hands. As permanent as the stones carved in ancient Greece and Rome. And I did it." The completed sculpture makes a statement that they can touch and see—full of stored memories from the workshop and from inside themselves. Here is lasting evidence of their ability to stretch in a direction they once doubted they could take.

II. Experience with Watercolor Markers

The Challenge: Take your own space and give yourself anything you want.

Materials Used: Several dozen watercolor markers, paint drop cloth (or bed sheets sewn together), miniature houses usually found in 5 & 10¢ stores around Christmas time (there should be at least two for each group member).

This experiment begins by spreading a 9' x 12' white drop cloth (the kind painters use to protect floors and furnishings) on the floor in the center of the room. The group is asked to join the leader at a nearby table on which is placed a collection of miniature houses.

Each house is different. Some are simple, one-story, thatched-roof huts, while others have several floors and rising towers. Group members are asked to select one or two houses that represent parts of themselves as they are now. Soon, the group is totally involved in examining the little houses and making those subliminal connections that finally lead to saying: "This house is me."

After the houses are selected, the participants are asked to remove their shoes and walk onto the drop cloth: "For the next hour this space will be your world. Walk about and become familiar with it. Find a place where you feel most comfortable and, when you are sure that it is where you want to be, sit down."

It usually takes several minutes for each person to settle into his/her own space. Then, a pile of watercolor markers in a variety of colors is placed within easy reach of each person seated on the drop cloth. (These felt-tip pens can be used to draw on a fabric surface without smearing and their bright colors dry instantly.) When everyone is ready, the leader says: "Take the space you want to claim as your own. Use a marker to outline your territory. Take as much space as you like and place your houses anywhere you wish within the space you take. If you run into your neighbor, you will have to work it out between you. There is only one rule—no talking, please.

"Once you have your space outlined, use the markers to give yourself anything you want—a front lawn for your house, a mountain range, your own ski slope, people, a money tree, a helicopter-port—anything your imagination can visualize you can give to yourself."

For the next hour, a dozen grown-up men and women lose themselves completely in the worlds they are creating. The drop cloth is transformed into a colorful panorama, as the blank spaces are filled with drawings of fences, cars, chickens, dogs, lakes, streams, lovers, armies, watchtowers, and whatever else anyone wishes. Men and women who have not sat on the floor to draw pictures since early childhood give themselves over with childlike abandon to the task.

When each person has finished filling in his/her space, the group is asked to assemble at one corner of the drop cloth. One by one, they share with the others what they have done with their space. One man has surrounded his house with a moat, another with a fence, and yet another has been content with no encumbrances. From time to time the leader may want to work with some persons individually. By helping them take responsibility for the space they have created and for what they have put down in it, the leader helps them become more aware of the parts of themselves visible in their space. Whatever is on the drop cloth, including where they placed themselves on the sheet and how much space they have taken for themselves, is in the "now" and relevant.

When the processing is completed, participants are told that they can take their "space" home with them if they wish. Scissors are distributed and each person proceeds to cut out his/her area of the drop cloth. Usually, most people take their space with them when they leave at the close of the workshop.

III. CREATIVE GROWTH EXPERIENCE WITH ARMATURE WIRE

The Challenge: Interact with another person.
Materials Used: Armature wire stapled to a wood base (one for every two participants).

Armature wire is used by sculptors to build the skeletal frame which is the first step in creating a direct plaster sculpture. The wire is strong enough to stand up straight without any support but also soft enough to be easily bent and twisted. For this experiment, a 10-foot piece of wire is formed into a "U" shape; the bottom of the "U" is firmly attached to a wood block measuring about 5″ x 5″. The result is a base from which two separate 4-foot wires rise straight up into the air.

To start the exercise, the group members are asked to pair up. When the pairs are formed, the leader places one armature wire assembly between each pair of people and says: "Using the wires you see in front of you, interact with your partner without speaking."

For the next five minutes, each person works with his/her own wire while experiencing the other person in the twosome. The partners may go their separate ways or they may become involved with one another. At an appropriate point, the leader asks the group to stop. He/she opens group communication with members about their experience. Some of the questions are: "How did you contact one another? How did you take space and give it up? Who was the leader and who the follower? Did you want to be separate or connected?"

Next the leader suggests changing partners. Again, after five minutes, there is a sharing session. "How was this time different? What was it about your new partner that made you behave differently? How were you the same in both experiences?"

The wire sculptures resulting from the exercise provide a graphic picture of how each person interacts with another. Persons who do the experiment four or five times with different members of the group and always find their wire (themselves) in the same characteristic position realize not only where they are but how they got themselves into the same position each time. Participants now discover the way in which they make contact, e.g., by enveloping the partner, or by moving away, or by knotting themselves up. To discover and acknowledge "where you are" makes it possible existentially to experiment with new ways of moving with the material and exploring another dimension of the self.

IV. EXPERIENCE WITH CRAYONS AND A CAKE BOX

The Challenge: Experience the inside-outside environment as a continuum.
Materials Used: Crayons in an assortment of colors, unassembled white cake box, scissors.

The leader starts by distributing the unassembled white cake boxes to the group. Before assembly, a cake box is simply a piece of flat cardboard with appendages on all four sides.

The leader indicates which side of the box will be the inside and which side will be the outside when it is assembled. Then he/she says to the group: "The inside is what is going on inside of you. The outside is what the world sees. Start drawing on the inside of the box and keep referring to the different folds and flaps as different parts of yourself. Find the child parts first. As you work on the inside, if things come up that show through to the outside, turn the box over and draw what comes through on the other side. If something starts on the inside and changes into something else on the outside, let it happen. You have scissors to cut through to the outside, if you want to."

Those are the instructions. What follows is an intensive experience in perceptual awareness. All participants become deeply involved in a graphic, multi-level conceptualization of where they are internally and externally in their life.

The box is there to be assembled or not to be assembled. For some people, the box becomes a house complete with doors and windows. Some have their boxes sealed tight. Some cover every inch of the inside and outside with pictures and symbols. Some leave large areas bare and unfinished.

For example, one man covered the inside of his box with pornographic pictures and then provided a peek-a-boo hole for viewing, contacting his voyeur, his hiding, and other secret aspects of himself.

A woman decorated the outside of her box with drawings of gaily colored Christmas gift wrappings while all the ugly things she felt about herself were inside.

Another woman remembered herself as a bratty child, sticking her tongue out at the world. She drew the big red tongue on the inside of the box and then carried it right through to the outside. She gave her box a big window so that she could "look in and see the bratty kid." What she saw when she looked into her box was not only a brat but also a fun-loving child. She felt that in allowing the brat to come out and be visible on the outside she had made direct contact with her enjoyment of her brattiness. "I don't have to be so serious all the time," she commented with considerable relief.

When everyone is finished, the leader draws a chalk circle on the floor in the middle of the room. Those who want to complete the Gestalt art experience are invited to come forward and put their boxes in the middle of the circle. The box has many parts, offering endless possibilities for work. Participants are asked to become these parts (similar to Gestalt dreamwork). Each member, by seeing and learning about the work of the others, becomes aware that what he/she does with his/her box is unique—as unique as each member is.

As members discuss their work, one at a time, each one of them and the observers learn over and over again: "I am who I am. I invent like no other, and I am my own person making contact with my external environment as only I can." Over and over again this concept comes to consciousness like a dream put out in front of us to see.

*   *   *

All artwork is one's personal symbol, as well as one's communication to the other. Creative growth takes place when that communication emerges spontaneously from within the individual and there is ample opportunity to process these manifestations of the self in a meaningful way. Marston Morse, the mathematician, once said: "It is only as an artist that man knows reality" (1958, p. 381).

To experience oneself in the creative act is to experience one's own aliveness. Instead of talking about what they *can't* do, members of a group discover what they *can* do. They learn how easily skills can be mastered, when proper instruction is offered in a supportive, non-competitive environment. They experience *the pride of creation*.

Another facet of working with art materials is the chance it provides the participants to experience the power they have to explore options and to change what they have created—if it is not what they want—into what they do want. Whether working with clay, collage, or even stone, there is the opportunity to undo what has been done and to risk the unexpected by exploring new possibilities.

A 19-year-old girl in one workshop had been piling layer upon layer of tissue onto the paper, working compulsively in her fear that any white paper might show through in the finished work. Later, when the group was sharing the collage experience, I asked her how much of the tissue she would dare take off her collage. Cautiously, slowly and painfully she stripped away one piece at a time. At one spot she came to the bottom layer and took the risk of lifting the tissue to expose the white, vulnerable part underneath. What she found, instead of the expected empty space, was an orange pool of color that had bled onto the paper from the tissue and entirely filled the "hole." Her catastrophic expectation of frightful emptiness was not fulfilled; in reality, there was no emptiness, and she found something unexpected. To enable her to release the energy blocked in the fear, the leader then asked her to become this orange pool of color. In the process of becoming the orange, she was able to experience the joy of the color, and in so doing owned some of her own colorfulness.

The sculptures, the drawings, the collages, and any other artwork produced can also stimulate the group; however at this stage it takes a good deal of initiative to use someone else's work for fantasy. For example, in one group a young woman had her designs on the floor. A young man who loved the shapes and colors began stating his own fantasy, which required some minor changes in the design. The young woman was enraged, feeling violated by his fantasy. This opened the door to exploring with her important feelings that might otherwise have lain dormant.

In the process of working with art materials, group members can add to a drawing, subtract from a collage, reshape a piece of clay, take out a negative in stone, explore endless possibilities for change. There are capabilities to fill in the unfinished parts, to create a new world of their own, to go back and change what has been before. In exploring whatever alternatives present themselves, they have an opportunity to experience how comfortable or uncomfortable they feel in the new experiences they choose to create for themselves.

Over and over again in whatever art materials are used, I find visible expression of the individual's polarities. There is the light side and the dark side, the weak side and the strong side, the death side and the life side, the child side and the adult side.

The polarities projected into the artwork are witness to the two sides of the person that are in conflict with one another at the moment. The child side wants to be taken care of and the adult side has babies who need to be cared for. The man who everyone expects to lean on because of his strength is in conflict with the side of himself that is weak and wants to lean on others. When these polarities emerge graphically in the workshop, I offer an opportunity to develop a dialogue between the opposing parts. Often mixed or ambivalent feelings emerge and can be worked through.

One group member, a strapping 6′ 4″ powerhouse of a man, chose to carve a small fragile stone. The stone became an expression of the small delicate boy within the powerful man. As the stone took shape, he was amazed that such a lovely, intricate piece of work could be created by his big, rough hands. The other people in the workshop came up to touch and fondle his carefully polished little stone and he finally was able to embrace his delicacy as well as his strength. At this moment the other group members personified the delicacy he had disowned, thereby encouraging him to own and integrate this side of himself. For the others, this meant also contact with their own delicacy and an opportunity to affirm or reaffirm it.

In the armature experiment, I sometimes suggest that group members work solo with both wires rather than pairing off for interaction. I recall one woman who completed her sculpture with one wire soaring off in a gentle arc while the other wire was bent over and twisted around the base and the lower portion of the free-flowing wire. It developed that the unencumbered wire represented the part of herself that yearned to reach out to people and the other wire symbolized the way she had been all her life—lonely, scared, holding down the part wanting to be free. In the dialogue that followed, the soaring part demanded in tears that the other wire be loosened "to set me free to move toward other people." This woman slowly untied the wire and reported feeling the knot in her stomach loosening at the same time. Having released the soaring wire, she turned away from the sculpture and reached out to the nearest group member. Moving from person to person, she embraced each in turn, and allowed herself to experience the outgoing part of herself.

*   *   *

One's art experience is one's reality, one's invention, as is one's life. The phenomenological approach to art produces the visual content that validates one's experience. I believe that all of us have the potential to reclaim what has been buried, to thaw what has been frozen, to find the excitement of play, adventure, sexuality and creativity.

Facilitating and being the inventor of art experiences, while using myself as an artist and Gestalt therapist, has outstanding rewards and it is an art work in itself. When, as a sculpture student, I first entered the Academia in Florence to see Michelangelo's "Slaves," I felt a spiritual energy that was indeed profound: Locked within this compressed stone was a vitality and life force that transcended its form. The metaphor of this experience keeps coming back to me. I believe that each of us has the capacity to create an inner and outer reality in harmony with ourselves and the world, and that we have the ability to emerge and change to new forms again and again.

8

Gestalt Movement Therapy in Groups

DELDON McNEELY TYLER

I should only believe in a God that would know how to dance ... I learned to walk; since then have I let myself run. I learned to fly; since then I do not need pushing in order to move from a spot.

Now am I light, now do I fly; now do I see myself under myself. Now there danceth a God in me.

FRIEDRICH NIETZSCHE, *Thus Spake Zarathustra*

Throughout history the art of dance has been associated with creation and healing. Most cultures exhibit ritual dancing in some form to mark the beginning of new ventures, to celebrate milestones of growth, or to express worship. Unlike smaller, more cohesive cultures, contemporary Western cultures do not give formal recognition to dancing as a healing process. Yet many individuals use dance to express depression, frustration, and hostility, as well as joy, sexuality and altruistic feelings.

The experience of using our bodies in new ways may promote awareness more quickly and energetically than verbal experiences alone. After introducing movement in therapy and training groups, I have often observed a responsivity in people who appeared to be rigidly holding onto some characteristic stance. These instances have encouraged me to develop techniques of movement and dance and to use them for various purposes in groups: as a source of pleasure, as a stimulus to self-awareness, and as a way of dissolving barriers to further experiment. In using movement in therapy, my theories, ideas and techniques derive from the four

105

major influences of my training: Freudian, Jungian, Reichian, and Gestalt approaches to psychotherapy.

Movement and music also became an integral part of my work because of their therapeutic effect on me. Many psychotherapists know the benefits of engaging in active sensory experience as a counterbalance to their work, which is usually intuitive and receptive.* A notable example is Carl Jung's experience with sandplay, whose soothing, balancing effect restored his perspective in times of stress.

For me, dancing unites and exalts the feeling and sensing functions, as I understand these functions in terms of Jung's theory of personality types; by merely continuing to dance uninterruptedly for a time, my intuitive function automatically involves itself. The effect on me is that what began as a pleasant sensation and expression of energy becomes more meaningful at a level connected to communication of feelings to others, life sustenance, and worship.

In Gestalt therapy terms, this means that I accept the music as environmental support to enable me to feel safe enough to let go of a fixed Gestalt, thereby loosening up and contacting my continuing needs and restoring the awareness continuum. If the thinking function is to be part of my process, it must be deliberately evoked by conscious effort; otherwise, there is no tendency to reflect upon or understand how or why I am dancing. It is enough: I am dancing, I am in It. However, if cognition is stimulated too abruptly, the whole rhythm of the experience may be halted.

On the other hand, if integration is to occur, the thinking function must be used. In fact, the current activity of writing this is one of the ways in which I hope to give form and sustenance to this belief. Movement and dance can be of great benefit without being analyzed, but the additional work of thinking through with participants the meaning of their experience through movement deepens awareness. Therefore, it is important to provide space for this in the therapy, as will be shown in more detail later.

Any therapy which involves specific attention to the body must acknowledge the contribution of the body therapists, particularly Wilhelm Reich. The body work in movement therapy varies from superficial, blandly stimulating exercises to intense bioenergetic work, depend-

* See Carl Jung's essay, "Psychological Types" (1971) for his discussion of the four personality functions which interact and develop in each person throughout life: intuition, sensation, feeling, and thinking.

ing on the goals and tolerances of the participant. Since movement therapy lends itself to many levels of work, the focus is different with different participants. The training of psychotherapists in movement group work, for example, requires some exposure to intense bioenergetic experiences, whereas in a short-term therapy or growth group, such experiences would be selected to fit the "group Gestalt."

In my approach to movement therapy and my way of exploring the emerging fantasy material, I have integrated Jungian and Gestalt concepts to such a point that I find it impossible to separate them in my description. In both Jungian and Gestalt therapy, one participates in dialogue with various manifestations of the Self,* grapples with the tension of opposites directly while experiencing polarities within oneself, and confronts archetypal images in the here-and-now. The amplification of unconscious processes by what Jung calls "active imagination" resembles fundamentally the Gestalt approach to dreams and fantasy material. The unique contribution of Gestalt therapy is an insistent focus on experiencing such integrative processes in the presence of and, importantly, with the participation of the therapist. Without that, therapy tends to become a reporting process of life lived somewhere else, a stultifying situation in which one may hide and comfortably maintain a neurotic position with the therapist's unspoken consent. For me the essence of Gestalt therapy is the integrative experience during the therapy session, and it is on this aspect of movement therapy that I will focus here.

In movement *group* therapy, another dimension is added to the dyadic process. It is possible to work in individual therapy using movement and music either occasionally or regularly, or to structure individual therapy around a primarily body-oriented approach. However, in my experience, the optimal circumstances for movement therapy are in a group whose members also participate in individual therapy. In the group, movement becomes a "megaphone" for the subtlest of inner experiences, and the contributions from creative sources are vastly enriched. It is, of course, impossible in any one session to cover all the possibilities for exploring newly discovered aspects of each member; these can be explored further in individual therapy. But the group, in addition to providing more stimulation, offers a setting in which family and peer-group experiences

---

* The term "Self" is used here according to the Jungian formulation and not according to the Gestalt definition, i.e., "The complex system of contacts necessary for adjustment in the difficult field, we call "self" (Perls, Hefferline, & Goodman, 1951, p. 373).

may be simulated for experimentation. This will become clear in examples given later.

For me, the most difficult and risky part of movement therapy is the assessment of the meaning of physical pain, especially in short-term groups. Participants are cautioned to recall and report old injuries and infirmities which may limit their motion at the start of the group so that these limitations can be taken into consideration during our work. However, occasionally I encounter persons without any obvious or remembered physical limitation who experience pain during the initial session. Such pain is clearly a caution to participant and therapist, and deserves careful respect. Usually it vanishes through some discussion and gradual entry into the pain-producing movements and fantasies. In a short-term group, however, if the pain continues or resistance to the work persists through several sessions, I recommend that the member leave the group and explore the resistance in some other mode of therapy. This is mainly in the interest of the other members and of the group-as-a-whole, for ultimately, given sufficient time, all resistance could be worked out through movement and verbalization in the group.

The movement group can be introduced at any level of psychotherapy and with a variety of goals. I will briefly outline two such levels to illustrate some of the ways in which movement therapy can be used.

THE MOVEMENT THERAPY GROUP WITH POORLY INTEGRATED PERSONS

At the most basic level of psychotherapy, when the person's task is to maintain conscious ground against the seduction of overwhelming psychotic content, how do we participate as therapists? Within the medical model we may maintain a distance, note the person's behavior, and prescribe appropriate treatment such as drugs or milieu treatment. In the Gestalt therapy model we contact such persons as they experience themselves and become part of their experience. In Gestalt-oriented movement therapy, we are not merely directive, but we present ourselves to the persons for imitation, for exploring physical boundaries, for developing a concept of their bodies. We encourage them to identify what they are feeling and how they look, and how they see themselves in relation to their therapist. We want them to get in touch with us and for a short time establish an integrated experience of inner and outer worlds. This may be done through any number of movement therapy techniques, but usually, at this level, the more structured, repetitive, and circular movements are most effective. The basic circle is a source of comfort and strength. Therefore, most of my group work with psychotic people occurs within a group circle.

When working with an individual who is psychotic, I may use massage and expressive dance, but only after careful assessment of how much physical contact the person wants or can tolerate. Simple exercises to music, games, and singing together are most valuable. The essential experience is one of emotional and cognitive contact between us, as a bridge from self-preoccupation to the arena of interpersonal relatedness. In movement therapy, that contact becomes primarily sensual. In a group, where more relationships are possible and the dependence on the therapist is diluted, participants experience disturbing feelings which are accepted by the group; they learn that they do not have to deny these feelings. The more security, the faster the healing; therefore, ideally there will be co-therapists or assistants to contribute to the security of the environment and a "manageable" number of group members. The therapists join the dancing, reveal fantasies, and participate actively.

THE MOVEMENT THERAPY GROUP WITH BETTER INTEGRATED PERSONS

When the participants have a clear sense of identity and are seeking to unblock creative energy from the unconscious, then movement therapy is a way of rechanneling physical and psychic energy. In our physical development and our formation of a self-concept, we follow propensities which become tension-reducing grooves, comfortable well-trodden paths, or super-secure ruts. Ruts, expressed in one's physiological and psychological stance, are given up only with a struggle. In movement therapy it is possible to approach this struggle with an attitude of play.

I conduct movement groups with better integrated persons in essentially the same way, regardless of the time-structure or the goals of the group. Usually, after an initial period of awkwardness, during which I discourage group interaction, I encourage progressively more active participation of members in revealing feelings, fantasies, and reactions to each other. In the beginning of a movement session I am quite active; as we proceed I initiate less, but remain available—mainly to guide the movement—while the group propels itself. To simplify things for myself, I think of each group session as having three phases: *warm-up, creative movement,* and *integration*. In the first phase, I encourage loosening of the body and suspension of self-consciousness; in the second, I stimulate creative, spontaneous body movement; and in the third, I help develop self-awareness, as together we examine, analyze, and integrate through action and words. In practice these phases overlap, necessitating continual decisions regarding whether to emphasize physical movement or verbal material.

The following description of these phases applies to various types of groups, such as a weekend growth experience, an ongoing therapy group or a professional workshop. The depth of the work can be altered to meet the needs and goals of any given group.

First Phase: Body-mind Warm-up

Even with very healthy and self-assured persons, encouragement and structure are necessary to create a feeling of safety in a group. Most of us have so thoroughly introjected injunctions against the public display of our bodies that some preparatory work is necessary before we can begin to allow the body to respond with spontaneity to moving impulses. However, once the initial stage fright is past, a wonderful freedom and joyousness replace it.

In a variety of ways I encourage group members to refrain from holding in their movements and their feelings. The stimulation of deep muscles by strenuous movement and deep breathing releases retroflection and thereby provokes sweating, belching, coughing, farting, sneezing, crying, giggling, dizziness, etc. I urge participants to freely indulge in these expressions of tension-release, even if they disturb others in the group. Furthermore, I ask that each person begin by concentrating on inner experiences without attending to what others are doing. Later it becomes important for participants to watch each other, imitate, criticize and cooperate, but not initially. In this way, a movement group differs from many verbal therapy groups.

In my opinion, the most essential element of all therapy is correct breathing. The breathing exercises with which every session begins vary according to the depth of therapy appropriate. In a typical group of inexperienced people we usually spend a few minutes at the beginning and ending of each session establishing a rhythmic, deep belly-breathing. Also, participants are instructed to inhale during extension and exhale during flexion when exercising or dancing. In a group with experienced members interested in intense bioenergetic work, quite a bit of time may be spent on breathing exercises using Reichian and yogic techniques.

After deep breathing and some warm-up exercises, stretches, or yoga positions, we begin with isolation exercises: Using stimulating music with strong rhythm, I take the group through a series of movements which isolate muscle groups, working first the head, then the neck, then the arms and shoulders, and so on. Through this process, group members become aware of where and how the body is blocking and holding energy; through repetitive motion and soft massage, either in pairs or by the therapist(s), we begin the loosening process. I see the total body as eventually involved in any one session, so that energies released are balanced, and stress can be compensated for in freer body areas before the session ends; we do not want to risk damaging muscles with repetitive stress or pushing through automated fixed responses.

Fantasies elecited during isolation exercises are elaborated, both verbally and in dance. For example, if a man shows special enjoyment of some arm movement, I may ask him to share his experience, placing him temporarily in the foreground of the group and amplifying the experience by having him repeat the movement until a fantasy accompanies it. Using the group to enhance the experience, I ask the others to give their fantasies in association to the movement. The same movement may elicit fantasies of digging, searching, laboring, building, burying, and so forth in group members; it will, however, have a clearly significant emotional meaning to the person in the foreground. Once the emotion is identified, the movement then can be resumed by the individual and the group, and rhythmically repeated in a cathartic and structured way.

Group participants often help each other with the maneuvers of isolation exercises, giving each other suggestions and encouragement. For example, a person with good capacity for chest motion may have just the right touch to mobilize another person who has difficulty in that area. The therapist has no exclusive claim on the talent of helping others to feel their unfelt parts; after all, therapists are by no means free of blind spots and need to allow others to fill in what they lack.

Usually during the warm-up we chant to promote the vibration of deep organs, and make babyish and animal noises to awaken deep associations. I welcome whining, growling, screaming, howling, hissing, and general zapping with sound. After years of suppressing whines and screams some people find it comforting to be supported in releasing these sounds. Others, however, may fear that this encourages animalism, lack of control, and a failure to live up to our highest nature. In response, I explain that by contacting the primitive within ourselves we are less likely to express it without awareness; we become familiar with these ancient parts of ourselves and able to make choices about how to express them. Our goal is not to revert permanently to primitive behavior, but to become aware of it within ourselves, see its value, and handle it constructively. Then we will be better equipped to understand and treat with compassion children, animals, and less developed persons. I recommend owning these disowned aspects of ourselves and expressing them in ways which do not infringe on the well-being of others.

Either in pairs or groups we do a good bit of mimicry and mirroring to make ourselves aware of the range of our expressions and how we limit this range in deference to a certain concept of character. For example, if we have defined ourselves as mild-mannered and rational, it will be difficult to find the musculature that expresses rage; if we have defined ourselves as chaste, the body language involved in the art of sexual seduction will be obscure. Thus, the group becomes a laboratory for experimentation with the development of self-expression.

Second Phase: Creative Movement

During the warm-up, spontaneous dancing or fantasy work often emerges, and it sometimes becomes necessary to explain or analyze. In general, however, the greater emphasis on eliciting imagery occurs during the second phase. In the context of pretending, playing, and dancing, we can bring back to ourselves parts that were disowned, abandoned, or imprisoned years ago, thereby enriching our personalities and enlivening our bodies. There are many imaginative exercises which stimulate fantasy and spontaneous dance. Here are some examples: dancing out a dream figure; exaggerating a motion or emotion; personifying in posture and movements an archetypical figure or a character who interests you; dancing as if you were a member of the opposite sex, or in many different sexual roles; acting as a person you fear, hate, or love; miming work, play, seduction, worship, and so forth. Music can be helpful in eliciting fantasy material, as it stimulates moods. Participants can move to the music in their imagination or through actual dancing. We may listen to soft, flowing music and allow ourselves to be carried by it to a receptive, passive attitude; then we can work with images and movements provoked by that attitude. By contrast, strong, loud music evokes assertive, active fantasy and movement. Whole sessions may be oriented around themes such as infancy, childhood play, feminine and masculine identities, birth and death. Whatever the theme, I put the structure at the service of spontaneity rather than the reverse. I use music, exercises, and suggestions to help the group members contact their own flowing movements; then, the more freedom they take, the better.

The importance of carefully gauging how far to take participants cannot be overstated. In exploring fantasy, as in breathing and warm-up, the members are aware of the time available, and the group's goals set limits for the intensity of the work involved. Even without probing, significant insights may emerge spontaneously and a person can have important and beautiful experiences with a well-structured, carefully limited approach.

On the other hand, the intensely powerful work of eliciting fantasy material and memories requires relatively experienced participants, sufficient time for working through and a commitment by the therapist to follow through until the protagonists are able to carry on alone or with another therapist. Moreover, no responsible therapist will start work until he/she has gotten to know the participants to some extent, and until the group has developed sufficient cohesiveness to provide a safe-enough environment.

Fantasy work which surfaces easily often emerges as a pleasurable experience, bringing with it a good bit of insight. For example, in moving to the fantasies evoked by the word "mother," a woman may find herself dancing out feelings which are close to consciousness about her relationship to her mother or about herself as a mother. While the experience may not provoke the emergence of any new or unknown content, it may sharpen her awareness of these feelings and contribute to an increased sensitivity to new facets of the relationship with her mother, her children, and herself. On the other hand, the same movement may evoke reactions of a different nature, such as a suddenly crystal-clear early memory of mother heretofore repressed, which carries guilt or anger— or unexpected tenderness and longing for mother—or the sudden awareness of the possibility or relationship with a Divine Mother.

As stated earlier, if we decide to explore in depth with one member a new or uncomfortable image, emotion, memory, or identity, we must allow enough time for a reasonable amount of working-through within the session in order to come to some sense of completion and closure.

Furthermore, while working with a person individually, the therapist also needs to remain aware of and in contact with the other group members. They may either stay in the background as an audience or be invited to participate in the process by, for example, picking up and portraying the same emotion. In either case, it is possible that some important memory or fantasy will be triggered off in one or more group members by the protagonist's work. These persons then need time and space in the group to work through their experiences.

Usually "difficult" fantasy material connects with physically repressed areas, so that expressing the fantasy in movement is awkward and involves the least flexible body areas. For example, a young man whose posture and movement revealed unusually tight muscles in the shoulders and upper back fantasized a paternal guide who taught him a dance. When he demonstrated the fantasy later, we noticed the strenuous arm and shoulder motions involved in this dance—which had been presented to him by a healing force within him. In order to work through this material, this man had to confront the problematic musculature. He also discovered some of the reasons for his rigidity in early conditioning and stress. In discussing his childhood fears with the group, he got in touch with the ways in which he had protected himself from those fears by becoming rigid, and how he continued to hold himself and behave as if he still needed to protect himself. By first acting out himself as a child, and then the feared persons of his childhood, he was able to discover and to integrate his own strength.

Third Phase: Conscious Integration

In this phase we reflect on what has occurred during the creative phase, discovering that there are various valuable aspects to that experience. Possibly the most valuable aspect is that, having exposed vulnerable and rejected areas of ourselves, we find that they are recognized and accepted by others. Also, the uniqueness of each person's response to the stimuli has created an abundance of material for communication, inviting exploration of the movements, ideas, and feelings that were experienced.

In this phase it becomes surprisingly easy to recapture childhood memories and to establish opportunities to be a child again in a way that permits experiencing and expressing polarities: The person who was always shy can now be a leader; the tomboy can experience being the group flirt; the jock can be a graceful dancer, and so forth. It is surprisingly easy to gain some understanding of, and compassion for, previously incomprehensible others, merely by walking in their footsteps and their posture for a while. It is surprisingly easy for a woman to empathize with a man when she has been a male for a while, and for a man to discover his maternal feelings when he has fantasized going through pregnancy and childbirth. Communication between marital partners is enhanced by such pretending, as is that of teachers and students, of employers and employees.

During this wrapping-up period, we not only analyze, but do most of our exchanging and trying-on of movements. Now the creativity of a group comes forth in offering suggestions and other help, as well as in inventing new ways to move. In this stage I consider it important to see that everyone, especially reticent members, is heard. Some participants have difficulty with the integration of thinking and feeling functions, so the therapist must confront and assist them.

This is also the time for unfinished work which, for one reason or another, was not attended to in the creative stage—for one member (or more than one at a time) to be the newborn of the group, or the dictator, medicine man, star, and so on. For a member who has always been reticent and has never been recognized or privileged, shouting commands to a group or choreographing and leading a procession can be a valuable experience, leading to growth in assertiveness. Similarly, for a high-powered executive, being "born" and nurtured by the group may be a balancing experience, expanding the range of "acceptable" behavior. (A particularly enjoyable way of providing this experience occurred to me after seeing an African tribal fertility dance. The "baby" crawls through spread legs of the group members who stand close together in a row; this is done with rhythmic music and a lot of swaying and body contact, and a great exhilarating commotion at the time of birth. This experience always brings forth important material relating to confluence, separation and contact boundaries, which can be explored further.)

During this phase we discuss where the stiffness and stress points in the body exist and with what psychic content they appear to be associated, and analyze how we keep movement from flowing smoothly. Actually, these observations begin in the isolation exercises and become more obvious as the sessions progress. A person becomes aware of tension areas through feeling sore in particular spots, through noting a lack of responsivity to a desired motion, or through the inability to imitate movements of another group member. And while it is never my goal for all to be equally limber or graceful, I do encourage all participants to stretch a little beyond their present range of motion.

Finally, this is the time for taking account of the fact that none of us is static, that we are in a continual process of change, and that with forethought and some attention to our direction we can attain some degree of choice about our future at any age and any level of flexibility.

9

The Gestalt Therapy Marathon

ELIZABETH E. MINTZ

We are in the midst of a Gestalt therapy marathon. This particular group, consisting of 12 participants divided about equally between men and women, is meeting for three days in a residential setting. We are in the middle of the second day and an atmosphere of trust and mutual concern has developed. Two episodes will be recounted, both chosen to illustrate what to this writer seems a unique advantage of this time format: Participants are able to try out at once new ways of being-in-the-world, instead of waiting until they reenter life outside the group, with the possible risk that they will once again choose old patterns of defensiveness and unawareness.

Susan, in her early thirties, wants to work. Her difficulty, as she sees it, is that she has a great need to care for other people, which is not only onerous for her but which, as she can see, is sometimes unacceptable and irritating to her protégés. Several other participants, who have been somewhat annoyed by Susan's solicitude for their welfare, confirm her description of her problem. In accordance with the Gestalt principle of polarities, which states that any extreme personality trait is almost invariably accompanied by an unawareness of the coexistence of the opposite trait,* Susan is invited to go around the circle and ask the other group members to do her a favor, give her something, or in some way take care of her.

In a ploy which will be familiar to every group therapist, Susan begins by making an attempt to sabotage the directions, pretending that she is

---

* This stratagem of requesting the client to enact the *opposite* of a pronounced personality trait, which I saw for the first time at Perls' Esalen workshops, would of course also be seen in pyschoanalytic terms as an exploration of material which has been rendered unconscious by defenses such as repression and reaction formation.

asking for something but in fact continuing to act out her pathological need to give and dominate. She makes such statements as "Do me a favor and stop putting yourself down," or "You'd make me feel better if you sat up straight." The group, not unexpectedly, very quickly sees through her ploy and without my intervention suggests that she begin again and accept the original suggestion.

The intensity of Susan's reaction would be astonishing to anyone who has not previously seen the terror which can be experienced when an individual abandons role-playing and reaches the level of experience at which she/he must either remain frozen or else reach a more authentic level of self-expression—the point which Gestalt therapists call "the impasse." Susan finds herself literally unable to speak. Her whole self-concept, her whole way of relating to people, has since childhood depended upon being a caretaker. The group watches in empathic silence as she stands gasping, with a slight body tremor. It is an enormous relief to everyone when she finally says, in a high squeaky voice, "Would . . . would . . . would you get me some coffee, please?" There is a burst of friendly laughter, and the group member to whom she has spoken goes immediately for coffee.

Thereafter it is somewhat easier for Susan to continue around the circle, though she has trouble thinking of requests. She is enormously supported by the friendly laughter, which helps her understand that there is nothing unacceptable to others in expressing dependency as part of her total self. As often happens when the trip through the impasse is successful, she ends the circle with a burst of joy, and is actually able to request and receive affectionate embraces from two or three participants.

Thus far, this episode is no different from any other successful episode in Gestalt therapy. It exemplifies the therapeutic technique of asking the protagonist to enact the opposite side of a polar trait which has been kept outside awareness; it makes use of the group as a therapeutic partner; and it takes the protagonist from the role-playing layer of personality into the impasse (the "dead" layer) and through the impasse into re-owning the trait—in this case, dependency—which had been denied. The group's support was important. I consider laughter (empathic laughter, never ridicule) as a powerful therapeutic instrument, since it helps the protagonist see that his/her fears of becoming aware and authentic are unrealistic.

However, the marathon time-format enabled Susan to carry her experiences a step further. Since the group remained together at all times, including mealtimes and recreation periods, she was requested to do "homework" during the remainder of the weekend. She must never get her own coffee, but must ask someone to bring it. She must ask for a floor cushion if she wants one. She must ask someone else to put a log on the fire if it was needed. And she must never, never offer to do anything for anyone else. This assignment, naturally, became a running joke, but it had serious value. It enabled Susan to see how ingrained her counterdependency approach to life had become and to test out new ways of relating in a variety of interpersonal situations. Of course, this was a humorous exaggeration of Susan's problem, but the humor helped to diminish Susan's anxiety and helped her to become more at home with the disowned aspect of her personality.

The second episode, from the same marathon, has to do with the overcoming of a specific phobia, the fear of water. Marilyn, a generally capable, middle-aged social worker, does not join the group in their afternoon swim at a nearby lake. Rather ashamedly, she reports later that she has never been able to overcome her fear of putting her head under water and of entering water over her depth; hence she has never learned to swim. Her college graduation had actually been jeopardized because she had been unable to pass one of the minimum requirements in physical education, swimming the width of an indoor pool.

Marilyn is requested to conduct a dialogue between herself, as Marilyn, and the water. As the water, she is very threatening. She says, "I'll overwhelm you . . . I'll choke you . . . I'll swallow you up." As Marilyn, she acts out of her terror. After she has expressed both the terror and the threat, she is asked to go around the circle, as the water, and threaten to choke and overwhelm the other group members. She is able to do this, at first with anxiety, then with playful enjoyment.

Marilyn's fear of being choked and overwhelmed was expressed quite fully, although its origins did not emerge. However, when the group went to the lake again the next day, Marilyn was able, with the help of another group member, to put her head under water several times. The next day she was able to swim several strokes in water over her head, and a few weeks later wrote proudly to say that she was now swimming every week.

The success of this episode, of course, depended partly on the chance circumstance that the marathon met at a lakeside setting. However, it is noteworthy that Marilyn's letter also included the information that she had attempted to learn to swim many times, with competent instructors and in the company of encouraging friends, and had never been able to overcome her phobia until the marathon.

Here, in addition to the opportunity of being able to try out immediately new ways of feeling and behaving in a group setting, are the special values of marathon groups, as I see them:*

> 1) Development of a sense of safety in the group, based partly on a growing awareness of the commonality of human experiences and partly on the feeling of mutual warmth and concern which nearly always comes to characterize these groups.
>
> 2) Intensification of the awareness of here-and-now experience, which is facilitated because group members are not required to return to the demands of daily life within an hour or two, as with conventional once- or twice-a-week therapy.
>
> 3) An opportunity to deal with the same emotional difficulty several times during the marathon, experiencing it in several ways, and, hopefully, at least reclaiming the energy which has been bound up in conflict and using it in the here-and-now.

These are powerful therapeutic forces and the Gestalt marathon is a powerful therapeutic instrument. Its prototype, of course, is Fritz Perls' famous one- or two-week workshop at Esalen and elsewhere. Many contemporary marathon therapists, however, do not follow Perls' approach precisely but instead prefer to allow time for free group interaction and upon occasion to involve participants directly with one another in role-playing and encounter exercises.

Moreover, the marathon time-format minimizes two of the limitations which, rightly or wrongly, are sometimes adduced by critics of the approach used by Perls: namely, that it is episodic in nature, dealing piecemeal with emotional problems rather than assisting the client to see the relationship between specific problems and his general life-style (Mintz, 1973), and that it does not offer the client a sustained emotional contact with the therapist (Bergantino, 1977).

These generalizations apply to most marathons, but every group is different. In 15 years of conducting Gestalt marathons, I have never been able to predict the way in which group members will interact or the

---

* Here the term *marathon* is defined simply as a time-extended group in which members remain together for a therapeutic experience from two to five days or even longer. My preference is to allow ample time for sleep, since I believe that defenses should be relinquished voluntarily in an atmosphere of trust and security (Mintz, 1971), rather than being eroded by group pressure and physical fatigue (Bach, 1966).

specific material with which individuals will choose to work—nor do I try to influence these choices. The Gestalt principle—that psychotherapeutic "work" comes from within the client himself and is not predetermined by the therapist—is relevant for marathons also. A marathon, therefore, is always a surprise. After having conducted a total of perhaps 200 marathons, I am still quite unable to predict what a specific group of people will do together or individually.

Psychoanalytic theory holds that, in the beginning and at the end, an individual psychoanalysis is fairly predictable, but that its middle course differs with each individual. This is true also of marathons. In the beginning, there is nearly always a period of what Gestalt therapists see as the first layer of personality, the surface layer of polite and meaningless exchanges about the weather, the transportation, and so on; it is part of the leader's responsibility to see that this phase is as short as possible, perhaps only two or three minutes. At the end, if the marathon has been successful, there is an atmosphere of great mutual warmth and appreciation, directed at least as much toward other group participants as toward the leader. The middle phase, the actual working phase, is always unique.

Here is a description of a Gestalt marathon, focused on the experiences of one participant, Janet, a personable woman in her early fifties, unmarried, headmistress of a school for emotionally disturbed children. This group consisted of 13 men and women meeting in a country setting, from Friday through Sunday afternoon.*

The first task of the leaders,** as I perceive it, is to help the group move beyond the surface layer of personality into an atmosphere of greater authenticity, which in turn gradually establishes a sense of safety in which meaningful therapeutic work can be conducted. My favorite opening, to which I have always returned after occasionally trying other openings, is to go around the circle with the simple instruction: "Tell the group something you really want us to know about yourself. Not necessarily your most painful problem or your deepest secret, but something you really want the group to know about you." Nearly always, the

---

* The question of whether or not marathon participants should be screened is often asked. My choice is for some preliminary screening whether through a brief interview, detailed letter, or the recommendation of a colleague (Mintz, 1971). Janet had come into the marathon through the recommendation of a therapist with whom she had worked individually.

** In this marathon my co-therapist was John Brinley.

non-specific nature of this request elicits responses which carry considerable feeling, and most group members reply by describing here-and-now anxiety, by stating what they hope to get out of the marathon or by bringing up a significant emotional problem.

Janet's contribution to the go-around appeared superficial, although it transpired later that it was truly a significant symbol. She said, with a rather coquettish evasiveness, "Well, I don't know . . . I'm not sure why I'm here, except I guess I thought it might be fun . . . but I was thinking, what do I want to work on? And I thought, snakes. I've always been afraid of snakes. So I thought, maybe that is what I want to work on."

In this initial go-around, participants are asked not to question or comment until everyone has spoken, after which there is a free interchange which enables the group members to know one another better and to express their feelings toward one another. Usually this initial phase of free encounter leads into intensive work with one of the participants. The participant who is working usually is asked to move forward into the center of the circle (group members sit on floor cushions rather than on chairs), a position which corresponds to the famous "hot-seat," the empty chair which stood beside Perls' chair at Esalen, in which a group member would place himself as a signal that he was ready to work. The center-of-circle position, used by many Gestalt group therapists today, has a different symbolic implication. It denotes that the group itself is a therapeutic agent equal in importance to the leader, and it gives the central participant a sense of being surrounded by supportive and benevolent energy.

The actual therapeutic approach, as used by myself and many other Gestalt group leaders, may vary, although it always is focused on bringing feelings, memories, conflicts and habitual characterological attitudes into an experiential here-and-now. In accordance with my belief that a basic principle of the Gestalt approach to therapy is *flexibility*, I freely use techniques borrowed from psychodrama, bioenergetics, encounter therapy, and transactional analysis, attempting to choose whatever method seems appropriate for *this* individual participant at *this* specific time. Sometimes the approach is intensive one-to-one therapy, differing little from what might be used in an individual session, although an effort is always made to end the therapeutic episode by bringing the participant back into contact with the group-as-a-whole. Sometimes the group itself becomes the primary therapeutic agent, offering feedback, confrontation and nurturance. In general, it can be said that the group represents external reality, while one-to-one Gestalt work affords the participant an opportunity to explore feelings which ordinarily lie beyond the bounds of full awareness.

In the particular marathon through which we are following Janet, she did not offer to work until several hours had passed, although she was empathic and attentive to whatever happened in the group. Finally, there was a lull in the group and another participant looked across the room and said to Janet, "Hey, there, what happened to your snake?" and Janet moved into the center of the circle.

As an exploratory approach, I began by asking a group member for a belt, to represent the snake; it would also have been possible to request Janet simply to visualize a snake, but I have found that "props" often help the protagonist to focus feelings. Janet, now, was asked to talk to the snake:

Janet: I don't like you . . . you're boneless. You're going to cling to me . . . to twine around my body . . Uggh! I don't like you, you scare me, you're so clinging . . .

When Janet was then asked to play the snake and to reply to Janet, her voice remained the same, rather dead and passive, and the content of what she said also was the same.

Janet: I'm going to cling to you . . . I'll coil around your body . . . I'll cling to you . . . you won't be able to move . . ."

Clearly, Janet was identified with the snake, whatever it might mean to her. A polarity had not been established between the clinging snake and whatever part of Janet's self was still beyond awareness. In accordance with the traditional Gestalt technique of asking the protagonist to do to others what he is afraid they will do to him, she was asked to go around the group and "play the snake." She complied, with some enjoyment of the playful situation, but without much energy, pantomiming snake-motions and repeating "I'll cling to you . . . I'll coil around you . . . I'll keep you from moving." Still no polarity.

"Would someone play a snake for Janet, please?" It is a source of endless delight and amazement to me that when a volunteer is asked to play a role, a volunteer almost invariably emerges who is exactly right for the part—not in terms of histrionic ability but in terms of meshing of the unconscious needs of volunteer and protagonist. In this instance, the volunteer was Pedro, who had hitherto been quiet and reserved, but who now suddenly revealed great perceptiveness. As the snake, he approached Janet stealthily and wound around her, coiling and clinging, with a sensuality which fell just short of being inappropriate for the group situation. Janet laughed in pleasure slightly tinged with embarrassment, and the group applauded.

Although I personally do not share the classical Gestalt position that interpretation by the therapist is *never* useful (a position which, in my observation, is occasionally disregarded by many other Gestalt therapists besides myself), I have often observed that the *group* reaction to a thera-peutic episode is often equivalent to an interpretation and carries even more impact. Pedro's "snake" elicited a pleased and embarrassed laugh from Janet, a spattering of applause from the group, and a few side remarks such as "That's a sexy snake!" In psychoanalytic theory, of course, a snake is frequently regarded as a sexual symbol, and this inter-pretation had clearly been suggested, though without conscious inten-tion on Pedro's part. Very frequently, spontaneous group interaction in itself suggests a dramatization of an interpretation which might well be offered in the most formal psychoanalytic tradition (Mintz, 1974), and it can be extremely efficacious. It was obvious that Janet, on some level, had become aware that her snake carried some kind of sexual significance.

We had not yet established the polarity or reached the impasse, but when Janet said, "I want to stop for now," her wish was accepted. Here is another advantage of the time-extended group; a participant who has made some progress in an area of conflict or of unawareness, but who does not feel ready to continue at the time, can stop temporarily and return later to the same problem. Theoretically, this choice to interrupt the work may be seen as resistance, in which case the participant usually shows signs of tension or anxiety; then I make an effort to help the protagonist become aware of the tension. However, the choice may also represent a healthy need to pause and integrate the partial awareness, or to gather energy afresh, in which case the protagonist seems relaxed and comfortable. Janet appeared relaxed and we were sure that she would return again to her symbolic snake. There were still two full days left.

In the next working session, a group theme emerged, having to do at first with parents' expectation for their children. Participants shared their anger at demands which they had experienced as unreasonable or limit-ing, their guilt over not having met these demands, and their hope that they could still live up to these expectations. Although some Gestalt therapists prefer to regard accounts of childhood experience and other experiences outside the here-and-now as non-productive "gossip," it is my belief that, especially in a time-extended group, it is extremely worthwhile for group members to share significant life experiences; it helps the individual gain perspective on his own life, it diminishes anxiety by the recognition that others have similar experiences and feelings, and it brings the group closer together. As the leader, of course, I seek opportunities to translate this verbal sharing of experiences into immediate therapeutic experiences, through a Gestalt dialogue, psychodrama or any other appropriate method.

In this session, Janet told us that her mother had treated her in a kindly, though overprotective, manner and had always seemed to assume that children are reasonable and can be controlled by rational appeals. Someone asked how her mother had handled the snake phobia, which had begun very early, and Janet was invited to answer this question through a Gestalt dialogue, playing the parts of both her mother and herself.

Janet: Mommy, I'm scared of snakes.
"Mother": Now dear, there aren't snakes in the house or garden and anyhow, they wouldn't hurt you.
Janet: But I dream about them.
"Mother": Then don't dream about them, dear.

As the mother and as the child, Janet's tone was almost identical. Again we had established no polarity; in psychoanalytic terms, the introjected mother was not perceived as ego-alien. We tried variations. Janet was asked to play mother at her best (good-mother) and mother at her worst (bad-mother), but these two roles emerged as very similar in their kindliness, rationality and detachment, and again Janet's voice and manner were similar as mother and as child.

In an effort to establish some distance from the introject, we asked for a volunteer from the group to play opposite Janet, first as her mother and then (switching roles) as Janet herself. And the same thing happened. As mother and as child, Janet used the same subdued voice. However, a new feature of the inner situation did emerge through gestures and physical contact: Role-playing herself, with a real person role-playing her mother, Janet moved closer and closer to the woman seated opposite on the floor, with a kind of stealthiness in the manner which was reminiscent of the way she had moved while playing the snake. Should I describe to her what I saw? Not yet, I decided; she would probably find the idea very interesting, but since there was still no polarity, my description would only be an interesting idea.

In therapy, especially with the Gestalt approach, the unexpected can be expected to happen, and now suddenly a memory from Janet's childhood broke through. To tease her, her five-year-old brother had hidden under the bed and had seized her ankle, refusing to let go. Janet, three years old, had been at first frightened, then pleased and excited by the little scuffle. Again we enacted the childhood scene, with a man from the group playing Janet's little brother. There was more feeling now, more aliveness, an expression of affection, and the episode ended in an embrace. Janet was delighted with the recovered memory, and told us that her relationship with her brother had been the happiest part of her childhood, because of the detachment of her parents. They had clung to each other, Janet said. It was the snake theme again, the theme of clinging, but again it seemed to me wisest not to point this out to Janet. Thanks to the time luxury of the marathon format, we could hope that eventually she herself would break through into awareness and integration of whatever the snake-symbol meant to her.

Here it is worthwhile to consider under what circumstances it seems best to ask the protagonist to play both parts when we are dealing with an unassimilated part of the personality or a toxic introject which may emerge as bad-me, top-dog, bad-mother, bad-father and so on. This, of course, is the well-known Gestalt empty chair technique, and it is usually the optimal choice when there is already some awareness of the inner split; that is, when some polarity has been recognized by the protagonist. When the protagonist plays both parts, the pure introject may emerge uninfluenced by outside stimuli.

However, there are other advantages in having a group member (or, in some instances, the group leader) play the role of the introject. An external symbol of the introject, another human being, may serve to establish distance between the identified, conscious, aware self and the alien, unassimilated part. Also, the role-playing member may intuitively pick up some aspect of the unassimilated part-self of which the protagonist is unaware, as Pedro had picked up the latent sensuality of Janet's snake-symbol. And finally, it often happens that certain attitudes toward the parental figure, or toward the unassimilated bad-me part of the personality may be revealed through the physical interaction between the protagonist and the role-player. For example, it occurs very frequently that when the protagonist is working with a conscious, verbalized wish to separate from a dominating or possessive parent, and when someone else plays the parent, the protagonist shows unmistakably by physical gestures, such as reaching out and moving closer, that he himself is holding on to the parental figure. This had occurred with Janet, whose physical movements when she was role-playing opposite a brother-figure and a mother-figure had strongly suggested clinging and dependency.

Very often, also, there are striking fringe benefits for the group member who plays the auxiliary role. Repeatedly, I have seen participants get into contact with important feelings of their own through role-playing a significant person in someone else's life. In this marathon, for example, the man who had role-played Janet's brother moved into an episode, extremely meaningful to him, having to do with his repression of his grief and guilt over the death of a younger sister when he was a child.

The marathon was now in the evening of its second day. In these groups, nearly always, a natural rhythm occurs between intense therapeutic episodes and spontaneous, natural discussion of life situations. Now, for the first time, Janet revealed something of tremendous importance in her life. For many years, she had been deeply involved with a man who, for reasons of his own, was unable or unwilling to leave his wife. At one time, she had actually declined the offer of a better academic position in another part of the country because it would mean separation from him. At the same time, she was extremely dissatisfied with the relationship, not only because of his commitment to his wife, but because the relationship in itself was not satisfying. The man was dependent, passive, and ungiving.

True to its reality-function, the group worked hard with Janet. Did she consider herself free to date other men? Yes, sometimes she had tried, but her lover was so hurt and so possessive! What did she gain from the relationship? Well, it was mostly that *he* needed *her*. And how long had it gone on? The answer to this question was a shocker. It was hard for Janet to reply. At last she admitted that this relationship had continued since her early thirties—a full 20 years.

The group questioned, argued, cajoled and reassured. Couldn't Janet understand that she was an attractive woman, a vital woman, that other interests would be available to her? Couldn't she see that she was being emotionally exploited? Wasn't she wasting her life? All this, presumably, was useful; Janet was receiving support and perhaps also was wanting to hear from the group what she had been saying to herself in secret, without full awareness.

"Why *do* you stay with him?" asked someone.

Janet's voice, by now, was less subdued and tentative. She said, "I always thought it was because I loved him. Now I'm not so sure. He—well, he *clings* to me!"

Now came the revelation. Janet's face lit up in the "ah-ha!" experience which is not only delightful for the participant (even if the insight is painful) but also for the whole group and its leaders.

". . . like a snake!" said Janet gleefully. The pieces of the jigsaw had come together, spontaneously, as a result of our two days of intermittent work. Now came an outpouring from Janet, and fresh revelations. She had tried several times to break off with him, but had always yielded to his importunities and to his protestations that he needed her. Right now, she told us, she was in a break-off period. She had told him good-bye. But she knew what would happen. He would telephone her, and she would give in again.

"I'm spineless," Janet said, and two of the group members finished her sentence.

". . . like a snake!"

"What will you do now?"

"Well I'll break off with him. For keeps." But neither my co-therapist nor I nor the group was convinced. It was time for a dialogue, which would take place by telephone, since this was how her lover always sought reconciliation.

As a beginning, Janet played both parts. As the lover, she was clinging, pleading and dependent. As herself, she began by being somewhat firm in her decision, but gradually weakened as "he" pleaded with her. There was, however, one wonderful unconscious slip. As the lover, consciously intending to say "please understand me," she actually said, "don't understand me." The group shouted with friendly laughter, but there was no sense of resolution. Janet's voice and manner remained almost the same when she role-played her lover and when she played herself. There was still no real awareness of her own inner polariy, no recognized separation between the healthy, self-actualizing part of Janet and the part of her which was clinging and passive, as represented by her lover and also by the symbol of the snake.

"Get up and stomp the snake," said my co-therapist. Janet complied, stomping on an imaginary snake. At first she was tentative, then gradually she gained energy, stomping harder and harder. She sat down looking flushed and vital, and now we could return to the telephone conversation with her lover, Janet again playing both roles.

This time, as the lover, she was able to exaggerate the passive, whining, clinging quality, and for the first time Janet's sense of humor—which had already been apparent in free group interaction—came into evidence in relation to her own situation. Her opening words, in the lover's imaginary phone call, were a caricature of her description of the man.

"It's only me," said Janet, in a self-deprecatory tone.

As Janet, she now sounded firmer and more energetic. "Oh, it's you! Why are you calling me?"

The dialogue continued. It was different. As the lover, Janet grew more and more clinging, less and less attractive. As herself, she remained firm. Her final words, "Good-bye, don't call again," were greeted by clapping from the group as she hung up.

The group now gave Janet the environmental support which she needed in rebuilding her life. They asked what plans she had for new activities, whether she would now be able to travel more widely on vacations, how she would find new friends. This was not difficult, since Janet had never been a recluse, and evidently had available to her many more resources, socially and professionally, than she had fully used. She was elated and energetic, but she accepted the warning that for the next few weeks, perhaps for months, she would perhaps be subject to occasional depressions and regrets. The group, as usually happens, functioned magnificently as the representative of reality.

On a cognitive and theoretical level, it was clear to my co-therapist and me what the snake meant to Janet in terms of her long, unsatisfying love-relationship. When she had announced to the group, in the beginning, that she would like to work on her snake phobia, she had actually given us the key to her problem, even though it might well have appeared that she was resistant and evasive.

If Janet's case history were to be reconstructed along theoretical lines, we can see that her dependent needs were never gratified in childhood, because of the rational detachment of her mother; she tried to cling to her mother, unsuccessfully, and instead found some gratification from her brother. The clinging and dependent part of her personality, however, remained unsatisfied. Thus, when she found a clinging and dependent lover, he served a double purpose. Not only did he gratify her "sick" needs directly, but he also represented the split-off part of herself which was clinging and dependent.

All this was clear, and since I believe that cognitive integration is not necessarily "elephant-shit," if and when it follows a genuine emotional experience, my co-therapist and I summarized briefly for Janet our perception of her situation. What remained still unclear was the meaning of the early episode with Pedro, in which he had brought out the implicit sensuality of the snake symbol, which had left Janet more relaxed and comfortable. She did, however, tell us (in response to group questioning) that her relationship with her lover had been sexually gratifying at first, but had long since ceased to be so. My own conjecture was that, for this reason, Janet's sensuality had also become split-off, and that Pedro's intuitive role-playing had not only reminded her that she was still a sensual woman, but also carried the implication that an attractive man might well enjoy her sensuality. This, however, was only a conjecture and I did not share my speculation.

When the marathon ended the next day, Janet continued to give an appearance of zestfulness and energy. She exchanged phone numbers with several group members and was looking forward to new activities. Several group members reinforced her decision not to yield again to her lover's importunities and she seemed firm. Several months later, she wrote to my co-therapist and me, saying that she had been able to maintain her independent position and was finding it enjoyable, although not easy.

Despite its extraordinary power as a therapeutic technique, the marathon time-format does have limitations and is by no means a substitute for the prolonged therapeutic experience provided by an ongoing group or by one-to-one therapy, which offers clients an opportunity to grow and change over an extended period of time with the support of a therapeutic relationship. The marathon is occasionally criticized as affording an emotional "binge" with little carry-over into subsequent emotional and behavioral adjustment. This criticism, in my opinion, is valid only in relation to untrained leaders who emphasize group encounter techniques designed to afford intense emotional experience, without sufficient attention to the group members as individuals.

My own profound conviction is that the optimum approach, which I have attempted to describe here, involves a flexible leadership with individual participants, and also involves the utilization of the group itself as a therapeutic force, principally as the representative of reality, but also as a supportive and nurturant environment. Here, indeed, I personally differ from some Gestalt therapists who interpret Perls' position as advocating total deprivation of environmental support. Here is an interesting technical and philosophical point. Having had the unique and magnificent experience of working with Fritz Perls, and having used what I learned from him in my own practice, I believe that the deprivation of environmental support applies only to the role-playing layer of personality, the phony layer, the acting-out of the mandates of the toxic introject. In Perls' work, when the authentic and aware part of the personality emerged at the end of a successful Gestalt episode, there nearly always occurred a friendly, sensual and celebrative bear-hug between Fritz and the protagonist. In marathons, the breakthrough of an authentic awareness, the successful trip through the impasse, often ends with embrace between the protagonist and group members. Environmental support is given to the person who is facing the pain of a trip through the impasse; environmental reward is given to the person who negotiates it successfully.

The ending of a Gestalt marathon is important. Most groups begin to show signs of separation anxiety within half-a-day of the group's ending. This may take the form of a sudden departure into superficial conversation ("I saw a movie which reminded me of . . .") or, more frankly, of a wish that the openness and warmth of a marathon could be directly carried over into the outside life, or of a need to exchange phone numbers and make further contact with the other participants.

There are specific technical ways to handle this separation phase. My policy is to devote the last two or three hours of a marathon to the question "What will I do tonight and tomorrow morning?" This question provides a bridge for participants between the ending of the group and their return to daily life.

A final go-around, which I adopted from Perls' ending of the Esalen workshops, consists of asking the question "What did you appreciate and what did you resent about this experience which we had together?" This question gives participants a last chance to express dissatisfaction or irritation with other group members, the leadership, or the working conditions. It also offers an opportunity to express affection and sometimes, on a cognitive level, to formulate whatever has been gained through the experiences of the marathon.

The marathon ends. Since separation is a part of life, and since facing separation is possibly one of the most difficult human experiences, I am deeply convinced that a marathon should end promptly at the pre-agreed time. If participants have been prepared for the ending, it is a significant part of the total therapeutic experience.

Section III

EDUCATIONAL APPLICATIONS

10

Educating for Autonomy: A Gestalt Approach to Higher Education

JOHN DAVID FLYNN

Consider the unqualified statement: A worthy and necessary aim of university education should be to foster the autonomy of each student. One implication of this view is that much of what passes as "educational practice" may, in fact, be anti-educational. There are also a number of other immediately interesting implications. Teaching would not qualify as educating unless the teacher were at least seeking to foster the autonomy of each student. Moreover, the educator's attempts would not count as successful in a given case unless each student actually chose to become in some way more autonomous as a direct or indirect result of the educator's intentions.

I think that college educators do have the responsibility to foster the autonomy of each student, that many teachers do not define their role in this way, and that even those who do often do not understand the process of moving someone toward autonomy well enough to be of much help.

It is with respect to this last problem that a discussion of Gestalt group process can be especially useful to educators. In my courses, I am aware of autonomy mostly by its absence. My students are not already autonomous readers, writers, discussants, interpreters and experimenters, and they rarely want to be. Yet, I want them to become more autonomous in these respects. My work, then, is to find or invent ways for them to become more aware of what is at stake and of how they can choose to have these abilities for themselves. Gestalt group therapy provides one model for doing this. Gestalt therapists have developed an effective "autonomogenic" group process.

By "autonomogenic process," I mean an enterprise which is organized both to foster awareness of an autonomous potential where that awareness is lacking and to encourage a movement toward that bit of autonomy. Gestalt therapists devise relevant autonomogenic experiments for both individuals and the group-as-a-whole which draw on the safe background of group supportiveness. The supportiveness itself has to be developed; it provides an optimal condition of autonomogenic experimenting. A group of people, initially relative strangers, will be more willing to work together toward greater autonomy when there is trust. Once a spirit of trust in the process has been generally established, the movement toward individual and group self-support can occupy the foreground of the therapeutic process.

I have found that this sort of Gestalt group approach to teaching is an effective frame in which to create and support each student's desire to learn autonomously. And because of the central role that imaginative experiment and group participation play in its method of working, it is likely to make the movement toward autonomy more enjoyable for both students and teachers.

This chapter falls into two parts. In the first part, I stand with those who regard educating students toward autonomy as both important in itself and as an antidote to the generally stupifying effects of socialization. I also explain, in general, what educating someone toward autonomy might mean. In the second part, I give some illustrations of how the autonomogenic structure of Gestalt group process might be used in a college course. I select a few typical educational issues, sketch out a systematic Gestalt approach to them, and then discuss some of the ways in which students can be motivated through individual and group experiments to move themselves toward autonomy.

I. EDUCATING FOR AUTONOMY

Although my initial claims about what autonomy means will have to be qualified and elucidated as we go along, I intend them to mark out a partial answer to what I consider the central question of the philosophy of education and of educational practice: What are the most desirable dispositions or states of mind for an educator to foster in a person?

In practice, the question is answered every day, well or badly, reflectively or unreflectively, by those who occupy the position of educator and who then, to some degree, affect the lives of people for generations. We try to answer it explicitly and reflectively because we want to have a clearer and more settled resolve about what is educationally desirable and what we need to know or do in order to accomplish this.

Education is always going on in human culture at every level of development. Education, in the sense of the relatively unorganized processes of socialization, is a brute fact of human existence. Each new generation is brought, often fearfully, unreflectively and resentfully, onto the tracks set down by the generations before. Each new generation is schooled to define a world and behave in that world in ways regarded as desirable by its predecessors, ways which they insist be regarded as desirable. In our social and personal lives we are each to a greater or lesser extent the product of the product of preceding generations. Our socialization generally produces an unreflective drift through history. Self-reflective education represents one of our attempts to take charge of this uncanny drift and govern it from the inside.

There are thinkers who do not regard the pursuit of autonomy to be the way to best try to govern history. Plato, in *The Republic*, thought that the majority of people were genetically unsuited to such a life, and Dostoevsky, through his demonic figure, the Grand Inquisitor, presents a characteristically ironic and ambivalent argument for the unreflective and unfree will. The inquisitor is speaking to Jesus, who has made an unwelcome appearance during the Inquisition in Spain:

> Didst thou forget that man prefers peace, and even death, to freedom of choice in the knowledge of good and evil? Nothing is more seductive for man than his freedom of conscience, but nothing is a greater cause of suffering . . . (1936, p. 264)
>
> . . . Thou didst lift them up and thereby taught them to be proud. We will show them that they are weak, that they are only pitiful children, but that childlike happiness is the sweetest of all . . . (1936, p. 266)
>
> . . . The most painful secrets of their conscience, all, all they will bring to us, and we shall have an answer for all. And they will be glad to believe our answer, for it will save them from the great anxiety and terrible agony they endure at present in making a free decision for themselves (1936, p. 269).

The Grand Inquisitor is not entirely wrong. When people have been "educated" to be dependent, autonomy is a burden and the process of reaching for it especially anguishing.

However, it was just cultivation and encouragement of free and authentic decision-making, defamed by the Inquisitor, which John Stuart Mill defended as the moral basis of democracy in his spirited essay *On Liberty* (1910). Mill argued that the fostering of this complex disposition (he called it "individuality") is, all things considered, more conducive to meaningful living than any set of legal and social constraints by which a person's choices might be shaped. He insisted that it is desirable, in education and elsewhere, to give:

> . . . the fullest scope possible to uncustomary things, in order that it may in time appear which of these are fit to be converted into custom (1910, p. 125).

Social progress, Mill thought, depends on the development of individual autonomy. The movement toward autonomy provides not only the opportunity for the best life of which the individual is capable, but also the conditions for the best life of which the culture is capable. Competition among the ideas of autonomous persons will strengthen truth and tend to root out error.

In rough outline, then, the idea of autonomy is the idea of being free to decide for oneself what one will do or be. Etymologically, to be autonomous means to be self-governing or self-determining. Now, suppose that I have an irresistible craving for chocolate ice cream and I indulge it. It was my want and I acted on it. Wasn't I self-determining and therefore autonomous? No. If the craving was irresistible I was not free not to choose it. This brings out a further aspect of autonomy: Not every choice of mine is autonomous just because it is mine. To be self-governing means not only the absence of obvious external constraints (a gun at my head, handcuffs, locked doors and the like), but also the lack of obvious internal constraints (such as compulsive desires and obsessive thoughts).

Is this what our notion of autonomy comes to? Am I autonomous when I am not obviously externally or internally coerced? If there were nothing more to it, autonomy would be widespread. It would characterize most of us most of the time. Yet this feels wrong or at least too simple: The unreflective drift of much of our ordinary life is non-autonomous even though we are not prevented from doing what we want and are not pathologically compulsive. We must probe more deeply.

The philosopher, Harry Frankfort, has developed some distinctions which will give us more leverage. The distinctions will frame the complexity of moving toward autonomy more clearly. Frankfort points out that I can have many other sorts of first-order desires besides compulsive ones such as my craving for chocolate ice cream. In addition, I possess two related second-order abilities which are distinctive of my being a person: 1) I have the ability to form second-order desires—to want to have or to be moved by certain desires to act; and 2) I have the even more important ability to form second-order volitions—to want certain first-order desires to be my *will*, i.e., to actually motivate me to act.

> Besides wanting and choosing and being moved to *do* this or that, men may also want to have (or not have) certain desires and motives. They are capable of wanting to be different, in their preferences and purposes, from what they are. Many animals appear to have the capacity for what I shall call "first-order desires" which are simply desires to do or not to do one thing or another. No animal other than man, however, appears to have the capacity for reflective self-evaluation that is manifested in the formation of second-order desires (Frankfort, 1971, p. 7).

> . . . when he wants a certain desire to be his will . . . I shall call his second-order desires "second-order volitions" (1971, p. 10).

We can use these distinctions both to explain my lack of autonomy in one sort of ordinary case, and to develop the idea further. Suppose I am a student who is disposed to ignore his work. As a result, I fail or do badly on an exam. I sincerely resolve never to ignore my work again. I want to have the will of a conscientious student. But, in fact, I do not change. This is a typical sort of case—and not only in education. My second-order volition is to do my work, but my effective desire, my will, is to continue to ignore the work.

This case reveals a number of things which are relevant to our understanding of the movement toward autonomy. It shows that a second-order volition to make a certain will one's own does not become effective just by resolving or deciding on it. In some cases I may have to go through a long process in which I continuously try to persuade myself, offer myself inducements, bribes, threats and so on before I am fully committed to wanting a new will. In education, this suggests that students will need to be given many opportunities to persuade and repersuade themselves that what they are doing is what they want to will to do.

The case also shows, more importantly, that I do not have free will. I have a will I don't want and I don't have the will I sincerely want. I have not been able to govern myself. To enjoy free will, for Frankfort, is to have the ability to have the will one wants. This is one level of self-governance. My actions and inactions, in this case, testify that I do not have this ability.*

We can now try to give more positive content to our original intuitions about autonomy. It appears that I am more autonomous or become more autonomous when I am able to go through a process of reflective self-evaluation to acquire the power of a free will. Frankfort thinks that this is all the freedom that a person could hope for:

> Suppose . . . that . . . a person enjoys both freedom of action and freedom of the will. Then he is not only free to do what he wants to do; he is also free to want what he wants to wants. It seems to me that he has, in that case, all the freedom it is possible to desire or to conceive. There is nothing in the way of freedom that he lacks (1971, p. 17).

This idea—if I have free will, I am free to have the will I want—is very close to the core of our intuitions about autonomy. But it is also ambiguous and potentially misleading. Interpreted in one way, I could be free to have the will I want and not be autonomous. Interpreted otherwise, if I enjoy free will, I would be moving toward autonomy. This difference is crucial to understanding what educating someone toward autonomy might mean. Let me try to spell this out.

As I indicated earlier, everyone is born into a particular position in the social fabric and provided with a language, habits of thought, emotion and motivation which he/she did not make or reflectively choose.

Yet my position in this world and yours are never neutral. Though I may be unreflective about it, I will to do (or not to do) this or that and my actions have consequences. For example, I do not *mean* to be opportunistic—that is simply the unreflective pattern of my life. It was the mood of my family, perhaps. I may not even be aware that my conduct could be interpreted in these terms. Yet that could be how others experience what I do.

In the larger sense, we would not want to say that I enjoy free will with respect to my opportunism. I am not really free to have some other

---

* I cannot attempt to do full justice to Frankfort's interesting analysis of free will here.

will. Since I am not even aware of the present tendency of my will *as* opportunism, I could not be expected to consider calling it into question. In this case, my lack of free will is also a lack of a certain freedom of mind.

Yet, in another sense, I might drift within my opportunism and still enjoy free will. This is the important ambiguity. It is true that from one perspective my explicit and reflective choices, my second-order volitions, can be seen to take place within a wider unreflective frame. But that is not my perspective. I did not originally choose my opportunism in a self-evaluative way, but I do reflectively decide where, when and how I am going to be opportunistic. I do have the ability to have this rather than that particular sort of opportunistic will if I want it. I can enjoy free will and yet be unreflectively opportunistic.

Obviously something has gone wrong. Our intuition is that being caught up in the orbit of some secondhand pattern of conduct is a mark of a non-autonomous person. We also indicated that enjoying free will was, perhaps, the core idea in autonomy. Yet here we have a case where a choice of will is both self-directed and also caught in an unreflective drift.

The way out is to distinguish between "internal" and "external" second-order volitions. My second-order choice can be made, as just indicated, from within the frame of a pattern of unreflective choice or can challenge that frame from outside of it. It is only in the second case that I am moving toward autonomy, because it is only then that my choice becomes genuine or firsthand.

What I am suggesting is that I approach autonomy only when I raise external questions and make external choices regarding some controlling and unreflective frame of reference or will. For example, I move toward autonomy with respect to my opportunism when I confront myself with a second-order volitional choice between that attitude and some different general pattern of motivation, such as a recognition of the rights of others. It is only when I come to frame and challenge the style of choosing or thinking which confines the range of my reflective choices within a non-authentic pattern that I begin to have a deeper and genuine ability to have the will I want. To the degree that we are unaware of the real possibility of alternatives to our established ways of being, we are not in a *position* to be self-governing in the deepest sense, to take full responsibility for our lives.

Can we now say that the more authentic my will becomes, the freer I can be *from* habitual patterns if I want to be, the more autonomous I become? Unfortunately, we are not yet out of the philosophical woods. There is one last consideration: Autonomy, in addition to entailing the core idea of authenticity, is associated with the notion of rationality. My will may have become more authentic when I confront one of my current wills externally, but this does not guarantee that my challenge to myself will be rational. A free will is not necessarily a rational will. Each step toward a more complete authenticity puts us in a position to take fuller responsibility for our lives, but it does not guarantee that we will use our new sense of possibility in any particular way.

> . . . a person may be capricious and irresponsible in forming his second-order volitions and give no serious consideration to what is at stake. Second-order volitions express evaluations only in the sense that they are preferences. *There is no essential restriction on the kind of basis, if any, upon which they are formed* (Frankfort, 1971, p. 13).

It is not unimaginable that I might grow up with an unreflective habit of kindness, that I might wake up one morning and decide to pursue a career of cruelty—just because it was one of my free possibilities. Nor is it inconceivable that someone might decide to take seriously, as a blueprint for living, the principles proposed by the "therapist" in John Barth's *End of the Road* (1969). The "doctor" in this novel suggests that the hero adopt the principles of antecedence, alphabetic priority and sinistrality: When it is a matter of choice between alternatives, either choose that which comes first, or the alternative which begins with the earlier letter in the alphabet or the alternative on the left.

If your intuitions tell you that a person who authentically chooses to live in these capricious and arbitrary ways in nonetheless autonomous, I would not know how to conclusively refute you. I am not sure myself whether there is anything to the intuitive idea of autonomy beyond the core notion of authenticity which I have developed here. However, I think that such persons are probably not acting very rationally, that there are probably alternatives which are more consistent with what they already want or alternative ways of thinking and choosing which they would prefer if they were acquainted with them. I do not see how we can claim to be moving toward full self-determination if we are not *at the very least* committed both to seek some consistency among our beliefs and principles and to be disposed to choose relevantly better alternatives to our present perspectives and choices if they should present themselves. As I understand it, then, persons become more autonomous to the extent to which they are able to judge, think, choose and act more authentically, as well as more rationally. In sum, this analysis suggests a number of important facts about autonomy:

1) It is possible for a person to become more autonomous in some respects and not others. For example, I may come to raise external second-order questions about the influence of my family on me, but not about the influence of my social class or my spouse.

2) There are levels of achievement in becoming more autonomous. I may have externally challenged my originally unreflective choices, but not challenged the authentic choices I subsequently made. Yet authentic choices can themselves become unreflective and auto-matized, and it is always open to us to raise external questions about the range of choices that even those new choices have come to confine.

3) The process of coming to be more autonomous in some respect and/or at some level involves a second-order volition to be motivated by rational independence in that respect or at that level. This is the minimal requirement of a search for some degree of consistency and relevant improvement which I suspect is characteristic of the move-ment toward autonomy in the fullest sense.

In general, then, what is it to become more autonomous? I must have more than a freedom from internal obsessions and compulsions. I must have more than the ability to will freely about matters that are internal to my present style of identity. To become more self-governing in the deepest sense, the sense in which I move toward the formation of an authentically rational self, I must 1) have the ability to raise questions and to make choices which are external to what I presently believe or will, and 2) be prepared to challenge myself on grounds of logical and factual relevance.

We always move toward autonomy against the background of some unreflective pattern of conduct. So working toward it will be a relative and not an absolute change. The movement toward authentic rationality will be difficult and asymtotic.

Rationality, and a choice between alternatives that is genuinely one's own choice, presupposes a full knowledge of the hitherto un-recognized causes of the confinement of one's choice to a particular range of possibilities. *Complete* rationality and *full* knowledge of every possibility open to us are an ideal limit at which we never . . .

could arrive. There are always the limits of our own language and culture, and of our own interests formed by social circumstance . . . self-consciousness must always operate on a given material . . . But everyone has the experience of coming to view some of his interests, previously regarded as inevitable, with a new detachment, as material on which his own deliberate choice can operate. Recognizing the sources of these interests, clearly identified for the first time, he confronts a new situation and has the means of deciding whether he should accept or, if he can, reject them (Hampshire, 1967, p. 256).

The goal of working through to this sort of relative autonomy has been thought of as one of the distinctive aims of higher education. Education can be the enterprise through which we awaken to new possibilities of living. If it is successful, we gain a critical or external detachment; we come to see our beliefs, attitudes and dispositions in the light of other and, usually, better perspectives. And we gain the abilities to engage in the sort of rational reflection and criticism which can result in consistent and informed, as well as authentic, choices about what we think and want to do.

This is the ideal of educating toward autonomy. The reality is that students are not consistently and systematically challenged to make authentic and rational educational choices, choices about acquiring the abilities, trying out the states of mind and developing the dispositions which educators have generally agreed upon as necessary for various kinds of autonomous activity. The reality also is that most students do not want to develop their autonomy. They are unwilling to assume full responsibility for their part in becoming more autonomous. This is not usually, at bottom, an active and externally reflective refusal; it is not an authentic choice, but rather an unreflective adaptive tendency to move in non-autonomous directions when a good opportunity arises. This should not be surprising. Most of us are taught from the beginning to seek approval and to avoid disapproval, and to manipulate others and ourselves to get what we imagine are rewards. Students learn early that parents and teachers usually do not want them to be autonomous; they learn that they will, in fact, be punished for not conforming to authority and that, therefore, the sort of authentic choosing which is necessary to autonomy requires too much of a risk in educational contexts.

As a consequence, many students will strongly resist invitations and demands that they be active makers in their own education. If they are initially tempted, they will become easily frustrated and fall back into old manipulative patterns unless the process is made interesting enough to involve them and unless they are given an adequate structure of support to sustain the risks and frustrations they will have to face. Deeply motivated resistance of students to taking charge of their own education is one of the main obstacles to educating for autonomy.

Usually it is not explicitly recognized that one of the first tasks of an educator who is interested in fostering autonomy is to address this problem of student will. In general, so long as the educational arrangements to which students are subject—the seating patterns, the organization of in-class discussion, the organization of communication in the evaluation of reading, writing, or whatever—are not reflectively designed to interrupt and discourage the typical non-autonomy of student learning patterns, they *encourage* them. As educators our unreflective habits of action are not neutral. *Our* drift, too, has direction. In our educational practices, we unavoidably take sides either for or against the autonomy of our students.

II. A Gestalt Approach to College Teaching

A Gestalt group therapeutic process is designed to foster autonomy. I want to indicate here how such an approach, adapted to the classroom, can become part of an overall course plan to encourage autonomous learning. In particular I want to illustrate how Gestalt experiments can be used to develop a systematic alternative to our traditional practice even within typical course and classroom forms. Gestalt therapeutic experiments awaken people from unreflectiveness and lead them to an awareness of nonmanipulative alternatives. They are situations which offer opportunities for increased awareness and responsible choice. They create what we earlier called "autonomogenic" opportunties—opportunities for authentic and rational choice.

Since I want to promote autonomous learning, I know that I am going to have to present my students with autonomogenic opportunities within a safe situation right from the beginning of the course. I want my students to see that I expect them to become authentically self-evaluative about how and what they want to learn and I want them to consider what they are willing to do to achieve it.

Initially, we can talk about expectations. In small classes, it is easy to "make the rounds" so that each of us can introduce ourselves by name and share our goals for the course.* I use my turn in the go-round to be as explicit as I can about my intention to encourage autonomy in a variety of ways. Since expectations change, I ask students to keep track of their goals in ungraded journals and to write about how they want to try to achieve them.

A teacher has many options in the beginning of a course to promote a general mood of support for autonomy. These are "ice-breaking" experiments and listening experiments which foster personal participation and an awareness of group process (cf. Pfeiffer & Jones, 1975). Since there are many discussions of how to do this in the literature I will not dwell on this here. What happens as a result of these experiments is that the class becomes a group.

There is one sequence of experiments I have used but have not seen written up so I will mention it here. I invite a class to consider a number of ways in which we might organize ourselves as a group:

1) Imagine that this is a very strict classroom situation. I will be an exaggeratedly authoritarian teacher who will come in and strictly lecture. I would like you to be aware of your response to this situation. Now line up in rows and remember not to talk unless you have a good question. And I will be the judge of that!

After a 15-minute experience with an authoritarian classroom, I introduce a permissive classroom.

2) In this situation, you make the rules. I will respond to questions but you will discover that I will almost always turn the questions back to you. What do *you* want to discuss? How do *you* think grades should be handled? What would *you* do if papers are handed in late? And so on.

As a result of this experiment and comparisons with what we had already been doing before the experiment, we are able to clarify the way we want to organize the course, at least for the present. We are able to jointly adopt an external point of view toward much of our previous unreflective conduct as members of this and other classroom groups. The results in increased autonomy justify the time invested.

---

* In large classes this can be done by breaking into groups and/or by writing out expectations and discussing them later. Also, "making the rounds" is a generally useful autonomogenic format. It can be used any time one wants to check something out with the group.

The ungraded journal format I mentioned is the core of a number of my courses; it serves to coordinate individual experiments of various types and to feed them into group activities.

The beginning of a course sets a mood or tone. I want to encourage as full a personal response from my students as is appropriate. One way is through fantasy. Here is an example of a journal assignment that raises an ethical issue: Will I do what is right if no one is looking? Does justice exist only as a social convention?

> Write a story in which you finish the following fantasy:
> You have just found a gold ring. You put it on your finger and twist it around to the left. Suddenly you discover that you are disappearing! You have become invisible. You twist the ring to the right and reappear again. Now you are aware that you have the power to become invisible at will.
> What are your first thoughts, feelings and impulses as you become aware of your power? What do you actually decide to do with the power? Without repeating yourself, briefly describe a few of your typical adventures. How do you decide to deal with the issue of keep-your secret from other people? Finally, what do you decide to do with the ring and why?

The fantasy experiment serves a number of purposes early in the semester. It is quite irresistible. Almost everyone gets personally involved both in fantasy and in the issue. A good fantasy reminds people that they have imaginations. The assignment says "It is okay to use your imagination here." It also helps me to get discussion going and to reinforce the personal contact which the name go-around had started. I generally break the class into small collaborative groups of five people. These groups remain stable if I want to encourage a sense of groupness and/or I shift their membership from time to time to encourage more people to get to know each other. The fantasies are shared in the groups. I guide the discussions toward a clear perception of the issue by questions which are prepared in advance and given as a task to each group. The educational rationale for as much personal involvement as we can appropriately foster is to have our students enter authentically into the issues we raise, or the scheme of thought we ask them to consider or the learning experiment we suggest, so what they think and do about it will matter to them. Creating opportunities for involvement inclines students to want to decide about these matters for themselves.

I have mentioned a number of experiments I have used to encourage group involvement and discussion. These are primarily process issues. But Gestalt-type experiments can be invented to structure authentic decision-making about course content, as well as about the process of coming to understand the subject matter. Sequences of individual and group experiments can be woven through a course to foster an authentic and rational choice to develop some basic ability.

Interpreting a Text: A Gestalt Approach

Most students are not good readers, especially of the difficult texts one finds in philosophy. They are tempted to avoid such readings if they can "get" what they need to know from my lectures or in some other way. They also become rightly frustrated by texts which they do not know how to enter. They lack an important skill. The educational problem typically involves both will and skill. I want my students to want to try on the schemes and perspectives in philosophy texts and I want them to want to be able to do it on their own.

I have gone through a lot of trial and error in my attempt to solve this problem. Here are some examples of what I have devised so far.

To interrupt the ineffective habit of passive and casual reading, I change the usual rules and expectations about reading from the beginning of the course. I emphasize that we are not reading books but encountering authors and that these authors are people we will be living with for a while. We have here an opportunity to get to know some very gifted people, people who have something to teach us—but we can meet them and understand them only if we make the special sort of effort that is involved in active reading.

> ... the operation of writing implies that of reading as its dialectical correlative and these two connected acts necessitate two distinct agents . . . Since creation can find its completion only in reading, since the artist must entrust to another the task of carrying out what he has begun, since it is only through the consciousness of the reader that he can regard himself as essential to his work, all literary work is an appeal. To write is to appeal to the reader to bring into objective existence the discovery which I have undertaken by means of language . . . the writer appeals to the reader's freedom to collaborate in the production of his work . . . (Sartre, 1965, p. 374).

Although I invite my students to view their reading in this way, I realize that they will need some support for their part of the collaboration. This is where I make clear how the ungraded journal format is the core of the course:

> The purpose of the journal is to help you to keep track of the important messages you hear in the readings and to keep track of your varied responses to the course. You will be asked to faithfully answer certain questions about the reading and the class discussions. You will also be asked to do short writing assignments which are designed to put you in a better position to appreciate the significance of what you read—for example, fantasy writing.
>
> Your journal responses will form the basis of small group discussion sessions prior to the lectures. The journals will also be collected every few weeks and comments will be made in response to some of your entries. The comments are meant to help you to read and think more effectively. I will ask you to reply to the comments to develop a correspondence with me about your experience with the subject. The journals will not be graded. They should be a place where you can feel comfortable, and try out new ideas. The only requirement is that you do the journal assignments fully and on time.

The journal is to be the safe place in which experiments can be carried out without significant risk. In large classes it can function as an analogue to the safety of small supportive groups.

Some experiments are designed to encourage a personal involvement with the material, as in the "fantasy writing." Students are asked to do fantasy writing when answering certain questions or to follow certain instructions in preparation for each discussion meeting.

> What most excited and interested you in today's reading? What windows or doors did it open for you? How do these ideas help you to see your experience differently or better? Given what you think is being said, what are your main agreements and disagreements?

> Perhaps you could organize your feelings and thoughts about these questions if you put them in the form of a letter to a close and comfortable friend. Or perhaps you would want to write a letter to the author him/herself.

The idea here is to involve students immediately in the question of what these ideas have to do with themselves, their own lives. There is always the potential of feedback to the group. In my responses I then encourage students to raise certain questions in class or to share a paper or to suggest other readings which might be of interest to them. Responses can also be shared in small groups to teach supportive group discussions.

Once students are involved, it is much more likely that they will want to understand what the author is saying. But such understanding comes only from careful reading and most students do not know how to do this. Structured experiments can be devised to develop this skill.

(a) What is the main point or claim the author is making? What is it that most concerns him/her?

    i) Cite a passage or passages that support your reading of that concern or claim.

(b) How does the author support his/her point of view (as you have stated it in (a))? What are the main reasons he/she gives to persuade us to have the same concerns and to think these reasons persuasive?

    ii) Cite a passage or passages that support your reading of the author's reasons or arguments.

(c) Now imagine that you are the author looking at what has just been written in response to (a) and (b). Do you find this to be a fair and penetrating summary of your views? What do you suspect, guess, imagine or know is missing? What do you think may be out of focus? Also, what do you find to be right on target or very close to what you would say yourself?

The sequences of these instructions leads to one pattern of effective reading. I try to challenge my students to choose this pattern as their own or to develop a better one. The last instruction, however, may seem premature. How can students criticize their own interpretations before they check them out with someone who knows? They can, to a degree. The instruction sets a standard. It raises the sort of external question that is necessary to autonomous thinking. It asks: "Have you given this reading a full and fair hearing?" We know, suspect, feel when we have not really grasped something, though we may not know exactly what we have missed or how we can handle it. It also introduces the perspective of the other, in this case the author, on what I, the student, have done, a perspective which is essential for identifying and taking responsibility for my previously unreflective actions and choices. I generally ask students to answer this question *after* the lecture/discussion as well, to say what was learned from the comparison, and to try to do things differently next time. If I do not see a change, I will prompt one by asking in the journal whether the student sees a change in his/her reading patterns. The opportunity to carry on this sort of development correspondence is one of the values of the journal format.

Let me illustrate this process of autonomonic development. For example, consider the chronic problem of student vagueness in writing. In many cases, a student would be willing to change but is caught in a habit which has never been adequately challenged by previous teachers. The typical instructional response to vagueness, if it is noted at all, is to scribble "too vague," "quite unclear," and "muddy" in the margins. This sort of gesture rarely accomplishes anything. For one thing, it is itself too vague to frame the student's problem in a clear way. (I recall one instructor whose only remark on a 'B' paper was "not what I expected.")

But more important, this sort of gesture is not part of a structured situation effectively designed to interrupt the educationally undesirable habit and to promote the authentic learning of an alternative. Student vagueness in writing and discussing is a chronic problem in education. Yet the experiments we continually use to address it are ineffective. In part, this is because we are not reflectively aware of our typical educational practices *as experiments*. They have become habits. We often forget to ask whether they are accomplishing their purposes or even if we any longer want to pursue the purposes they are accomplishing. We forget that they are our own choices and that they can be changed. In this case, the implicit purpose of our putting criticisms in the margins is to encourage greater specificity in writing. As an experiment, it does not work; it leaves too much leeway for students to remain attached to their habitual tendency. Since the remarks do not call for any developmental response, they can usually be safely ignored. And even if they are taken seriously as a signal that there is a shortcoming here, there is no structure of support to bring students to a concrete awareness of how their writing is vague, what vagueness fails to accomplish that greater specificity would accomplish, and how they can do things differently. This experiment does not provide the opportunities for students to raise external questions about vagueness, to confront their impasse, to make a second-order volitional choice to want to be more specific, and to try out an alternative will.

I want an educational situation which will provide students with opportunities to confront their vagueness and other issues of understanding and skill development. I realize that if I want to create autonomogenic situations, I will have to change the usual rules and expectations concerning evaluation. Instead of assuming that my critical comments are a one-way impersonal signal that something has been done poorly, I will require that they be treated dialogically. I don't want my evaluative efforts to be ignored. I regard my comments as a bit of correspondence, like a letter. I expect a response. This is what is behind the new rule that I want my students to keep a journal in which they reply to my questions and instructions even if this response is disagreement. The journal will be a safe place. As stated earlier, it will be checked for completeness, but otherwise ungraded. It will be used to work toward the understandings and skills required for the course. But for now consider how it might be used to address the specific problem of chronic vagueness.

Given this journal framework for evaluation, suppose Pam hands me a number of vague papers in a row. She hasn't responded to simple suggestion. I now have the option of using the evaluation of her paper as an occasion for Gestalt-type developmental work. I want her to see her tendency to vague writing more clearly and move her toward authentically choosing to be more specific. First, I indicate some consequences of her action; I say how her lack of specificity led me to doubt her understanding of the material. I isolate a portion of her paper and replace vague terms and phrases with more definite ones to give a sample of what I want her to try. I ask her to summarize and compare the messages in her version and in mine. Perhaps I ask her to take another portion of the paper, underline the vague spots and make the substitution herself. I might ask her to have an imaginary dialogue with the author quoting from the text to encourage her toward a more specific understanding of some topic. Then I propose that she work through a sequence of experiments like the following:

1) Write a two-page paper on X in which you try to say everything as vaguely as possible. (Exaggeration often leads to a clearer awareness of what one is doing and how one is doing it.)

2) Take my position as a reader of this paper. Imagine that you are the teacher evaluating this piece of work. Make specific comments and give the paper a grade. (This is the stage of external reflection and evaluation as well as additional practice with the alternative.)

3) You will be evaluated on how clear and specific you are about

the defects of the paper. Be sure to give reasons for the suggestions that you make to the writer. (This provides an opportunity to confront the issue and to work through it.)

Since vagueness in writing is a pervasive student problem, this sequence, or some variation, can be given as a journal assignment to almost everyone in the class at some appropriate time. Students can be asked to form small collaborative learning groups to exchange their deliberately vague papers and evaluations for evaluation by others. Evaluations and the reasons for them can be compared, discussed by the group and the criteria of definiteness in writing clarified by the instructor. Students usually learn a great deal from these exchanges. They often come to see possibilities of judgment, perspective, and choice that the instructor would not think of.

The general idea of the "safe" setting of journal correspondence and the associated group work is to help students to become more skillfully self-evaluative about their own interpretive activity. Each experiment supports this movement toward asking external questions of themselves about their interpretive ability and about their interpretations.

A review of the journal responses and small group reports also makes me aware of generally shared misunderstandings and misinterpretations of the subject. This can be worked on with the group as a whole. I have found role-playing and role reversal very useful for this purpose, especially when we are ready to integrate what the author has to say. This experiment is often useful:

> I announce ahead of time that the author (Sartre, Kant, or whomever) will be in class next week and that they should prepare questions that they would like to ask. The questions need not be restricted to the meaning of the text, but can include other issues to which this philosophy may be relevant, even personal issues. Of course, the philosopher reserves the right to not answer or to turn the questions back to the questioner.

The role-playing experience is usually very lively. I use it to address many of the misunderstandings I see in the journals by asking the students to switch roles with me for awhile. They (some or all) become the philosopher and I become the question-asker. I can then ask precisely those questions which I see have been puzzling them. As a spin-off, it is possible to break the class into smaller collaborative groups and ask these groups to work on the questions for awhile and then report back.

The dramatization of an author in class ("now you be Sartre") puts everyone in the position to match the performance in class with the author's script as it is presented in a text. Did this performance capture what Sartre means by "bad-faith"? Was it true to the text? We can shuttle back and forth between our play and the author's own words to find out.

Another effective method of dramatizing a concept is to ask how that concept applies in the here-and-now. The group and its activities often exemplify exactly what the author is talking about. Was anything that any of us just did an example of bad-faith? Bad-faith is not just a word in a book or a concept "out there." It is right here in our midst.

The journals are also used for student evaluation of the class sessions, of the course as a whole, and of the journal assignments themselves. This is a systematic way of underlining the value of group as an individual process. I ask students to offer these evaluations spontaneously as a matter of course, but I also specifically ask for them in class. It always seems odd to me that so many educators ask for evaluations at the end of a course when it is too late for them to use them to revise it. The evaluations, as well as everything else in the journal, can be a rich source of correspondence, class discussion or group experiment, and an occasion for suggesting individual experiments.

Although there is often no substitute for actually performing an educational experiment and seeing what happens, I often find it useful to anticipate and possibly revise what I am considering by first rehearsing it myself. I have saved myself and my students a lot of wasted effort by doing what I intend to ask them to do ahead of time. Just as I ask my students to put themselves in my place to encourage their independence, so also I can put myself in their place through role-playing, to encourage a needed detachment from my own preconceived and favorite ideas. This can be done with a good friend or colleague. We run through a new educational experiment, switch back and forth between the role of student and teacher, look at the form of life we have just created, and then see what we want to do. We run through a proposed circuit of awareness to see if it will actually lead students toward the confrontation with an authentic choice.

CONCLUSION

Although we don't always have a reliable person to help us reflect on and work through our educational decisions, it is often useful to pretend that we do. Let me close by suggesting a fantasy experiment for educators. The experiment is designed to provoke educational reflection and to encourage Gestalt experimenting.

Suppose that you have access to the latest educational computer, the ideal interpreter (I.I.). You punch into the computer through a sophisticated electrode connection so that I.I. can be with you at every moment. The computer functions as the ideal observer and interpreter of all your course-related activities. It has the capacity to see what you are doing, its likely effect upon students and every actual and possible, better or worse, alternative from every presently imaginable educational perspective. So if you wanted to know what Socrates or a Zen master or the best people in your field would do in your place, the I.I. could answer you. You could use I.I. to explore what is happening when you have your best times as a teacher or what the alternatives are to the way you usually introduce a theme or try to develop a skill. In short, you can ask about anything that you want to know about teaching individuals or groups.

Now suppose that you have all the time that you need to concentrate on your teaching. Have a series of dialogues with I.I. from the stage of course planning to the end of a course in which you ask the questions you most want to ask and receive the computer's answers. Remember that you can question from any imaginable perspective. Actually write out these dialogues.

My experience with experiments like this is that they function much like yogic warm-up exercises. They begin to stretch my educational imagination. They put me in touch with my tensions and cramps as an educator as well as the places where I feel good. Since the questions come so much more easily than the answers, the experiment leaves me feeling the need for more stretching. I find myself looking for solutions to the unfinished situations I have created. I begin to find new frames through which to interpret my present practice and I begin to feel intimations of an impasse between what I now do and what I could do. I feel motivated to try out some new things. Getting an experimental attitude is something like "getting religion"; it creates enthusiasm.

I have been arguing that if students are to enjoy the systematic support they need to move toward autonomy, an experimental approach is essential. The Gestalt therapeutic tradition is a rich source of experiments and of experimental strategies for both individual and group educational work. The general consequence of having teachers in the classroom who do not know how to lead groups, who are not regularly involved in supervision or peer-group sharing and who, consequently, are hardly aware of the group and individual processes which they initiate, is that these inadequacies become obstacles to the student's potential for being educated. At best, this is a repetitive cycle of lost potential. At worst, it is a negative spiral in which those who have been already oppressed and "disadvantaged" by a lack of genuine education suffer the most for being at the furthest remove from the reach of the teacher's immediate awareness. But this need not be so. Education can be practiced so that both teachers and students share the excitement of awakening.

11

Contact and Boundary: Creating a Nontraditional College Classroom

RONA GROSS LAVES

Everyone manages his energy so that he makes good contact with his environment or he resists the contact. If he senses that his efforts will succeed—that he is potent and that his environment is capable of nourishing return—he will confront his environment with appetite, confidence and even daring (Polster & Polster, 1973, p. 70).

As a teacher interested in the application of Gestalt principles in the classroom, I first ask myself: Is the traditional learning environment adequately supportive of students' efforts at contact and autonomy in learning, or is it possibly repressive of these efforts. And if it is repressive, how does this come about? Process provides the key to change.

What I see, hear, and feel in the traditional classroom is the dull thud of resistance, the closed door, the closed mind. Students report that they are confused and lost, that the material is over their heads, boring, baffling, arcane, and irrelevant. The teacher is frequently described as arbitrary and unsympathetic, distant, disinterested, and again, most often, boring. I take my students' complaints seriously, as a description of their experience of the classroom as an unsafe, unnourishing environment which cannot support autonomy.

Boredom is, in fact, the defining quality of the experience of many college students, who spend four or more years in the formal educational system without even the expectation of good contact. These students live in a kind of frozen, alienated relation to the knowledge which they must

Many thanks to John Flynn who was involved in the formulation of this chapter and who helped me to envisage it.

somehow absorb, with a vague, persistent apprehension of the teacher's expectations which they must somehow meet. Discovering what it is the teacher wants is the direction of the students' efforts, leading to the ritualistic demonstration (on an exam or a paper) of what the student has learned. By the end of the semester, the successful student has swallowed, more or less uncritically, the teacher's attitude or perspective in much the same way that the infant introjects the parents'. And while introjection may be necessary, even desirable, for the infant who does not yet have the capacity to make certain kinds of critical discriminations, it is certainly deadening for the adult.

Even the most ardent advocates of the use of a Gestalt approach to therapy and to living create an uninspiring picture of the learning situation, in which they assign a passive role to the learner, who is seen in a fixed, uncreative, and noncontactful relation to the course content:

> Introjection of the dull and unimportant material of the required course may be healthy when one has the chance to spew it forth and relieve himself of it on the final examination (Perls, Hefferline & Goodman, 1977, p. 249).

But introjection results from spoon-feeding or force-feeding, and it is inferior to assimilation as a mode of contact with that which is novel. The novel-other (another person, a new idea, a perspective or attitude) which is assimilated becomes part of the learner. But material which is introjected is easily and willingly given up (or regurgitated, as students aptly say) on the final exam, *precisely because* it has never really become part of the learner. Introjection is not only an unpleasant experience for the learner, but it is an inefficient and wasteful method of education.

This introjection which is the students' response to limited opportunities in the classroom for autonomy, contact and assimilation results in forced dependency and resentment. Excitement is transmutated. Now we can see that the chronic anxiety with which students approach the classroom is excitement turned back upon itself, i.e., retroflected excitement. This transformation of excitement is engendered and encouraged at every turn in the traditional classroom, most particularly by the nonparticipatory lecture format which excludes the student from involvement, obviates contact, and renders assimilation difficult, if not impossible.

In addition to the passive position which the student is thus encouraged to take, the following implicit rules of the classroom contribute to non-support and alienation. First, individual experience is disregarded and excluded from the definition of legitimate knowledge. Objectivity is the rule: reactions are irrelevant. Secondly, competition among class members is encouraged by the imposition of an artificially-generated scarcity economy of successful outcomes in which one student's success proportionately reduces the possibility of success for every other group member. In this way the energy of the group is turned back on itself, so that a potentially supportive environment is transformed into a divisive one. This particular fact of classroom life constricts the possibilities for using the classroom group and the interactive experiences of its members (group process) constructively to support the individual's learning experience.

We now have a picture of the student who is encouraged to be passive and is probably resentful of this position. The classroom arrangement which I have described renders support from others, as well as self-support, unlikely. Any excitement which the student feels must be quickly checked because the classroom environment is not safe enough to permit experimentation or support assimilation. Some of the most typical symptoms of the ossification of learning in the traditional classroom are a result of the students' detachment and alienation from each other, from the teacher, and from the substantive course content. From the students' perspective, then, *nothing happens* in the classroom. Students, for example, often report the peculiar sense of reading their class notes for the first time before the exam, as if they were written by someone else. Students who have introjected a great amount of material for a course rarely remember it after the paper or the test. When anxiety is intense and debilitating in the face of evaluation, students often go blank on an exam, or when speaking in class. At the extreme, students drop out of school either formally or, more likely, informally, by coming to class stoned, by falling asleep, and in numerous other ways seeking refuge from the anxiety that arises out of non-contact and non-support.

Symptoms of the students' failure to assimilate the course material take a variety of forms other than forgetting. The student may not be able to deal with the material creatively. Questions or assignments which require the student to look at the material from a new perspective may result in confusion. At a minimal level, students may not even be able to put into their own words the perspective or idea which they are articulating. They may demand to be spoon-fed, and be angry when they are not. We now have a self-perpetuating system which effectively subverts personal autonomy and which substitutes in its stead conformity and introjection. This approach to teaching cannot accomplish learning, because contact and assimilation are necessary components of any learning experience. Nothing less will work.

Having survived a traditional education herself, the teacher frequently has no idea how or why many students do not survive it; and therefore she has little insight into how to prevent alienation and failure in the classroom. But if she pays attention to the quality of interaction between herself and her students, she may note that contact is tentative, sporadic, muted, and unclear. Behind students' questions often lie hidden agendas and manipulations. The actual activity of the student (as opposed to the apparent activity of learning) frequently has less to do with the assimilation of an ongoing present than it has with a variety of internal activities such as rehearsing, fantasizing, projecting, and playing-out or avoiding the expectation of failure and rejection.

The Classroom Gestalt: Process and Self-Support

The teaching situation, like therapy, is a series of potentially contactful arrangements in which one person challenges the other(s) to move more or less gradually from environmental support to self-support. The Gestalt experiment describes and provides a model for this movement from unawareness to awareness to decision or redecision. The end result of the successful Gestalt experiment will be increased autonomy and self-support. In the college classroom, the teacher can provide a means and a forum for experimentation and growth. The teacher's attitude is important in that it reflects the positive expectation that this movement can occur and is desirable. Without interference, the organism has a tendency to form a good Gestalt in any ongoing present situation, to come into contact with the novelty and to assimilate it. The experience of the contact-boundary is the experience of the self-in-action, which is "an exciting, choice-making experience" in which ". . . customary things are out, and artful decisions become a necessity (Polster & Polster, 1973, p. 103).

Teaching is an activity at the contact-boundary. The teacher presents the novel-other in a way which will encourage assimilation. As a teacher I aim to have some designated effect on the contact-boundary of my students. In the language of teaching, I want my students to increase their horizons, to sharpen some specific ability, and to gain some increment of independence in learning. I want to turn the learning process over to the student. Therefore, part of the teaching task is to teach process and awareness of process.

In defining the goal of my teaching as personal autonomy or self-support, I want to arrange it so that at the end of the semester I am no longer needed by the student. That is, the student who accomplishes the course goals will be functioning autonomously with respect to the material and will, if interested, be able to continue functioning in this way. She/he will be able to assimilate new bits of information, to reason effectively, and to have a creative involvement with the material. In pursuit of this goal, I try to lead my students from passive introjection of the body of knowledge to active confrontation, assimilation, and a clear perception of the material.

However, usually, in the first minutes of the class, I have all the evidence I can possibly want that my students are ready, even willing, to swallow whatever I say and to do whatever is required to get a grade. Students rarely question the relevance or purpose of an assignment, a text, or a grading procedure which I establish. I suspect that this results more from passivity than from trust in me. I take this passivity as symptoms of lack of involvement and alienation from the process of learning. My students do not come to class with a clear expectation of what they want to learn; neither have they established for themselves an acceptable minimum standard for learning. They expect that, as in the past, these definitions are solely the province of the teacher.

I try to interrupt this habit which most students have acquired in the educational system. To do so, I first bring the habit into awareness by asking students to make their expectations of their role in the learning process explicit. Then the habitual behavior can become an object of decision and change. Once my students become aware of their passivity with respect to the classroom, they begin to glimpse the possibility of change. Sometimes it is useful to turn the frame slightly:

> What are your expectations of my role in the classroom? What criteria would you use in assigning a grade to me as the teacher? Specify how I could earn an "A," a "B," "C," "D," or an "F." How does an "A" teacher differ from an "F"? Now specify your standards for acceptable teaching in this course.

I try to create an environment of safety and a climate of plenty in the classroom. I tell my students that there is no arrangement in my classroom for some of them to fail simply and only because of their standing vis-à-vis other students in the classroom. My teaching is "student-centered," to use Rogers' (1951) term, and I urge and encourage students to rely on themselves and on one another for support and feedback. I offer myself as a resource person and as a facilitator. I offer my students a partnership in the learning process.

I recognize and value my students' experience, as I do my own. I consciously use myself and my experience in the classroom. I venture opinions and express reactions; in so doing, I model and validate the relevance of personal experience in the classroom. Usually my students respond in kind.

Because I attempt to maximize excitement, experimentation, and support, and to minimize alienation and competition, I rely on group approaches rather than individual ones, whenever possible. I see the classroom as a potentially supportive community, and as Polster and Polster (1973) note, ". . . in a community where good contact is prized, more people will be likely to learn to accomplish it well" (p. 303). The support of the group, the excitement of good contact, and the possibilities for experimentation and feedback facilitate learning, as does the opportunity to learn through the experience of others and to resolve or accommodate diverse or contradictory interests through a supportive group approach.

Contact between students is ordinarily thought to be a waste of class time and to compete with, rather than augment, the teacher's goals. However, I believe that the natural interest and spontaneous excitement which students experience in contact with one another can be useful in teaching. Learning occurs in a social context and can be facilitated by it. In fact, of course, it is impossible to eradicate the social context of learning in the classroom by rules which restrict interaction among students. Under such circumstance, the teacher becomes the object of a kind of forced attention which in time results in boredom and is antithetical to learning. Rather than restrict opportunities for interaction in my classroom, I open the avenues to contact. For example:

> The seating chart which is being passed around is for your use. Fill in your name and telephone number. This list will be available to everyone in the class and will be posted on the board. Think of the other students in the class as resource people whom you can contact if you have a question or an idea you want to discuss.

Sharing ideas, working on group projects and presenting class reports are all traditional ways of harnessing the excitement of contact in the classroom. Less traditional, perhaps, is giving students permission to help one another. Study groups in which students discuss their ideas, problems, questions, and reactions to the material make use of *all* of the class resources and demonstrate that support and help are available from other students.

RESISTANCE

Particularly when a teacher is trying to ameliorate habitually passive approaches to learning, she is likely to encounter resistance. Students who are used to being spoon-fed may balk when they are asked to participate in the learning process. They may complain that the teacher is not doing her job, that they are not getting anything from her, etc. The teacher must be prepared to lead the students to an awareness of their expectations and, it is hoped, to a reformulation of them in a way which requires the students to be active participants in their education.

> On the first day of class students can be asked about their expectations for the course and how they plan to reach them. Frequently, students will have only vague plans or goals, and even more vague ideas about how to reach them. This is a good consciousness-raising exercise in itself.

Students can then be asked to come in with concrete plans and a means to effectuate these plans for the next class. Fantasy and imagination can be an aid:

> Imagine that you are the teacher in this course. What material would you want to cover? How would you go about doing this? How could you involve the class in this task? Would you want to do this, and if so, why?

Early in the semester, the entire class, or several subdivisions of it can be gathered together to write the syllabus, to establish a method of evaluation, or to create learning contracts which take advantage of all of the resources that the members of the class have to offer.

> Spend this class working out a learning contract with your group. Discuss with them your learning goals and listen to the goals of others. Then decide what you want to contribute to the learning

experience of your group. (When this phase is completed, students can be asked to examine their plans and contributions in the light of those of others in their group, e.g., what does the student's learning contract reflect about her/him.)

COMPETING GESTALTS: EVALUATION AND REQUIREMENTS

I am aware that students have a great deal on their minds when they first enter the classroom, and much of it has to do with evaluation. I have found it useful to address myself to this issue very early on and to be as clear as possible about expectations, methods of evaluation, requirements, goals, work loads, and so forth. The issue of evaluation must be recognized as salient for students. If not directly addressed at the outset, it will persist and reemerge as a competing Gestalt throughout the course. I emphasize the students' responsibility for outcomes and try to have students plan for a grade, rather than to anxiously wait to receive one:

> What grade do you want in this class? What grade do you expect? If there is a discrepancy between the two, is there anything *you* can do about it? As concretely as possible, imagine and list what you will do to get the grade you want.

I try to have students experience support from other students and to provide support as well:

> Is there anything in your learning plans that you think someone else in the class can help you attain? Go around to three people in your group and ask each one to take on a task for you for the next class. The other person may agree to help you or may decline. (The way in which people go about carrying out tasks, or what tasks get done, and for whom, can all be useful and informative to the group.)

NOVELTY, EXCITEMENT AND THE ATTRACTIVE FIGURE

Contactful teaching takes advantage of excitement in the process of assimilation of the novel. A technique, approach or attitude toward teaching which is creative, unusual or new stands a greater chance of attracting attention and involvement than more traditional, fixed approaches which will tend to evoke habitual, passive responding from students. I try to be aware of the ways in which my students' excitement can be harnessed toward the assimilation of the material I present, and how the excitement at the contact-boundary can be used to encourage students along each step from environmental support to self-support. Doing so often involves finding or creating experiments that provide the subjective link to the abstract course material.

Any technique or approach which involves students personally in the substantive material is more likely to elicit good contact and to compete favorably with other Gestalts and agendas which the student brings along into the classroom. Experiential exercises are likely to be more effective in creating a lively figure. Rather than defining the term anxiety, I would demonstrate it with an exercise proposed by Stevens:

> Close your eyes, and keep them closed until I ask you to open them. In about three minutes I am going to call on one of you to stand up and tell this group of strangers about yourself honestly and in some detail . . . Between now and then I want you to imagine that you are the one that I will call upon. I'm giving you a chance to rehearse and decide what you will say . . . Actually imagine yourself standing in front of the group facing the people here . . . What will you say about yourself? . . . Now get in touch with your physical existence. What is going on in your body? . . . What tension, nervousness, or excitement do you feel? . . .
>
> Now stay in touch with your physical existence and notice any changes that occur as I tell you that I am not going to ask anyone to stand up and tell the group about himself . . . Be aware of what happens in your body now (Stevens, 1971, p. 225).

Another way of involving the student personally in the substantive course content is through fantasy and imagination. I may, for example, ask students to imaginatively communicate with, or become, the person behind the theory or idea which we are considering:

> Write a letter to Sigmund Freud. Tell him your reactions to his theory of personality, tell him what you like, or don't like, how things are changed, or tell him about yourself. This is your opportunity to communicate with this important person—so make sure you say what's on your mind. Then give your letter to another student who will answer as if she/he were Dr. Freud.

* * *

> Imagine you are able to see the last sentence in Viktor Frankl's journal. What is this sentence? What would be the last sentence in

your journal in the concentration camp? Is it similar to Dr. Frankl's? How does this sentence reflect your life philosophy?

* * *

Make a tape recording of an imaginative phone call to Carl Rogers. You only have enough money to make a ten-minute call, so be sure to accomplish what will satisfy you. Another student will take the part of Dr. Rogers. Try to represent his response as you would expect him to be.

The effects of competition and cooperation may be discussed, or they may be demonstrated by the use of an exercise developed to assess strategies of risk-taking. For example, Pfeiffer and Jones (1971) propose a zero-sum game called "Prisoners Dilemma" as a group evercise which can be employed to explore ". . . the relative merits of collaboration and competition and the effects of high and low trust on interpersonal relations" (p. 53). A zero-sum game is one in which the gain of one team (or person) is achieved at the expense of the other team (or person). In this respect it resembles many aspects of our everyday social functioning in a competitive society. Zero-sum games may be used experientially to demonstrate diverse aspects of group problem-solving, consensus-seeking, polarization, discrimination, information-sharing, management styles, and so forth.

Assignments which encourage a critical, creative, and contactful approach to the material will foster assimilation. The following example illustrates an innovation on the familiar classroom technique of debate. In this example, a critical attitude is fostered, along with the opportunity to make contact with other students, through listening, exchanging roles, and through being heard and represented by others:

A designated number of students engage in debate on a particular issue. The students are then asked to reverse positions, so that student A must now represent student B, and so on. There is no limit, except time, to the number of perspectives which can be represented in this way.

A variation on this design can involve several students interacting from different perspectives in a role-playing arrangement, using alternates to express what they think is unsaid, to finish the incomplete thought, to extend what has been said, or to illuminate a blind spot. In the process, the teacher may use any number of psychodramatic techniques, such as freezing the action between participants, or having feedback from the group, or using directors.

Role-playing is a valuable method for involving students and for personalizing the material. Its novelty as an instructional method and the drama of its unplanned, serendipitous enactment of the abstract principle make the role-playing situation a lively and attractive figure. Students can role-play a situation from one perspective and then from another. In situations where students are practicing a skill to be applied at some future time, role-playing has the additional advantage of providing a safe forum for feedback and the development of skills.

SKILLFUL FRUSTRATION

The principle of the unfinished situation pressing for completion can be usefully employed in the classroom. Teachers typically create a great deal of unfinished business in the process of teaching. Much of the frustration experienced by students in educational settings can and should be avoided, but frustration can be employed skillfully by the teacher to coax the student on to a more self-supporting position. A problem that the teacher creates and presents for solution is a good example of how this is done, even in traditional classrooms. When neither anxiety nor other Gestalts are competing for the student's attention, the unfinished situation, thus presented, can be a compelling and lively figure.

I'd like to emphasize two things about skillful frustration. First, what is frustrating does not necessarily have to be painful or anxiety-producing. Secondly, there must always be an element of surprise in skillful frustration, otherwise predictability overtakes the momentum of the demonstration. Students can be frustrated into more self-supporting positions in many ways, and the ways are not nearly as important as the goal: independence in learning. Thus, in order to make my students more independent learners, I may ask them to grade their own exams while all the time they were expecting me to *give* them the right answers. Their grade may depend on their ability to grade their own exams, rather than on the exam answers *per se*. For a term paper, I might ask students to give me the answer that Freud might have given to his detractors (rather than asking them simply to repeat the criticisms of his theory). I might ask the chronic-questioner in my class to teach the next session, requiring her to begin to answer questions, rather than always ask. The point here is that whenever the teacher sees dependent or passive behavior on the part of students, she must begin to interrupt it by frustrating this behavior in whatever way possible.

WHEN ALL ELSE FAILS: AWARENESS OF NONCONTACT

As Stevens (1971, p. 158) suggests, "Anything can be done with awareness or without awareness," and I am suggesting that awareness and contact are processes which can bring vitality and excitement to the learning situation, and can extend the boundaries of what can be learned and how learning can occur. But the recognition or awareness of human events in the classroom may involve acknowledgment of boredom, of difficulty or of unease. If I am aware of my students' boredom, in spite of my conscientious effort and fervent wishes that my students be inspired and involved, I can at least address myself to what is and work from there. If my students confirm my observation that they are bored or overloaded, we can take a boredom break:

> I'd like you to tell two other students in the class what you'd rather be doing right now. Try to give the other a picture of what you would like to be doing and how you would feel. Listen to the other student tell you what she/he would rather be doing right now. Give and get some feedback from them.

Spending 15 minutes of an hour lesson on a boredom break is probably more productive than exacerbating student boredom with more noncontactful teaching. In any event, it is surely wasteful of my energy and probably destructive of morale to insist that students pay attention when they have other things on their minds.

CONCLUSION

I've provided you with some examples of how I have utilized Gestalt concepts and the Gestalt experiment in my classroom. This approach has convinced me that boredom and alienation are not only unnecessary concomitants to education, but that they are antithetical to it. It is said that the first step to revolution is the ability to envisage it. If as a teacher I decide that I will not settle for the usual level of student passivity when excitement can exist in its place, then I have taken the first step in the direction of change. What I have done as a result of this decision has been contactful, exciting, and psychologically real for me, and by example, by contagion, and through contact, has become so for my students.

12

Gestalt Therapy Training in Group

BUD FEDER

The Pine Barrens is a peaceful, quiet, small-piney, almost deserted area in southern New Jersey, noted for abandoned iron mines and meandering, shady streams for canoeing—gentle and rust-colored from decayed pine needles. When I first entered training in Gestalt therapy with Laura Perls in New York City in 1971, all of New Jersey felt like the Pine Barrens as far as this type of therapy was concerned. I was the only trainee at the New York Gestalt Therapy Institute who both lived and worked in New Jersey. Gestalt therapy was relatively unknown to the established professional community and carried a stigma of quackery and superficiality. (Gradually I was to learn that many younger professionals and students were familiar with and enthusiastic about it, though only minimally exposed to it experientially.)

When I completed my training three years later and was elected to full membership in the New York Institute for Gestalt Therapy, the situation was only slightly different. It was then that I decided to offer experiential-didactic training in a weekly group to mental health professionals in the area. That particular training group continued for four years until June 1978 and it is my experience with this group that I shall describe in this chapter.

I have described the context in which I offer training, because that context was one factor prompting me to develop the model I employ. This model—pragmatic in essence—suited me, since I am essentially a pragmatic person. So I see here a blending of the needs of the local situation and my own style.

Still, what were and are my purposes in providing such training and what benefits did I expect and discover for both myself and my trainees? Why offer the training in group? What specific training model do I employ, and what special pitfalls are encountered? Within this model what responsibilities do I assume and what do I leave for the trainees to assume? After answering these questions, I will describe a sample session to illustrate my training approach and experience.

PURPOSES

For me, the lonely Gestalt therapist canoe-camping out in the Barrens, this training had the following explicit and implicit purposes:

> to enable trainees, committed to Gestalt therapy or not, to develop their skills locally;
>
> to enable beginning therapists to sample Gestalt therapy experientially and theoretically in depth;
>
> to provide a therapeutic experience for trainees, something indispensable to their overall development as professionals;
>
> to provide trainees with an opportunity to work under supervision and with immediate feedback;
>
> to provide me with an interesting and challenging professional activity;
>
> to provide me with an opportunity to spread the "word" about Gestalt therapy.

BENEFITS

Over the four years of doing this, additional benefits, not originally envisioned, have accrued for my trainees and me:

> development of personal contacts (friends, colleagues, lovers) both for the participants and for myself;
>
> development of a network composed of individuals and of subgroups, which various members and I myself have utilized in professional and recreational ways and in moments of personal crisis;
>
> development of a Gestalt Association of New Jersey, which I started at least in part because of the positive experiences of leading training groups.

WHY GROUP TRAINING?

Gestalt therapy training is offered in classes, seminars and in groups, so why did I choose to do training in group? At the outset my reasons were:

1) More variety of approach and method is possible due to the variety of personalities and interactions in a live group.
2) Group offers an opportunity for trainees to practice on each other.

Additional reasons from hindsight are:

3) In group I can also teach Gestalt group process and Gestalt group therapy as well as Gestalt individual therapy.*

4) Through the group process, important subsystems and spin-offs are more likely to accrue.

THE MODEL

My training model is a very simple one: I treat the bulk of the session just as if the people are clients, assembled for regular ongoing therapy; the final portion of the session, though, is reserved for reviewing the therapy segment. Typically, in a weekly group session, this means 1¾ hours are devoted to therapy; the final 15 minutes are used for cognitive review, discussion, theorizing and feedback. I rely on the natural unfolding of the group's development to provide trainees with opportunity to experience and to cognitively explore the essential aspects of a Gestalt therapy group: group character, group energy, group stages, group safety and danger, subgroups, contact impediments and factors which facilitate exploration at the contact-boundary. Ideally, the elements, aspects and qualities of a Gestalt group, already described in earlier chapters of this book, are present, noticeable and experienced in our own group sessions. For the last 15 minutes, members are encouraged to discuss and question what they've been living through and to conceptualize it in Gestalt terms.

Pitfalls

This model has a few built-in difficulties. Among these are:

1) *Professional gossip*—At the beginning of sessions there is a tendency to rap about professional items, such as job openings and

---

* Since little emphasis on group process was given by either Fritz or Laura Perls, I did not realize initially how important this aspect would become for me. Only gradually, as I pursued my career as a Gestalt therapist, did I realize that the group process knowledge, which I had acquired previously in my work as a group therapist, could and needed to be integrated with my Gestalt approach.

recent workshops. As in any group, it can be understood in terms of contact and safety issues, but with a homogeneous group of professionals, this gossip seems more pronounced.

2) *Premature cognitive processing*—A member may interrupt the group during the ongoing therapy process by discussing or asking questions about a technique or event in cognitive terms; again, contact and safety issues are often involved, as well as others, such as competition.

3) *Overemphasis on therapy*—Members, and the leader, often become caught up in and empathetic toward the personal issues being worked on, and are reluctant to "waste any time" on "intellectualizing" or "mind-fucking" at the end. Occasionally, with appropriate flexibility, I allow the therapeutic process to continue for the whole session, omitting cognitive work during the last segment. This is justifiable only when special pain is being felt or an imminent breakthrough is in the works. There is always plenty of important therapeutic work to do, and unless exceptions are held to a bare minimum, the cognitive aspect of the experience can easily go by the wayside. In my experience, in their enthusiasm to work on personal issues, group members hardly ever watch the clock and request to stop therapy and to begin the cognitive segment. This task, appropriately, falls to the leader.

Therapeutic Responsibility

Because I conceptualize the training model as learning through personal therapy, I accept those responsibilities which I consider appropriate for me to assume in my role as therapist (Feder, 1978). That is, I distinguish here between my role as a classroom teacher or seminar leader, for instance, and my role as therapist. As an example, when I might overlook lateness in a class or seminar, in this situation I feel a responsibility to raise it as a therapy issue. And, for another, more practical example, I believe it is appropriate to cooperate in third-party insurance payment for these sessions, which I do not do for supervision, either individual or group.*

Member Input

Beyond the basic structure of group size (I prefer eight members), length of time, and division of time for therapy and cognition, I leave

---

* I might note here that in fliers announcing these groups I am very careful to point out that the groups are based on learning through personal therapy.

most of the other elements of structure to the members. That is, it is their training group and I see it as their responsibility to get out of it what they can and want. So if a member wants to experience running a session, or to do some dream work with another member, or do any other kind of work, it is up to the member to put that desire out and negotiate for its happening. This places responsibility for growth where it belongs and is quite consistent with the Gestalt approach. Sometimes, of course, this leads directly into therapeutic work, such as when a member feels scared or resentful over this issue, or when a member tries to manipulate me in an effort to avoid this responsibility. For instance, I have often found members very scared to work publicly, either leading the whole group or doing some individual work in a fishbowl. Almost invariably this can lead to productive work regarding old familial expectations, as well as current self-expectations.

A SAMPLE SESSION

Over the course of a training group, whether it lasts for years or for a time-limited period (occasionally I lead semester-type groups), a great deal begins, develops and closes. Here I will describe one session which illustrates my approach emphasizing, among others, balance between individual work and work with the group-as-a-whole, time for therapy and time for processing, members' responsibility for use of the session and awareness of the group atmosphere. This session, like most of my training group sessions, has four obvious phases: *gathering, checking in, working* and *processing*. Each has its value for the individual member and for the group-as-a-whole.

Gathering

The group meets late in the afternoon. Everyone has worked all day and is a little tired and a little hungry. Usually, just prior to the session, I am busy working with a regular client in the office where the group meets. Members who arrive early, however, know they are welcome. So some enter the building—a large, warm house—and drift back to the kitchen. Water is hot, makings for coffee and tea available. By group time, about half of the members have rapped over tea or coffee for a little while. I finish my session, we bring the urn, as well as some nibbles, into the group room, and soon most of the trainees have arrived, said hello, and settled down on the floor to start the session. We have gathered

gradually, and a sense of group—the familiar whole-more-than-its-parts—
has emerged. Also, the openness of the house-office and the provision of
edibles are designed to help promote a positive atmosphere and contribute to a sense of safety in the environment.*

The Round

We begin by going around, checking in. Often I go first; sometimes
someone else feels urgent—then that person takes the initiative. We
briefly say whatever we want about what we're feeling, anything that's
happened which we want the group to know and/or if we want to work
this session. As mentioned earlier, this is sometimes a bogged down phase,
in which members distance themselves by going on at length regarding
professional matters. Today, for instance, Mark tells us too much about
his new clinic job, the clinic's policies and problems, etc. I interrupt and
get us moving again. Good old reliable, eager Celia indicates she wants
to work on a dream, so we all know we're in for a treat: something rich
and meaty and poignant. Then Paul says that he is experiencing a vague
sense of discomfort. He wants to work, although he's not sure on "what."
(Members typically feel they need a "problem" to work on, and only
gradually learn that, as Pogo says, "We have met the enemy and they
is us.")

Otherwise there is a low energy level as far as requests for work time. I
note this, but decide to keep my observation to myself for now. I'm a
little tired, and down too, today. I have a hunch but figure it'll come out
in the works if I'm right. My hunch concerns some developing competitiveness and irritability within the group since Sam's entry a few weeks
ago. I keep it to myself to let it percolate to the surface, and to provide
members with the opportunity of feeling and handling their own disturbances. The paucity of requests for work time indicates a strong
possibility that the group is no longer considered a safe place to work.
Although I consider a direct confrontation on this, possibly using the
"safety level index" (Feder, Chapter 4, this volume), I decide to wait.

At any rate, we've made some contact and are ready for Celia's dream,
which Paul and Celia agree will come first during work time, since she's
clear on what she wants to do and he's not. Often, in a session when

---

* For greater detail on safety and danger in the Gestalt group, see Chapter 4 in this
volume.

the group atmosphere feels safe, there is a heavier demand for work time and the competing members usually negotiate as to who starts. Sometimes they even determine an order and the amount of time allocated. I do not interfere in this nor do I see to it that the order or time allowances are followed through. I let the members take their own responsibility for this. Sometimes, though, I utilize this negotiation process to get into therapeutic issues, as when a member characteristically bows out of the competition or insists on going first.

Working

Celia tells her dream. As expected, it's a "goodie," replete with vivid detail, including some homosexual aspects. Celia is motivated to get something out of it; she tells it in the present and gets in touch with some feelings as she does so. Mark (Celia's "twin" in the group in the sense of having entered it simultaneously with her and of having since then experienced a kind of sibling warmth and kinship with her) begins to work with Celia on her dream in a sensitive, productive and supportively confronting manner. Still tired, and satisfied that Mark's interventions are good, I watch. Solid work is done as Celia gets in touch with both parts of the homosexual duo. Family relationships are explored and become clearer. Celia is emoting, Mark is helping—and Sam is fidgeting.

After a while Celia feels finished. Paul is vibrating to Celia's work, and to our pleasure (because he rarely does) states clearly and directly what's happening for him. He shares something of his feelings and thoughts. Energized and nurtured by Celia's work and Paul's directness, I pick up the intervention ball and begin the therapy dance with Paul. Momentarily my attention is very focused on him; for a while I'm relatively unaware of the rest of the group. But Paul isn't. Sam is playing with the belt of Celia's coat, teasing her—and distracting Paul. Paul gets angry and calls Sam on his behavior. Sam responds defensively, blaming Paul and me for his boredom, attacking my intervention and making a pitch for an alternative transactional analysis intervention which he thinks would have been better. Mark rises to the bait and tries to get into an intellectual discussion with Sam on this point. Sam is condescending; Mark gets furious. They argue and bicker. When they stop—unresolved and angry—Tom says he can't trust the group anymore and may quit. The group is stunned and hurt and worried, and for a few minutes, everyone expresses reactions to this sequence of Paul-Sam-Mark-Tom.

Processing

At this point I notice that it is time to stop personal work and start processing, and despite our heavy involvement in the fracas between Mark and Sam, and the strong reactions of Paul and Tom, I suggest we do so. There is a strong current of resistance: Members know that on occasion, when positive work is going on which I think can be finished in a few more minutes, I relent and omit the process section or postpone it until the beginning of next week's session. Tonight, though, I am convinced that this issue cannot be resolved quickly. Another 15 minutes of work will still leave us a long way from home and processing will have been lost. So firmly, if reluctantly (since I too am troubled by this fighting within the group), I stick to my guns and explain why I think we should process. The group acquiesces.

It isn't easy, though, as Sam (now appropriately) voices his opinion that a particular TA method would have been much more useful than my Gestalt intervention with Paul—Mark flares up at Sam again, upbraiding him for rudeness and deviousness. I call us back to the issue, not the person, and request some thinking on what happened in terms of the group-as-a-whole as well as the individuals concerned. For the next few minutes I act as discussion facilitator. My style is to encourage thinking and integrating; after the group has given its opinions, with very little time remaining, I offer my ideas on the experience. Members are, I hope, left with the impression that it is up to them to decide for themselves what happened. My idea—that the Sam-Paul-Mark-Tom excitement was an outgrowth of a recent upsurge of competition and mistrust in the group—is only one of several and not presented as *it*. I elaborate briefly on the Gestalt concept of working at the contact-boundary, the relation of the group climate to this work and the identifying phrase "safe emergency" as it applies to the group situation. Since this work is very unfinished and the group needs to do a lot more regarding it in the next few sessions, I don't get into much personal detail, since this would amount to making unproductive interpretations.

The session ends a few minutes later. A difficult phase has begun for the group which will take some time to work out but which, if done with integrity, blending the experiential with the didactic, will prove valuable both therapeutically (emotionally) and cognitively. We part, troubled by what has happened and already anxious in advance about our next meeting; but I, at least, am also pleased that the group is lively and percolating, for this liveliness is essential if we are to obtain the training value which we seek.

As I reread the above, I realize that an important affective aspect of the training group experience is not communicated. This is my own emotional involvement with the group. This, my first training group, began with four people, grew to 12 the second year, shrunk again, then stabilized at eight. The group, this changing group, whose only constant was me (although one charter person continued in it for 3¼ of its four years) had a wholeness and an energy that made it often for me the highlight of my professional week. It is this energy, this wholeness, this strength and pain and joy in the *group-as-a-whole* that I'm trying to emphasize here. The names Sam-Mark-Paul-Celia are only a string of names, but to me those words conjure up an image and a feeling of "the group"—and with it the process: the creation, the existing and the ending of the group-as-a-whole which I'm trying to describe and share, because above all else the importance of this process is what I try to convey to my trainees and myself.

Section IV

COMMUNITY APPLICATIONS

13

Intensive Gestalt Workshops: Experiences in Community

RUTH RONALL

No man is an island. . . .

JOHN DONNE

In the summer of 1950 I spent six weeks at the Tanglewood Festival, singing in the Festival Chorus. It was the Bach Centennial and we performed the B-minor Mass and many of the cantatas. We also sang the music of other composers, medieval through contemporary. And when the Chorus was neither rehearsing nor performing, I listened to other units playing. So, from early morning until late into the night I was surrounded by music, immersed in music. I talked music, felt as if I were eating, drinking, smelling music, and music often followed me into my dreams.

This summer in music has been the only experience in my life that compares in intensity with the experience I have had in intensive Gestalt workshops.

*   *   *

For the past seven years I have been leading intensive Gestalt workshops—for training in Gestalt therapy and for personal growth—in the United States and Europe. Most of these are one-shot, time-limited groups, lasting from two or three days to one or two weeks, which are sponsored by a variety of institutions, or sometimes by individuals. Occasionally I also lead a training week or weekend for an ongoing training program or for a team. Most of the time, however, I work with groups consisting mainly of strangers: persons unknown to each other and to me.

179

Group composition varies: The training workshops are attended exclusively by members of the helping professions or students; the personal growth workshops are open to "anyone interested"—and that often includes professionals with or without their partners. Some of the growth workshops are arranged for couples only, others for couples and singles. Participants are adults, ranging in age from their early twenties to their late sixties or early seventies. The maximum number of participants is 20, the minimum 10—most workshops have around 16 members, which, for me, is the optimal number.

As a rule I lead these workshops by myself. When I work with a co-leader, I choose her/him carefully to ascertain that she/he shares my basic philosophy and approach to groups.

While the size, composition, length, location and function of the residential workshops vary, they all have these elements in common: complete absorption in the here-and-now; development of a high degree of intimacy; and passionate involvement in the task or theme. First-timers often remark that they never before experienced anything quite like it.

The opportunities for experimentation with time and space, with fantasy and play, with music, dance, and art, and with environment not only are more numerous than in ongoing groups, but also assume a different quality, *inviting* one, as it were, to become imaginative and creative.

Opportunities for contact are more varied, as are the opportunities for withdrawal. Inevitably, the group becomes cohesive fast, and intensively so, usually so much so that it tends to assume the character of an ideal, unreal, "island" community. A German term for this phenomenon is "Klausureffekt"* which I translate as "retreat phenomenon." While this retreat phenomenon occurs to some degree in any kind of residential workshop, irrespective of theme, type of leadership, or method used, it develops with increased speed and intensity in Gestalt workshops because of the excitement generated and the creative energy released by the Gestalt approach.

However, the forces inherent in such an intensive situation, exciting as they may be, are not beneficial in and of themselves. A very cohesive group may create rigid boundaries to exclude the outside world—which is pronounced as "bad"—and refuse contact with the environment, be it the workshop's host environment, home, or the world at large. Simul-

---

* Prof. Dr. Peter Peterson, Hannover, personal communication.

taneously, the group may tend to exert pressure on those who do not conform to the quickly established norms and, finally, it may exclude— or at least try to—a member who does not appear to fit in with the rest.

At first I was not fully aware of these hazards, although I did become uneasy when a group was overly enthusiastic about our special way of being, or seemed to feel that we had found a new form of living that was vastly superior to all others. Soon I realized, however, that I had to pay serious attention to those group phenomena that might spell exclusivity, superiority, intolerance, and elitism, since they were nothing but indications of an attempt by the majority of the group to create and maintain confluence. As Laura Perls (1976, p. 224) states: "Convention and conformity insist on a *confluent* attitude *within* the fixed boundaries, a taking for granted of sameness and agreement, of being *one*—a "we"-ness without the I and thou—the acknowledgment of the other and oneself as separate individuals. This blurring and ignoring of boundaries apply not only to society at large . . . but particularly to the interpersonal relationships in marriage and the family." And, I might add, to the interpersonal relationships in intensive workshop groups.

Once I recognized this, it became clear to me that, in order for the group to become an optimal environment for learning and growth, we would need to create a climate of inclusivity rather than exclusivity, inviting each person to find a way into the group and to feel safe enough to stay. This means that once a person has joined the group he/she will not be excluded, either overtly or covertly. No matter how an individual may differ from the rest—be it in terms of physical functioning, intelligence, education, color, creed, belief system, or whatever—no matter how much he/she feels different, feels an outsider—for its duration the group is to become his/her home and community and he/she can remain with us in some way acceptable to all.* Naturally anyone can choose to leave us. But I encourage a full and open discussion in the group before such a decision is made final.**

I am putting the main stress on the group-as-a-whole making room for

---

* There is one exception—the individual who is or threatens to become violent— since in such groups we do not have the means to cope with violence.

** I am aware that my passion for inclusion is related to my experiences of being excluded from the age of six on: first, when I was the only Jewish child in class in public school in Vienna, and was ostracized by the other children; later, throughout the time I lived in Vienna, i.e. until 1938, when I had to leave Austria; and even to this day when there are "restricted" areas everywhere in the world, in fact right here in the United States. This I believe does not make my efforts less valid.

the individual, and not so much on the individual making a place for him/herself. This is because of my conviction (borne out by theory and personal experience) that the group-as-a-whole has enormous power for better or for worse. Of course, each individual needs to create his/her own space. However, he or she can do so freely and fully only if the group-as-a-whole maintains "the elasticity of . . . it(s) boundaries" (Perls, 1976, p. 223) and thereby makes room for everyone who wishes and is able to remain in it. By the same token, if the group boundaries remain permeable, the group maintains contact with its surroundings. Thus, by creating a climate that allows for differences within and without, the group can be a nurturing environment for each member—the leader included—and is in turn supported and nurtured by its members and by its environment.

In such a group members not only learn and grow freely, confronting their environment with zest, but they also live together in a climate in which differences and conflicts are neither blurred nor wiped out. When boundaries are recognized, there gradually emerges a sense of belonging, a sense of community.

My efforts to promote this sense of community are based on the following premises:

1) Anything that improves the quality of contact within the group and between the group and its environment-at-large supports individual growth, group cohesion and a sense of community.
2) The more the leader and the group members are aware of, and share responsibility for, group process, the better the chance for a community spirit to develop.

As a Gestalt therapist, I focus on, bring to awareness and work with disturbances at the contact boundary with individuals, intragroup constellations and the group-as-a-whole. As a group leader, I realize that this is not enough: I also need to be aware of and use group process. Therefore, I have developed over the years an approach to group leading in which I use Gestalt principles as my basic frame of reference and integrate these principles with concepts from other sources, primarily Theme-Centered Interaction (to be described below). Moreover, my approach is geared to utilizing the specific features of the intensive workshop, such as the opportunities afforded by living together for a predetermined time. I have formulated my approach in retrospect and am presenting it in the remainder of this chapter. It has grown slowly out of my experiences in

many different kinds of workshops with hundreds of incidents that have
occurred and problems that I have solved with my groups, using theoretical concepts, my own and my groups' ideas and, last but not least,
common sense. While I cannot name all the sources of my approach to
group, I do wish to acknowledge the two main ones:

The first is Alfred Adler* and especially his concept of "Gemeinschaftsgefuehl," a term which has yet to be satisfactorily rendered into
English. ("Social interest" or "social feeling," the two terms most frequently used in English, do not adequately express its meaning, and can,
in fact, be misleading. The best translation I have found so far is "social
embeddedness" by Alfred Farau.**) It is precisely this sense of social
embeddedness, of community, which characterizes a Theme-Centered
Interactional group experience and which I try to foster in all my
workshops.

The second is Ruth Cohn and her Theme-Centered Interactional approach*** to group leading. The aim of this approach (and the essence
of its philosophy) is to create a climate and to promote a group process
in which participants take responsibility for giving and getting what
they want, and become aware both of their autonomy—their ability to
make choices—and their interdependence—their need for, and the effect
they have on, one another—as well as of the necessity to continuously
balance one's own needs, wants, wishes and actions against those of
others. Ruth Cohn formulated this principle in the ground rule: "Be
the chairman of yourself" or "Be your own chairman," later changed to
"Be your own chairperson" (Cohn, 1969; Ronall & Wilson, in press). In
the group this means: Try to give to this group and to get from this
group whatever you want to give and get—in terms of yourself, the
others and the theme or task. This has remained my ground rule for
group leading—and for living.

THE WORKSHOPS: PROMOTING A SENSE OF COMMUNITY

Planning the Workshop

When I plan a workshop I keep in mind the major elements of a

---

* I was introduced to Adlerian theory early in life by my parents, and many of his
concepts have remained essential to my thinking to this day.
** Personal communication.
*** Theme-Centered Interaction (T.C.I.) is taught at the Workshop Institute for
Living-Learning (W.I.L.L.) in New York City and other major cities of the United
States, Canada and Europe.

group (cf. the concept of "the Globe," Cohn, 1969, p. 24) and how each can contribute to the kind of community spirit I have in mind. These elements are:

> Sponsor or sponsoring organization;
> The theme or task of the group;
> The people comprising it—group composition;
> Time—the specific group time, and time in history;
> Place—in all its dimensions (geographical, housing, etc.);
> Leader(s) and leadership.

My workshops start with a *sponsor*—be it an individual or an institution—and with a theme, which I usually discuss with the sponsor.* From the beginning, my negotiations are geared toward obtaining as wide a range of participants as possible—heterogeneous groups work better. For example, if the *sponsoring organization* is a church, I will try to make sure that people other than members of that particular church are admitted; if it is a hospital department, I try to ascertain that participants are representative of different disciplines and different levels of management.

The *theme or task* becomes active as a focal point for the group only while the workshop is taking place. However, its function, especially for personal growth workshops, is important: The better and more succinctly I formulate a theme, the more likely will participants come with a clear purpose and thereby have more of a common interest and goal.

Group composition is determined by the sponsoring organization and the task or theme. For example, training workshops are for members of the helping profession only. Also, the sponsor may select the people who are to attend the workshop. Personal growth workshops, however, are for the public at large, and in these I prefer to try to reach as heterogeneous as possible a population: adults of all ages, races, creeds; singles and couples; professionals and lay persons. I also avoid screening by the sponsoring organization or by myself. I want the groups to be formed at random and to represent a "slice of life." I prefer to be surprised by the picture I find, rather than to be reassured by a "balanced" group with approximately equal numbers of women and men; blacks and whites; young and old; etc. The unscreened group makes for variety, is more exciting, and is representative of society at large. It presents a greater

---

* Of course, leaders can sponsor their own workshops; I prefer not to do so.

challenge to reaching the goal of creating a sense of community and a safe and nourishing environment for all.

When, next, I decide on the *time*—both the time of the year and the length of the workshop, I again consider how these aspects can be used to contribute to the building of community: I pick a time when most people are likely to be able to join, such as a holiday weekend or vacation time. The length of the workshop is determined by the population: Training workshops can run for two weeks, whereas personal growth workshops usually last no longer than five to seven days, so that they do not become too expensive for prospective participants in time as well as money.

Having no choice about the historic events that are taking place during my workshops, I must at least keep myself and the group aware of current events that may affect some or all of the participants, such as a strike in their home town, a kidnapping, or war. The Yom Kippur War, for example, affected a training workshop that I led in Switzerland from beginning to end: It brought some of us closer together and provoked the group to deal with such issues as anti-Semitism, the holocaust, hatred, self-hatred and guilt.

The *place* of the workshop is usually determined by the sponsor. Nevertheless, I do state my preferences and make recommendations to the sponsoring organization regarding the minimal essentials: At least one large room for work, some indoor and some outdoor play space, comfortable sleeping accommodations and a quiet surrounding. All of this should be as *inexpensive* as possible ,so that nobody will be excluded or exclude him/herself because of cost.* The most important contribution to the well-being of the group and to the growth and development of the community as far as the place is concerned is made by the "host"—that is, the person(s) who run our meeting place. Their feelings about and attitude toward our kind of workshop, and the extent to which our philosophy and life-styles are compatible are of great significance.

When given a choice, I often opt for simple accommodations and simple food because the owner-manager understands what we are about and will give us freedom to move, to expand our boundaries, to exchange our experiences with him and his staff. I still remember my first Gestalt training workshop in Europe: We stayed in a first-class Swiss hotel, had

---

* The relatively high cost of these residential workshops has bothered me ever since I have first become acquainted with them, since it contributes to elitism. (I know only one way toward ensuring equality of opportunity: a scholarship system.)

rooms with bath and elegant service, but our only work room was in the main building and was furnished with costly period furniture and an antique clock that ticked away our time. We had to move to one of our bedrooms in the annex in order for one of our group members to be able to scream! Since then I prefer simple accommodations that allow us freedom and an opportunity to develop a sense of being at home.

As for the *leader or leaders,* their main contribution to the community spirit doesn't start until the workshop is in session. However, in the course of time, my emphasis on group process has begun to bear fruit and is becoming known to the circle of people who come to my workshops. As a result, people who are interested in that aspect of Gestalt work constitute a group core willing to work on the community aspects of a workshop.

Leading the Workshop

During the workshop, I continue to be aware of the major elements that make up the group. However, their relative importance changes: The *sponsor* comes into the foreground mainly in the very beginning and towards the end of the workshop. At that time it is important to bring into the open the participants' connection within and toward the sponsoring agency (for example, that of a team within the agency that sent it to the workshop) and feelings about administrative requirements, such as a questionnaire that has to be filled in or a report that has to be written. The question of who pays for the workshop is also an important one to be explored. However, disturbances around these issues, once they are handled, usually recede into the background fairly soon, to be brought back in a new form only towards the end, when participants prepare for "back home."

Group composition and internal group structure are also of greatest significance in the beginning stage, although we need to remain aware of new alliances, especially newly formed couple relationships, throughout the time we are together. However, it is in the beginning that I make group structure (subgroupings, previous relationships, etc.) transparent in order to promote a sense of security.

The overall *theme,* though always in everybody's consciousness becomes background to subthemes, either of a personal nature or of the kind that promote and support the group process.

Space and *time,* however, which in ongoing groups are of relatively

minor significance, assume different dimensions in time-limited residential groups—essentially because there is continuity between working
and living time, and between working and living space, and therefore no
break in the group process. This offers such opportunities for experimentation, for learning and teaching, and for creating a sense of community,
that time and space remain in the foreground for me throughout the
workshop, yielding important material for our work.

The *leader or leaders* (the person) and their *leadership* (the approach
and philosophy) have, of course, a great impact on the workshop and on
the kind of community that develops. Although much of what I am or
do can be seen from the context, I will begin by describing how I experience myself as a leader and the style of leadership I aim to develop.

Finally, there are various other aspects of a workshop that contribute
to a sense of community or lack of it. These are described at the end of
this section.

Leader

> A Gestalt therapist does not use techniques; he applies *himself in*
> and *to* a situation with whatever professional skills and life experi-
> ence he has accumulated and integrated. There are as many styles
> as there are therapists and clients who discover themselves and each
> other and together invent their relationship (Perls, 1976, p. 223).

While I use techniques, such as "go-arounds," "dynamic balancing"
and "the empty pillow," and introduce "ground rules" which I shall
describe soon, these are all part and parcel of my life experiences in
groups, and I use them neither mechanically nor rigidly. My primary
sources of support and inventiveness for the tasks of leading the group,
attending to group process and working with individuals are within
myself and in my awareness of what support is available to each member
from within and from without, that is, from other group members and
from the group-as-a-whole. Thus, in each workshop we invent and develop a way of living together which is unique to that particular group.

I am a participant-leader. From the moment the group has assembled
and the actual group process has started, I become involved: I introduce,
encourage, support and *model* the kind of communication and activity
that promotes a sense of safety (see Feder, Chapter 4, this volume)
through directness, openness, self-disclosure, and through avoiding and
discouraging secretiveness, gossiping, and the formation of closed sub-

groups. As a participant-leader, I share my feelings, needs and wishes, and acknowledge, for example, that I am here not only to give but also to get something from the experience. It is my task to lead the group, to teach, and to be available to the participants. I can fulfill this task best if I also take care of myself. For example, when I am quite anxious and tense (which is often the case in the beginning of a workshop), I state this to the group during one of the first go-arounds. Some people are disappointed and angry; others are relieved. Whatever the response, one piece of ice is broken: I have not met some people's expectations (that I am always calm and collected) and nothing terrible has happened.

Furthermore, quite early in the life of the group I say that I will unavoidably make mistakes and I invite all of us to examine them and to learn from them. Again, some members get angry: They want a perfect therapist-leader. Yet I become more relaxed: I have lowered the group's unrealistic expectations by giving all of us "permission" to be imperfect.

In this way, as the first session progresses, I become increasingly "transparent" (Jourard, 1964), and thereby encourage others to move in the same direction.

Quite early, I also demonstrate respect for my own as well as for other people's boundaries. I make it quite clear that neither I nor anyone else will be forced to answer questions or abide by all the rules. This spells considerable relief for many participants, especially for those for whom this is a first experience with Gestalt therapy. And the fact that I include myself promotes a sense of equality.

I listen and respond with my personal reactions rather than with interpretations, long before I have started to introduce the corresponding "ground rule." I am careful, however, not to overload the group with my concerns and I use "selective authenticity," a term coined by Ruth Cohn (Cohn, 1969-70), in sharing my disturbances. On the other hand, I watch out that I do not get stuck and thereby hamper the whole group's progress. Therefore, throughout the workshop, I need to balance between sharing too much and too little. I measure this by estimating the climate of the group. If the group seems stuck, the interaction feels sluggish and the people's mood is down, I first search within myself to see if I am holding back something that concerns and may affect the group. For example, I might discover that I am annoyed with one of the participants, and then try to express this in a way that relieves the group without hurting or harming the particular person, primarily by not blaming him or her for annoying me. If I manage to do so, I have been acting as a model of self-disclosure and of being "straight" with others, and I have demonstrated that it is safe in this group to express one's difficulties.

I invite criticism and also ask people to let me know when they are uncomfortable about something I do or say, for example, if I come too close to someone physically. Through such feedback I do not have to guess and do their work in addition to mine. Thus we become partners: I am a teacher/learner and the group members are learners/teachers, and this benefits all of us. Usually I am enthusiastic and enjoy myself as much as I can, letting the group know when I am interested or when I am bored, where I am and where I want to go. I use my sense of humor whenever I possibly can. Good, warm laughter is refreshing and healing. I do use irony—it provides spice—but sparingly; sarcasm is used only with paradoxical intent. (Sarcasm is essentially toxic and should therefore be used in homeopathic doses only.) Often I am playful, and by allowing the child in me to come alive I stimulate others to do the same. For example, several years ago I bought a small stuffed rabbit made of real rabbit fur as a toy for myself. When I took it with me into the group, it aroused—to my surprise—the interest of all the participants way beyond their mere curiosity as to what was sitting on my lap. They wanted to touch and to stroke it; they imagined it saying things they wanted to hear, thus projecting their own needs for contact and nurturance onto it. In this way, "Randolino" became my "co-therapist" and "co-leader" and has been traveling with me since. Symbolizing playfulness and warmth and providing comfort, he is a piece of environmental support for the group and myself.

Leadership

Throughout the workshop I introduce and explore Gestalt concepts, beginning with the emphasis on the here-and-now and continuing with the concepts of contact, withdrawal, contact boundary, support, figure/ground, unfinished situation, and so forth. Within the context of an experience, the process of conceptualizing results in assimilation, nourishment and growth. This is equally true whether the workshop is for professional training or for personal growth. The difference lies in the rhythm: In personal growth workshops the processing takes place as the occasion arises; in training workshops there is time scheduled for processing and conceptualizing, although, of course, much spontaneous processing and teaching/learning take place too.

In both training and growth workshops there is a balance between individual therapeutic work and work with the group-as-a-whole. In either case, work raises the level of trust and intimacy in the group: A person who volunteers to work individually thereby expresses trust in the group and moves toward greater intimacy; by the same token, if the group-as-a-whole works on some group issue, it becomes a safer ground for an individual to risk exposure and intimacy. Moreover, each therapy encounter releases excitement previously interrupted by anxiety, and this is one of the reasons why Gestalt groups become exciting and intense, and why Gestalt therapy, whether with individuals or the group, increases group cohesion and a feeling of community.

* * *

In the course of the first few sessions I announce the basic ground rules of "confidentiality" and "no violence." The latter may seem quite unnecessary to some who take it for granted that we do not use violence. On the other hand, it does reassure others—especially those who are afraid of losing control and those who have experienced violence in their lives. The rule of confidentiality is also taken for granted by most. Yet we have often had useful discussions about episodes in other groups when confidentiality was not observed, exploring the issue thoroughly and coming to some agreement as to how we are going to handle this problem, knowing that confidence lapses do occur and have to be taken in stride.

Then, gradually, I introduce ground rules of communication, which are partly taken from theme-centered interaction (Cohn, 1975, translated into English in Ronall and Wilson, in press) and partly resemble as well as overlap the rules used by some Gestalt group leaders (for example, Levitsky and Perls, 1970, and Zinker, 1977).

Ground Rules of Communication

Be your own chairperson.* This means take responsibility for yourself. Do not wait for others to invite you to speak out. Speak, assert yourself, but always with regard and respect for the others around you. (This is not the same as "doing your own thing"!)

Disturbances take precedence.* No one can be truly present while

---

* These two "rules" are existential postulates (originally formulated as "ground rules"), in T.C.I.: We, are *indeed*, our own chairpersons—autonomous and interdependent—and disturbances do *indeed* take precedence. The rules bring these two aspects of the human condition to *awareness* and thereby enable us to make conscious choices.

preoccupied with internal or external distractions. Such unacknowledged personal distractions stifle the individual and the group process. Often a simple statement of the disturbance is sufficient to enable the person and the group to return to the theme or task. Sometimes, however, the disturbance needs some individual work on interpersonal relationships within the group before there is sufficient relief for continuing the group-as-a-whole. *Note*: This second "rule" is of extreme importance in residential groups. If a sense of safety is essential to Gestalt work in ongoing groups (Feder, Chapter 4, this volume), it is of even greater significance in a residential group. Whatever disturbs the sense of safety in a session will, if not resolved or at least brought out into the open, be carried into the in-between time and may develop into a problem out of proportion to its real significance. Therefore, from the very beginning of a workshop, I keep aware of interpersonal disturbances and begin to train all members to focus on such disturbances and to bring them out into the open.

Speak for yourself. Make "I-statements." Don't hide behind generalizations, generalizing pronouns, such as "everybody," "one," "you"; they are essentially indicators of, as well as contributors to, confluence; they provide a spurious façade of commonality and deprive you of a chance to test out the validity of your assumption or conclusion.

Ask as few questions as possible. If you do ask a question, state your reason for asking it. Avoid the "interview."

Give your personal reactions to, rather than interpretations of, others. Interpretations often involve hidden agendas and create resistances.

Side conversations take precedence. Inasmuch as they are a form of disturbance, they are usually important and very often related to the theme or task. A participant talking to his/her neighbor is likely to be quite involved in the theme but may need help towards further and more open participation in the group process.

Only one at a time, please. Nobody can hear more than one statement at a time—verbal interactions have to be consecutive.

If more than one person wants to speak at the same time, let each make a brief statement about what he/she has in mind. The decision as to who speaks first, second, etc. is made by the speakers themselves, *rarely by the leader* (unless the leaders is one of the speakers) based on a variety of criteria, such as urgency, group interest, and so forth.

When you address someone, look at him or her rather than at the rug or out the window, so that you can observe the effect you have

on that person, and can gear your statements to the other's capacity
to take in what you are saying.

*Conversely, when someone addresses you, be aware of the effect the
person has on you* and let him or her know how you feel about his/
her statement to you.

Be aware of your body signals as well as of those of others. For example, if you are getting a headache while someone is "lecturing,"
state yourself. On the other hand, if you see someone yawn or wiggle
while you talk, pay attention to that person's signals.

Respect other people's wishes for space or for being left alone. Do
not crowd in on someone. Even if you feel the other person "needs"
you—allow him or her to make the decision to ask for, or accept, support. This is especially important for touching, holding, or going
after a person who has left the room.

I introduce these rules gradually, one by one, as the occasion arises
(and I don't always introduce all of them as "rules"!). I make a point of
observing them myself as well as reminding others to do so. Gradually,
group members take on this task and by the middle of a workshop most
people have integrated these rules and their meaning, thereby becoming
more and more independent of the leader in taking care of group process.
In this way the rules serve to promote self-support, autonomy and a sense
of self-responsibility and mutual responsibility, and contribute to a sense
of community.

I stress, however, that rules can be abused as well as used, and that these
are not iron rules. It would be ridiculous, for example, if nobody were
ever permitted to make anything but "I-statements." Moreover, if a person, for whatever reason, is either not willing or able to remember and
observe these rules of communication, he/she must be allowed to continue
to participate in his/her own way.

> For example, in a personal growth workshop, John, an engineer—
> quite compulsive and unrelated to his feelings—disregarded our
> reminders and continued to speak in generalities making pronounce-
> ments about "one," "everybody," and "nobody." It was clear to me
> that, at this moment, he was quite incapable of involving himself in
> any other way, and since many participants became impatient with
> him, we discussed this and agreed that while our rules of communi-
> cation were preferable to us, nobody need to adhere to them rigidly.
> As a result, he was able to stay for the one-week workshop, partici-
> pating in his limited way. Both John and the group-as-a-whole had

gained as a result—John by having been accepted as he was, the others by having practiced acceptance of difference, and also by getting a great deal of recognition from John.

Such a group experience also increases the sense of safety and belonging, for if one member can be accepted with his own different style of being, so can others.

The Sponsor, Group Composition and Group Structure

The beginning sessions of a workshop are always devoted to the process of exposing and exploring the group composition and its inner structure, starting with a theme such as "Sharing Who I Am and Why I Am Here." This not only gives us a chance to find out what people's expectations are and to respond with some correctives when they are way off (which happens often enough), but it also is the first occasion to bring into focus any expectations a sponsoring agency may have for the participants.

For example, members may be expected to bring back a report or give a presentation. They may have agreed to these conditions under some pressure and are now angry, anxious, upset. This offers an opportunity for individual work, or work with a subgroup (that particular team, i.e. all who are affected by this requirement). They may, for example, be invited to have a dialogue with the person within the sponsoring agency who "made" them accept this requirement, or even with the whole department, as they imagine it. Or perhaps they will have a dialogue with the report (as yet unwritten). Often other members join, having had similar experiences and feelings on another occasion. The result is a lessening of the disturbance and a beginning sense of commonality.

In personal growth workshops, the "Who am I?" theme may cover a whole session. I may suggest that each person give not only his/her name, but state how he/she feels about the name. This enables all of us to remember the names more quickly and, more importantly, it brings into focus the person's sense of identity, background and history—feelings about parents and siblings, about a cousin or aunt after whom someone was named, stories of migrations, feelings about having lost one's home or one's mother tongue. The sharing of such emotional material provides support for good contact and soon a sense of group cohesion begins to emerge.

The second or third session is focused on making the internal structure of the group transparent. The theme I use for this purpose is "Revealing whom I know and how I feel with that person here."* At times it is sufficient for members to simply state verbally who has known whom before and what their connections were and are. Occasionally, however, there are intricate networks emerging within the group and then I use nonverbal means first, such as group sculpting,** to bring into visible relief what the subgroupings in this group are, and let people explain them only later.

In a training workshop a whole training group (part of an ongoing training program) was present except Sam, the leader and sponsor of that group. I had noticed listlessness and a desire to cut short the workshop—quite unusual in my experience—had commented on it but had not received any enlightening response. When I suggested that the group sculpt its history, that is, how it had become *this* group, by starting with the earliest members, later members joining in order of appearance, it became clear that the earliest member, the founder (Sam), was missing. We used a hat stand to represent him, and all members gradually joined the sculpture, clutching the empty hat stand in the center. I then invited the group to address the hat stand (Sam) one by one, telling him how they each felt about him and his absence. A great deal of anger was expressed, not only about his absence now, but about his habit of coming and going as he pleased. The sculpture then was dismantled, and "Sam" put in a corner; "we can do without you!" was the message. The group continued to work with much more excitement and vigor. Moreover, the members were then able to relate to me in a more open, contactful fashion, and to accept me as their leader for the weekend.

In another workshop, organized by an existing peer group of eight, who had invited another six people to join for a "Gestalt week," it became evident to me very soon that I was dealing with two groups: the "in-group" that had invited the others, and the "out-group"— the invitees. The in-group seemed covertly hostile and exclusive. Also, I noticed considerable tension among its members. When I suggested that the host group members sit on the floor, they agreed only reluctantly and then were surprised to see how their positions

---

* I discovered the importance of this theme in a workshop which I co-led with Dr. Wolfgang Gerstenberg of Hannover. In that workshop, half the people left in the middle. We found out later that the people who had left were all members of an organization which was inimical to the one that had sponsored this workshop, and we concluded that they had come in order to undermine our work. We both decided then that from now on we would try to discover the connections between participants at the beginning of a workshop—before it is too late.

** A modification of Virginia Satir's Family Sculpting and of the group dynamic sociogram.

on the floor reflècted their relationships with each other, complex relationships at that, since they had been working together for several years and there had been intermittent love affairs among them. They explored these relationships to the etxent to which it seemed relevant at that moment and were then able to literally "make space" for the other people present, including me, by shifting their positions on the floor. More relationships were then made visible, the internal structure of the group became transparent, and we were on the road to becoming one group.

While the internal structure of the group at the beginning of the workshop needs to become transparent as early as possible, this does not mean that later on it can be ignored. It rarely remains stable. New relationships are formed, be they friendships or enmities, and old alliances are dissolved. These changes can become disturbing to the group-as-a-whole, if they remain "underground," that is, if they are not openly explored in sessions. For example, if two people fall in love, it is useful for them and the others to explore the meaning of this new relationship in terms of their patterns of choosing partners and dealing with partnership. Such exploration more often than not throws light on their relationships at home. Furthermore, as such newly-formed relationships often arouse competitiveness, jealousies and feelings of abandonment in others, these, too, then become material for work. Therefore, whenever there are important changes in the group constellation, I encourage participants to bring out their feelings about these changes. This does not mean that I support tactless questioning or "cross-examining." There must be respect for the intimacy of any relationship. However, we may encourage a "new" couple not to sit together all the time during sessions, so that their energies are not completely bound up with each other. And before the workshop ends, they will most likely want to work out whether it is desirable for them to continue their relationship, if so how, and if not, how to terminate it in the most constructive and creative way.

If such a relationship remains secret or is ignored, or if it is supported or undermined silently, it may block the energy flow and can weaken the cohesiveness of the group—as does *any* secret. If, however, it is explored in the group-as-a-whole, the couple can be accepted and jealousy can be expressed as well as joy—all feelings are kept flowing.

*   *   *

Couples who come together into a "mixed group" (consisting of couples and singles) often bring stability, provided they are in good contact with each other. I remember Virginia Satir saying in a workshop, "True intimacy knows no exclusion." Truly intimate couples are open to others and contribute much to cohesiveness and sense of community. Couples who are in conflict, on the other hand, are often a strain on each other and on the group-as-a-whole.

> In one of the workshops, such a couple, Erica and Peter (not married but considering marriage, and in the process of separating from their previous partners) repeatedly brought their disturbances into the sessions—Erica her jealousy and her fear of being abandoned (Peter was quite flirtatious), and Peter his fear of being engulfed by her. At first the whole group was interested and participated with enthusiasm in the couple's attempts to work through their fears and their catastrophic expectations individually and jointly. After a while, however, many in the group felt drained and tired, and confronted Erica and Peter with the fact that they were, after all, a couple "in formation" and were neither in need nor in a position to resolve all their difficulties during this workshop: Although they had only partially resolved their conflicts, they had confronted them; there was better contact at the boundary between them, some sense of completion and some new process going on. They agreed with this and to their own and the group's relief they also agreed that they need not strive for complete and total solutions. After this the group was able to continue to work with more ease.

Couples are not the only constellation that requires special attention. Other preexisting dyads (or triads, etc.), such as supervisor-supervisee, employee-boss, mother-daughter, brother-sister—and all sorts of "indirect" relationships (people who had heard about each other)—must be brought to the awareness of the group, and disturbances resulting from them need to be worked on throughout the time the workshop meets. I have had strange experiences: For example, Adam (ex-husband of Eve, who is now Robert's wife) unexpectedly met Lili (ex-wife of Robert) in a workshop, and the group had to deal with the avalanche of feelings generated by their encounter. We all survived and benefited because we were able to live through the passionate feelings of pain and anger at their respective ex-spouses, aroused by their encounter.

Of equal importance are "outsider" positions, such as those of the clown or the scapegoat. Whenever I notice a person remaining in either of these roles (or in any other fixed Gestalt) for any length of time, I consider this a group problem, an impasse, and examine it with the group. First, what is the present climate: Is there a sense of rigidity? Of authoritarian leadership? Is there unexpressed hostility toward me? Toward anyone else? Are there disturbances among group members that need airing? And so forth. When the ground has been cleared, I move to the figure: I search for the partner or partners who represent the other side of the outsider position, the polarity: for the scapegoat—the persecutor (usually the remainder of the group, including me); for the clown— the "King," "Queen," "Court," or "Audience," and so on. And then both sides take in their projections. The group takes in the "evil" (whatever that means at the moment) projected on the scapegoat; the scapegoat, in turn, takes in the "goodness" projected on the group. Now, the outsider can take his/her place in the group, the group has gotten through the impasse and, for the time being, the community is healed.

In summary, the internal structure of the workshop group needs to be focused on not only at the beginning, when it is most obviously necessary, but intermittently throughout the duration of the workshop, to prevent disturbances from remaining "underground," undermining the sense of safety and trust and, thereby, the work and growth of the community. Defining exactly which aspects of a relationship need to be discussed openly in the group, and which do not, is quite impossible. Essentially, each participant must determine this for him/herself. But if the climate is one that invites openness, most people are able to handle these problems with sensitivity and tact. With those who cannot do this, or with those who, unawares, assume outsider positions, the leader takes the initiative in order to enable the group to get through the impasse.

The Theme

To describe fully how I use themes to support and promote the group process and the development of group cohesion would require a chapter in itself. Here I will mention only the main aspects.

While it is certainly possible to lead a personal growth workshop without a specified theme beyond that of "Personal Growth," a theme such as "Journey of Discovery" (open-ended) or "Owning the Disowned Parts of Myself" (dealing with polarities) gives the group focus and a frame: It offers something participants can recognize ("I never thought I could feel jealous and feel good about myself at the same time!"). Also, by referring back to the theme over and over again, leader and participants remain aware that this is meant to be growth through concentration on a particular area, rather than therapy. Since a specific purpose within the overall goal of personal growth is provided, it becomes a point of common interest. Finally, the theme adds a dimension to group process, enabling participants to do their own "dynamic balancing," a key concept in theme-centered interactional group leading (Ronall and Wilson, in press) which denotes a process of shifting focus from individual participant to group-as-a-whole to theme and so on and so forth, to avoid overemphasis on one of these points. In this way, the theme is a handle for participants and leader alike, reminding them of their common purpose, and, since it is accessible to all, it furthers equality and promotes group cohesion.

In training workshops, the task—training in Gestalt therapy—is the theme. However, I use subthemes in the beginning and at the end (as described elsewhere in this chapter) and I also use a theme for processing sessions, such as "Reviewing What I Have Experienced Today—and Exploring It in Gestalt Therapy Terms." Such a formulation invites both an experiential and a didactic exploration of the preceding work, making processing lively and exciting and, by providing a focus, promoting group cohesion.

In personal growth workshops, subthemes emerge and are used sometimes for one session, or two, or for a whole day. Occasionally, the group splits into subgroups to work on the formulation of subthemes, and sometimes the whole group works on this task together. In either case, the common task requires cooperation, and the process itself, as well as the sense of accomplishment on having created a clear and well-sounding theme, promotes a sense of community.

Place

> Spontaneity is the seizing on and glowing and growing with what is interesting and nourishing in the environment (Perls, Hefferline & Goodman, 1951, p. 231).

Since the place in which our workshop meets becomes our environment "for the duration," work-play-sleep-eating space and furnishings, as well as the food itself, are significant to our well-being and thereby to the development of a community spirit. If our accommodations are uncomfortable or if we feel unwelcome, we may huddle together, close off our surroundings, or spend energy on dealing with our discomfort. We may develop a stance of *"us* against *them."* By contrast, if our hosts are in tune with us and make an effort to meet our needs, we will be glad to maintain contact with them, and contact among ourselves will be around our own issues. Thus our boundaries can remain flexible and open within and without.

Beautiful scenery invites hikes and exploration or play or work outdoors and this is nourishing for each person and for the group-as-a-whole.

> In a workshop with the theme of "Discovery" I spent a session with the whole group on a steep mountain side exploring ways of contacting one another and withdrawing, of moving, of being still, of experiencing the earth, and the wind. We discovered new plants, flowers, herbs, stones, new sounds and new views. We came back to work in the usual circle, glowing, invigorated and energized.

> We used the environment in a different way when we spent one of the beginning sessions of a training workshop outdoors on a meadow, exploring the theme of "Distance and Closeness": First we walked slowly toward and away from each other, giving each other non-verbal signals on how far or how close we wanted to be, testing our skills in giving and receiving such messages. Gradually we walked faster and faster until we were running. When we returned to our room, we processed this experience to see to what extent each person had succeeded in getting closer or keeping distance from others, as he/she wished—and in the process were able also to allay some of the anxiety about getting "too close" or being "left out"— boundary issues important in that stage of the group.

Sometimes, the group affects the space: We have often managed to change our environment to suit our needs, provided, of course, that our host gave us permission. Moving furniture, removing doors, erecting partitions, and painting pictures to decorate bare walls—such joint activities stimulate imagination, awaken playfulness, and promote a sense of cooperation and responsibility for, and pride in, common achievement, all promoting and supporting a sense of community.

The location of the workshop relative to the group members' home base is another aspect to be considered: if the workshop takes place close to the home of some of the members, we need to deal with their families', their employers' and their own expectations that they can go home for visits—be it for special occasions such as birthdays or conferences or for the day off. This interferes with the cohesiveness and flow of the group and of course makes it impossible for such persons to use their "in-between time" for encounters and other experiences with the rest of the group. The same is true for visits by members' relatives or friends, since members then tend to withdraw from the group-as-a-whole for most of their visitors' visiting time.

This does not mean, of course, that all contacts of this nature are seen as disturbances. Some are necessary, some simply pleasant, some both. But I do elicit information about any plans of this nature, as well as about a planned early departure, at the beginning of the workshop for, since the whole group is affected, we need to work this through together. Such discussions bring out clearly how the whole is affected by each of its parts and raises members' awareness of their interdependence. As a result, people sometimes change their plans in order to stay with the group.

Time

While time of the year and length of the workshop are quite important, the most significant aspect of time in a residential workshop is determined by the fact that we work and live together in the same place. This fact not only creates a different experience of time but allows for a different use of it.

As my training and experience had been in open-ended ongoing group therapy, I at first felt I was "cheating"—that is avoiding group process—when I started a workshop with a meal or an informal get-together over coffee,* or when I used a recess or free time for dealing with disturbances or for spontaneous work. In fact, I considered all work done outside sessions as "illegal," helping the group avoid its conflicts. Gradually I realized that by refusing to recognize the recesses as "life space," I was avoiding a piece of reality—namely that group process continues whether the group is in session or not. I then conceptualized the sessions and free time together as the "Gestalt" of the residential workshop: the figure of work against the background of recreation, of being together. The sessions are the *primary but not exclusive* time for the foreground purpose—work. Important work takes place during free time, and by the same token some play or fun is often introduced into work sessions. Thus background and foreground shift frequently and flexibly.

There is, however, another shift that occurs when we live together: recreation and informal, unstructured being and living together, while primarily background to the main purpose of doing Gestalt work, assume considerable importance. Many people have less difficulty working than playing. They can make contact more easily in the structured situation

---

* Because people often come from far away, I had instituted these informal beginnings initially in order to permit latecomers to drop in casually without disturbing the first session.

of the sessions than in the free hours between. They dread the evenings or the days off. They do not know how to make contact informally, spontaneously. They feel hurt, excluded or ostracized. Therefore, so that no one feels or is left out and so that the sense of community which has been growing in sessions can be carried on outside, I frequently bring the theme of free time into the foreground during sessions. Essentially there are two ways in which I do this: 1) I keep aware of how free time radiates into sessions and I encourage the group to do the same; 2) I occasionally pre-structure free time by suggesting some common activity, or an experiment. But, whether I have suggested some structure for the in-between time or not, disturbances, excitements, boredom, anxiety, encounters, loneliness, etc. must be brought out into the open during the next session or they will remain "underground" and undermine our sense of safety and thereby our work. Therefore, at the beginning of each session, we pay attention to who sits where, who sits with whom, who is late or missing, who appears absentminded, depressed, and "not fully there." And I remind all of us to be aware of and to work through or at least bring out into the open "unfinished business" which started in free time, even when such "business" seems to have meaning to some of the members only.

> When the whole group had spent a break at the beach, Jane came back with a sullen expression. She said she was disappointed with Gary (a casual friend): While the group was sunning itself he had "just talked"—to anybody, not to her specifically—and spoken in generalizations—"holding forth." Jane, who had been working through a disturbance with Gary in the preceding session and had felt closer to him than previously, had expected continuing intimacy, more "I-statements"; in fact, she acknowledged she wanted only one kind of contact with Gary: spontaneous and authentic, close and intimate, all the time. Gary was not ready for this, nor did he want to be. He felt Jane was asking too much of him. Jane still sulked; she needed considerable work until she finally realized the demands which her expectations put on others and the disappointment she was bound to create for herself. The others, ready for the theme, now picked it up as a group theme "Closeness and Distance—Balancing My Needs and Yours," working on it for the remainder of the session, clearing the ground for greater awareness of freedom and safety in our community.

Naturally, I must be aware of my own experiences in recesses and how they affect me when I return to the session. This includes encounters with group members, letters from home or friends, telephone calls, "restless" rests, etc. And I share my disturbances or passionate involvements with the group for the sake of my own well-being as well as the group's, although with "selective authenticity." In this way I keep my own contact (and withdrawals) as flowing and undisturbed as possible, and cut down to a minimum feelings of being excluded or exclusive.

There is another way in which I use free time: a typical Gestalt group experiment carried out in a session can be continued during free time and reported on in the following session.

> Tim does not ask for what he wants but expects the others to guess and offer it to him, and feels neglected when they don't. In a session, he goes around the group asking for something from each member; having concluded this successfully, and feeling pleased with his willingness to risk and the rewards he gets for doing so, he is now given the task of asking for what he wants at the dinner table. In the session after dinner, he reports on his experience and gets feedback from his table companions on how he came across. He learns he tended to appear rather impatient, somewhat demanding; at the same time he gets recognition and support for continuing to risk and to be straightforward.

Conversely, an experiment started in free time ("I wanted to see what happens when I let someone else lead me") can, in the next session, turn into a series of experiments for the whole group on the theme of "Leading and Being Led."

Or, in training workshops, I may suggest during a meal that we experiment with chewing, or—if the mood at the table does not invite such experimentation—that we take some bread to the next session to experiment with then. Around these experiments, I introduce the concepts of dental aggression, destruction, annihilation, assimilation and introjection, and discuss the parallels between physical and emotional or mental hunger, and between styles of chewing food and chewing thoughts (Perls, 1969).

Finally, a person who concluded an experiment in a session and is pleased and proud of him/herself ("I can hardly believe I could tell this secret to you all!") can enjoy this fully and get continued support from the other members during the next break.

In this way, the context for the "safe emergency" (Perls, Hefferline & Goodman, 1951, p. 287), that is, for the Gestalt experiment, has been extended from the session (structured work time) to the "in-between" (unstructured living time). To paraphrase Redl's term (Redl & Wineman, 1962), it becomes a "Life Space Experiment," in the most natural manner, with group members as peer therapists. In this way, the group expands its boundaries from being a group-for-working to being a group-for-living—a community.

Another and different aspect of time is its structure and the use I make of it: At the beginning of the workshop I prepare a visual scheme of the total workshop time along the lines of the "week-at-a-glance" calendar, showing sessions and free time, days off, and the ending, and I prepare a schedule for the first half of the workshop. In training workshops we also schedule processing sessions, usually at the end of the day, in the beginning sometimes every other day. We discuss the prepared schedule in the beginning and later we decide together on how to use the remainder of the time. Discussions around scheduling and use of time are opportunities for getting into authority issues (who decides what in this group) and for joint decision-making; they mark a beginning in group cohesion.*

There are still other uses of time. One is the creation of special events —celebrations—throughout the workshop. These may be birthdays, anniversaries, national holidays of the country in which we happen to be, or religious holidays that fall into that particular season. For example, we once celebrated Chanukkah and Advent in a workshop in Germany using the same kind of candles, as our theme became "My Festivals and Yours." We may also celebrate a participant's especially important discovery or recovery, such as that of his/her mother tongue. Such celebrations cement our sense of community—as they do everywhere in the world.

A highlight is the festive evening that announces the ending phase. This festival does not take place on the last evening but on the evening before. A great deal of emotional involvement and excitement—and sometimes upset—is generated during such an event, and this requires time to be worked through—more than just a day. For the preparations, small groups take responsibility for different tasks, such as decorating the rooms, drinks, food, music, etc. Depending on the group's state and wishes, the evening can be a "happening" with no preconceived idea of what we will do, or it can be structured. We may have a theme, such as "Owning and Enjoying the Child in Me" (which once landed us in a Kindergarten complete with imaginary sandbox) or "Discovering the Devil in Me"

---

* In my groups, as in all TCI workshops, we always work towards consensus, or, if that isn't possible, compromise.

(which resulted in a colorful and noisy evening in Hell, enjoyed by all and bringing up important material for work the next day). Sometimes we just eat and drink and play and dance together. The success of this festival hinges on the degree of community spirit that has developed, and the extent to which we have become a community can be measured by the way such a festival proceeds. Happily, many of these festivals in my workshops have been lively, exciting, original, creative and satisfying to all. But what if they do not turn out so well? The failure then becomes grist for our workshop mill, and this is where the importance of the next day and evening lies. We thoroughly process the festive evening, encouraging negative as well as positive feedback. And if only one or two persons felt bored or "out," we explore how the system—the group-as-a-whole—shares responsibility for this. Quite often, this results in an important discovery of the means whereby the outsider creates, supports and maintains his position by ignoring, not trusting or refusing invitations from others, by creating a situation that excludes him, or at least allowing such a situation to persist without protesting. The last evening offers a chance to try out a new stance.

Toward the end of the farewell festival, George, severely handicapped by polio, was sitting in a corner while the others were dancing. Although for most of the time, one or two of the dancers, including me, took turns in keeping him company, I felt rather uncomfortable, for it was because of his handicap that he had to remain on the outside looking in, so to speak. I also suspected that this indicated some lack of community spirit, although I could not pinpoint it: After all, there had been, prior to the dance, other activities that he had been able to join, and I did not feel that everybody was obliged to give up dancing to accommodate him. So where was the snag? The next day, the whole group acknowledged discomfort. We then examined the role George had played in contributing to this situation, by, for example, not participating in the preparations, and found that the others, who were annoyed but did not acknowledge this, had unawares ignored his problem. Had he taken part in the planning, they could have discussed together what to do about dancing, and might have found a creative solution, such as inventing a sitting dance or a rhythmic game. Furthermore, we looked back at our experiences before the festival and, to the relief of all, aired our feelings about the way George had used his handicap to get our attention (being late, in obvious pain when looking for a seat, etc.) and to avoid contact. And although this was by no means the first time that his handicap had become the theme, he became more sharply aware of how he had isolated himself, projecting his rejection on us and experiencing himself as victim of our rejection. We, on the other hand, gained awareness of the degree to which we had been in collusion with him: We had avoided contacting *our* feelings about him and about handicaps, ours and his. At this point, George began to cry and with deep feelings he told us what it was like for him to live with this permanent disfigurement and handicap.

That evening I introduced the "Magic Shop" (a modification of the psychodrama warm-up game) and George, to our surprise and delight, became the star of the evening, this time getting our attention not for acting the humble victim, but a powerful, arrogant man, who demanded what he wanted—and got it!! And that evening —the evening before the workshop was over—George joined our community fully and happily, as an equal.

Endings

For the remainder of our time we prepare the ending of our community. Themes (the order may vary) are: "Finishing Unfinished Business Here," "What Do I Leave Here—What Do I Take with Me?" "Re-Entry: What Do I Find at Home? What Do I Bring with Me from Here?" We may work on these themes by simply sharing our expectations or I may use a guided fantasy or psychodramatic work to deepen the experience and to allow feelings to surface.

Many people are fearful of good-byes and close up long before the workshop is over, long before the final session, trying to avoid the experience of ending, the departure from their newly-won friends, the ending of this, our self-created community. Whenever I become aware of this I work with these people toward achieving a more contactful ending process. I bring in my experiences in migrating—taking roots and then picking up to take new roots elsewhere and saying good-bye so often. And just as a great deal of work can happen in the last few minutes of a session, so it can be in the last hours of a workshop.

Themes, like "Holding on and Letting Go" or "Endings—New Beginnings" are useful in supporting us to give up this group, to let this community die.

The last session is reserved for saying good-bye: First while we sit in the circle, each person takes his/her turn to say good-bye to individuals and to the group-as-a-whole. Then we break up and, in the room in which we have worked throughout the workshop, we say good-bye to one another individually. Then we disperse into all directions.

We finally meet over lunch, informally, the way we had met first over dinner or coffee—no longer the group.

And then we depart . . .

Space does not permit me to describe all the other possibilities available in a workshop to promote a sense of community. Here, I will mention only two: language and art material.

Language

Throughout the workshop, but especially while people are working individually on an internal split or on an unfinished situation from their childhood, I listen carefully for signs in their speech patterns, rhythms, or accents, indicating that they are not comfortable in the language they are using, such as sudden halts, pauses, stammers, or gross foreign pronunciations and grammatical errors. When I notice any of these, I ask them to say something in their mother tongue. Usually, their first reaction is protest: No one will understand them if they speak, say, Czech. Or, if they are native Germans or Austrians and have been speaking German, they are perplexed: They *are* speaking their mother tongue— so what do I want? To the first protest I respond that we will understand the "music" and thereby the feeling tone of what they are saying; besides, they can tell us the content later. To the others I explain what I mean by mother tongue, namely the exact dialect or familial variety of a language they heard and spoke as children.* Some still object, but, sooner

or later, most are willing to "try on" their childhood language and then, more often than not, something dramatic happens.

> In a training group, a Hungarian who, up to that point, had kept at a distance from the group, burst into tears after she had had a dialogue, in Hungarian, with her father. She then revealed that she was a political refugee, and told us of her flight from Hungary, of her panic as she crossed the border into Austria, a teenager, all alone, running, running. . . .
>
> Until then, she had participated as a therapist, discussing mainly professional matters with us. Now, for the first time, she was sharing

---

* Central European regional dialects show much greater variety than those of English spoken in the United States.

something personal, deeply meaningful, and with this, she made her first real contact with us. When she had completed her story, she had finally joined the group. That evening she began to whistle and hum Hungarian folk tunes—and to her delight some of us joined her. Later she taught us to dance the Czardas.

Similarly, in another workshop, a Greek woman taught us Greek folk dances, after she had, in Greek, dramatically taken leave from her grandmother, whose death she had never before accepted.

The situation is somewhat different with people from Switzerland and German-speaking countries. In the German parts of Switzerland with its many dialects, most people dislike "high" German as the "schoollanguage" imposed by authority and are relieved when they are invited to speak their own dialect—their mother tongue—needing no coaxing, just the assurance that the others in the group are willing to make an effort to understand them. Educated Germans, however, are often used to speaking "Akademiker-Deutsch" (the German of academe, a language which is grammatically correct, dry and lifeless) and find it hard to give it up, although it necessitates their holding themselves erect, stiffening their necks, freezing their facial muscles, jutting out their jaws, squeezing their lips, and speaking through their noses, so that their whole demeanor appears stilted and always dead serious. Speaking their mother tongue releases them from these retroflections, loosens up their faces and necks, sometimes the whole upper part of their bodies, and brings out anew long-forgotten qualities, especially humor and mischievousness.

In a training workshop, a pastoral counselor, a native of Berlin who had been living in southern Germany for most of his adult years, changed from being permanently serious, dull, and closed to people and thoughts, to a vivacious, intelligent, very funny and likeable person, after he had given us a brief lecture in his native "Berlinese" dialect. In gratitude for this transformation he translated, or rather transposed, the first few pages of Laura Perls' paper (1976) into that dialect. He demonstrated by his witty formulations his understanding of every subtlety, and earned the group's well-deserved admiration, when he read it to us during our farewell party.

In listening to these dialects and foreign languages I guess a great deal from the context and from facial expressions and gestures. I also ask for translations when necessary and encourage others to do the same. Thus, I work toward people's freeing themselves by using their mother tongue at least for part of the time, and faces relax, voices drop and become resonant, eyes become clear, and postures straighten out. Moreover, as people contact their childhood language, other parts of their childhood become accessible to further work.

The effect on the group-as-a-whole is profound: To witness a person come to life as he/she contacts and re-embraces his/her mother tongue and, with it, a piece of home, is a deeply moving experience. Usually, the whole group is spellbound while this happens. Other people's memories of home are evoked and exchanged, and the mood becomes mellow. Some may hum a folk tune—always evocative—or later dance a folk dance. It is as if, for a while, the group becomes a home for many homes—a place where no one is a "foreigner."

In addition to experimenting with real languages, I also introduce gibberish or language games, some remembered from my childhood, some picked up in various professional contexts, others invented ad hoc, to help loosen up an individual or a group-as-a-whole when there are expressive difficulties. All of these playful experiments, such as scolding or cursing with a nonsense word, by using appropriate affect, or acting out a dialogue or a skit with the figures from one to one hundred, giving them meaning through tone of voice, facial expression and gestures, shake up and loosen habitual speech patterns and language taboos. They create a playful environment in which participants become less concerned about being refined, correct and exact, and more interested in inventing, trying out and practicing their own, unique ways of expressing themselves. The result, for a while, is often chaotic: A Tower-of-Babel kind of atmosphere which releases creative energy and invites us to contact the novel in our own and in other people's expressive modes. We keep what is useful and leave behind what we no longer need. As individuals and as a group we have expanded our boundaries.

Art Materials

Since I am an art therapist I cannot use art materials systematically for therapeutic purposes. However, I enjoy drawing, painting, cutting out paper, and playing with clay or plastelene, and I introduce art materials into my groups to promote playfulness and risk-taking. Usually, the material is just available, and is used occasionally by individuals or the group without much attention from me, for example in the preparation of happenings or festivals, for decorating a room, or for costumes and masks.

However, a few times I have used art materials to deal with disturbances with totally unexpected results.

In a personal growth workshop a woman came to sessions evidently drunk, and became a serious disturbance to the group. Confronted with this, she agreed to give up drinking "for the duration," but was afraid that her withdrawal symptoms, specifically her tremors, might become a new disturbance. Indeed, these tremors, primarily in her hands, appeared the first morning she was sober and she was in considerable distress. Noticing this, I suggested that she select something from the art materials lying in the corner of the room. Without hesitating, she picked up a few pieces of colored plastelene and within minutes had created a charming little rooster. She was extremely pleased and completely surprised. She had never before touched plastelene or clay. The group, visibly touched, encouraged her to use her newly discovered talent, and she continued to "play" with plastelene until the workshop was over, producing many original little sculptures. She also remained sober, her "shakes" subsided soon, and she was able to participate in the group process. She had joined our community.

Sometimes, when working on a theme, I use art material as well as other objects to stimulate participants' imagination, and thereby to free them for better contact with each other.

In a workshop with the overall theme of "Freeing Creativity"* one of the subthemes was "Making My Dreams Come True." For this session, participants were asked to bring from their rooms one or two objects they would enjoy using or have others use. We then put all these colorful objects—scarves, stoles, blouses, skirts, sweaters, pictures, photographs, newspapers, magazines, colored paper, scissors, paints, brushes, crayons, and so forth—in the middle of the room. Small groups were formed. Each decided on a dream to make "come true," chose material for this purpose, and within an hour all the projects were completed. The results were truly amazing. They included a scene in paradise, with Adam and Eve in perfect bliss; an opera that spoofed our workshop; and a fashion show in which six women modeled the latest "freedom garments," such as see-through blouses and "almost topless bathing suits."

The whole group was exuberant, as one dream project after the other was exhibited or performed. More importantly, this experience welded us into a creative community for the remainder of our stay together.

---

* My co-leader in this workshop was Klaus Vopee of Hamburg.

Conclusion

In my idea of a workshop community I want all of us to feel welcome and at home, to feel secure enough to show ourselves as we are now, and to risk all kinds of new behaviors to discover the novel in ourselves and others. We grow and change without pushing ourselves or one another, knowing that there is no need for pressure.

Every member contributes to the welfare and enrichment of the community according to his/her ability. There is no hierarchy. All members have the same rights and powers in the decision-making processes for the group-as-a-whole, except for the leader or instructor, who has to make certain decisions by virtue of his/her training and ensuing responsibilities. We do not always love or even like each other, but we respect one another's differences in values, in tastes, and in behavior sufficiently not to disturb and, most importantly, not to ridicule one another. Nobody is rejected because of a handicap—be it physical or emotional, chronic or temporary. Conflicts are handled openly and without violence, and when the parties to the conflict cannot resolve it alone, a third party is invited to help arrive at consensus—or, if that is impossible, compromise. The same is true in decision-making for the group-as-a-whole: We are not satisfied with a majority decision; we strive toward consensus or compromise.

We discourage secrecy, yet respect privacy and each person's "space"; we can trust each other not to pry—and we can wait for full openness and authenticity to develop gradually. We trust time, and we trust the group process.

We have fun—we laugh and we play. We celebrate and sing and dance. We cry and mourn. We love and we hate. And we value our life.

But is this type of workshop not a luxury? A kind of pseudo-work-vacation? A camp for adults, affordable only to the privileged few? Do our efforts have an impact beyond the workshop itself—on the community at large? Many participants ask these questions. My answer is that I do not know how these workshops affect the community. I do know that many people return home having acquired not only new skills for their profession but a taste for this kind of life, and a process with which to continue it—with their families, with their teams on the job, and, perhaps at some point, with the communities they live in. Many come back for more and often bring along their partners. In this way, slowly, more and more people are infected with this spirit and spread it beyond the confines of our workshops, which, thereby, serve a purpose beyond that of training or personal growth.

For me personally, leading intensive Gestalt workshops on two continents and trying to create a sense of community in them has become a continually exciting adventure. Workshops are never dull, often difficult, usually full of surprises and always rewarding. I have learned much that has enriched my practice and my personal life. And when I look at a map—especially of Central Europe, where I have held most of the workshops—I see it dotted with familiar places that contain familiar faces, often the faces of dear friends.

I have regained my own mother tongue, which I had never forgotten but had refused to use fully once I had left Austria, and with it I recovered a wealth of memories of my childhood and youth—poems, songs, stories, scenes, and episodes—which I had buried as I had buried that part of my life.

I have much to be grateful for. Most of all I am grateful for having become part of a network of people—in Europe, in the United States and Canada with whom—diverse as they are—I share common interests and common values.

14

Exploring Sex Roles in Gestalt Workshops

GINGER LAPID

In my Gestalt workshops we come together, be it for three hours, three days, three weeks or three months, for a common purpose—to explore and experiment with sex roles and sex-role stereotypes. Some of the questions we address ourselves to include: What are our sex roles at the present time? How did we develop them? Do we still want them? Which aspects are no longer satisfying and growth-producing for us? What are we *able* and what are we *willing* to do to change our sex-role attitudes, behaviors and values?

Ten, 20, 30, or 80 people come together as a learning community, where participants have the opportunity to recreate both themselves and new social possibilities. "Sex-Role Workshops" have been composed of students, teachers, members of public and private organizations, or simply of people who are interested in sex-role awareness and change. Various races and both sexes participate in these workshops, which are also problem-solving communities. Personal, interpersonal and social problems related to sex roles and sex-role stereotyping are explored, as are the interrelationships between the personal, interpersonal and social aspects of sex-role problems. The sex-role concerns which individuals experience as personal problems are always interpersonal issues as well and, therefore, can be explored at the group level.

It is through personal sharing and group interaction that the social context of sex-role socialization and sex-role stereotyping emerges. The group can be viewed as a microcosm of society; differences and similarities with respect to sex roles are made explicit, are explored and understood. Then change becomes a viable option.

As I reflect on these workshops, various aspects of the total group experience emerge. Each of these aspects has an impact on the personal growth of individuals, on the relationships between group members, and on the growth and development of the group as a whole. I shall describe three of these: figure-ground, polarity, and contact-withdrawal.

I. FIGURE-GROUND

Gestalt therapists are concerned with the organism in context, with the individual in the environment. When individuals cannot or will not distinguish themselves from the environment or differentiate between various aspects of their environment, their experience becomes all indistinguishable background. The more the organism grows and develops, the more it is able to differentiate foreground from background. A person's wants, needs, interests, awarenesses and fascinations begin to merge as the focus of attention.

In Sex-Role Workshops, a goal for the groups as a whole, as well as for individual group members, is for sex role to become "figure." As a result, after leaving the group and while functioning in their daily environments, group members have become aware of sex roles, perceiving them clearly at relevant times. In my workshops, I have observed a wide variability in the degree of clarity with which groups members perceive sex-role concerns as figure. In fact, some have concerns which are related to sex-role stereotyping, without any awareness of the connection.

For these people, issues of sex-role stereotyping are firmly embedded aspects of the undifferentiated ground. A woman, for example, may feel inadequate for not being petite or cute, yet have no awareness that this standard of femininity (which she has introjected*) comes from the cultural sex-role stereotypes. She has received this message from her family, significant others, peers, the media and the culture in general. Becoming aware of the social context in which these feelings of inadequacy developed may relieve women and men from blamatory attitudes towards themselves and others with regard to previously personalized sex-role issues. An awareness of the social context also enlarges group members' perspective: For example, having to be petite and cute also goes along with being doll-like, being helpless, needing protection, and acting more

---

* Introjection is the "mechanism whereby we incorporate into ourselves standards, attitudes, ways of acting and thinking which are not truly ours . . . We have moved the boundary between ourselves and the rest of the world so far inside ourselves that there is almost nothing of us left . . ." (Perls, 1973, p. 35).

like a child than an adult. These and other aspects of female sex-role stereotypes will not be chosen by women who want to be full, creative, healthy, adult human beings.

Helping people explore and understand the societal context of their previously personal concerns is one of the *most satisfying* aspects of leading Sex-Role Workshops. Bringing this background into clear focus, through personal, interpersonal and group exploration, is a significant experience for the participants, which enables them to see themselves and others in a different perspective.

Another type of person who attends my workshop is the one for whom sex-role stereotyping remains an almost continual, rigid figure which rarely recedes into the background. This rigidity can be seen in some people who are strongly in favor of "traditional" sex-role stereotypes, as well as in some who are adamantly opposed to them. These people are often primed to react to what is said and done as a personal attack on themselves and their world-view. They frequently anticipate negative, even hostile, reactions from others to what they say and do. They are "ready to trigger" in a defensive manner, to expressions, statements and behaviors of others in the group. What fascinates me is that an antagonistic symbiotic relationship develops between those who attack traditional sex-role stereotypes and those who defend them. To continue their current attitudes and behaviors, they need and feed off each other. As an example, when a "traditional" group member (female or male) says "I don't understand why some girls (referring to adult females) get so upset when men open doors for them; men are supposed to do this," members of the opposing force are likely to respond angrily to the position stated, as well as to the speaker. This antagonism quickly escalates.

II. POLARITY

Polarization between those strongly in favor of and those strongly opposed to traditional sex-role stereotyping is not uncommon in Sex-Role Workshops. The resolution of the polarity represented by these factions is critical to the growth and development of both the group-as-a-whole and individual group members. If the antagonisms are either not dealt with explicitly in the group or are addressed in a manner which increases the polarization, the group is likely to be laden with covert or overt hostility, lack of trust between and among group members, and lack of mutual support. Group members will be guarded in what they say and express, take fewer risks, and experiment less. This wary (rather than open) group behavior will usually arrest group and individual growth. As a result, individual and group backlash often occurs in ways ranging from simple resistance to group experiments to subtle or overt group sabotage.

Simultaneously, this very polarity contains the seeds of diversity and energy which can be used productively to enhance group development, thereby creating a safe ground for individual growth. It is from this very dichotomy that group members can experience and assess their responses, behaviors, discrepancies and sex-role-related attitudinal and behavioral patterns. From these experiences emerge awareness and significant growth.

As a group leader, I have a strong impact on the effect of group polarization on group process. Although a feminist myself, I attempt not to ally myself with one side of the polarity or the other; maintaining a facilitative position allows me to guide the group with a measure of objectivity and makes it more likely that my guidance and input will be accepted by the group. This is no easy task. What has helped me, however, not to align myself with a particular position is having participated in consciousness-raising and therapy groups where I worked through many of my own emotional responses to sex-role issues.* Also, through the experience of leading numerous Sex-Role Workshops, I have gained perspective on group members' statements and feelings at various stages of the consciousness-raising process. I tend to accept participants' responses, even if I don't agree with the sentiments or points of view expressed, since I see them as part of a developmental process.

To constructively utilize group conflict, I introduce several explicit ground rules into my workshops. Some of these are: 1) All participants have the right to have and express their own opinions and feelings; 2) all participants have the right to be listened to in the group; 3) all participants are to take ownership of their opinions and feelings by beginning their statements with "I think," "I feel," "I want," or whatever "I statement" is appropriate; 4) all participants are to take responsibility for the statements behind their questions. For example, a question such as "Why do women demand all the benefits of equality but still expect me to pay for them?" may get transformed into the statement "I resent women who demand equality with me but who are not willing to pay their way." The group then can deal with the explicit statement, rather

---

* Maintaining this objectivity is easier for me to do in workshops than in intimate relationships!

than get involved in "answering" a rhetorical question. By observing these ground rules, an atmosphere is promoted in a group so that dialogue and appreciation of differences are respected.

In dealing with polarization, I have had the most success and seen the most growth when I focus directly and explicitly on what is happening within the group. Usually I find that those directly involved in the polarized conflict are angry, resentful, defensive, hurt and sometimes frustrated, while those not directly involved are also frustrated but also anxious, confused, fearful and sometimes disinterested. As a rule, I deal with those directly involved first, giving them space and opportunity to express themselves within the group. This is often enough to resolve the conflict. As an alternative, I may ask opposing group members to participate in a role reversal. If the polarization involves a significant number of members, I often use the following "fishbowl" technique:

> One group sits in a circle in the middle of the room and discusses what they are experiencing, feeling and thinking in terms of the conflict. The other group sits around the inner group and listens. When the group in the middle has finished, a short time is allotted for the outer, listening group to respond to what they heard, saw and experienced. The inner group listens as the outer group shares their responses. The two circles then reverse positions and repeat the whole procedure. When the second cycle is finished, the two groups then come together for total group sharing.

The content of the "inner group" discussion is determined by the needs, concerns, attitudes and behaviors of the group members involved in the sharing. For example, in one of my workshops I noticed that the majority of men were harboring covert resentment, possibly in response to having been blamed by the women in the group. I suggested that the men form an "inner" circle in the middle of the room and I asked them to express their resentments toward the women in the room and women in general. This unleashed previously bridled energy in the male group. The women, who were observing and listening, were sitting on the edge of their chairs and seemed ready to jump in with what I sensed was a slightly disdainful attitude.

When it was the women's turn to be in the middle, I imagined they were expecting me to ask them to express their resentments toward men. I shared my expectation with them and they concurred. Because the women had aired these resentments during the beginning of the session,

I felt and told them that doing so again would be redundant and counter-productive. I suggested they experiment with another approach, to which they agreed. I asked them to pay attention to how they were sitting, with special attention to their body language and the attitudes conveyed thereby. I then asked each woman to give a here-and-now statement to go with her posture. After this round, I suggested to the women that they imagine they were men and change their body posture and manner accordingly. Again, I asked each woman to give the here-and-now statement which went with the new body posture.

There resulted a discussion among the women on how in our culture their lives might have been different had they been born and raised male. This included thoughts and feelings on opportunities missed, paths not taken and regrets. They then moved to explore existential questions regarding their sex-role identities and potentials. The men were genuinely moved by the women's feelings about their disadvantaged position. When the total group reassembled, warm, genuine contact was established among all the members.

While increasingly intense interaction often facilitates the resolution of polarity in a group, structured separation is an alternative, particularly if the group has been together for an extended period of time. Uninterrupted prolonged interaction may result in overload for the group. One method of structuring separation is to suggest that members write in journals. Another is to call for a break. Many conflicts have been resolved over coffee, in the bathroom, and so forth. Those in conflict often rush toward each other to discuss and exchange their ideas. After the break, when they feel refreshed, people are usually more open and willing to deal with the conflict.

III.   CONTACT-WITHDRAWAL

A group leader needs to be sensitive to the contact-withdrawal patterns and needs of the group. In Sex-Role Workshops, as in other groups, I often observe people entering with "contact-withdrawal ambivalence": On the one hand, they want to make contact with others; on the other hand, they feel awkward, fearful, shy and uncertain.

To deal with this initial "contact-withdrawal ambivalence," I often structure beginning sessions in such a way that they offer participants the opportunity to work alternately in small groups and in the total group. Small groups tend to eliminate some of the participants' anxieties.

The smaller the group, the safer and freer members feel to experiment, especially at first. Also, through small group sharing they make contact with a few people at a time. However, after having worked in small groups for some time, participants are encouraged to share some of their responses with the whole group. In this way, they make contact with the rest of the group and differences and similarities between them emerge more clearly. To give you an example: I start out by asking members in the total group to tell about their personal, interpersonal and group concerns. Next I ask them to write their expectations, best hopes and worst fears—personal, interpersonal, and for the group. Then they are asked to assess the relationship of these concerns to sex-role issues and to share their discoveries in small groups.

Although the contact-withdrawal ambivalence is resolved, Sex-Role Workshops, like all groups, exhibit contact-withdrawal cycles. These are evident in each session and in the workshop-as-a-whole.

By the time a Sex-Role Workshop ends, the group has usually become a more self-directing and self-supporting entity, having taken increasing responsibility for its wants, needs and purpose. Most participants leave such a workshop with heightened awareness of their own individual sex-role stereotypes, as well as those of others and of society in general. Many feel encouraged to expand their roles and to experiment with new behaviors. Having discovered through self-disclosure in a supportive environment what they have in common with others, as well as what is unique for each, they are better able to accept their own and other people's differences.

Interestingly, I often see the greatest gain in sex-role perspective and awareness among those who come into the group saying skeptically that there are really no problems. They leave the group with sex role as clearer, more flexible "figure." Group members with an initially rigid sex-role "figure" become more flexible in the process and gain a measure of freedom from limiting sex-role stereotypes. And as becomes obvious in Sex-Role Workshops, none of us is totally free from sex-role stereotyping.

15

Identity House — A Gestalt Experiment for Gays

PATRICK KELLEY

At the cutting edge of gay consciousness in June of 1965 there was an after-hours club in Greenwich Village called The Stonewall. "This club was more than a dance bar, more than just a gay gathering place. It catered largely to a group of people who were not welcome or cannot (sic) afford other places of homosexual social gathering . . . 'drags' and 'queens' had no place but The Stonewall" (Teal, 1971, p. 29). That a drag queen "threw the first stone" (literally a beer can) during the police attempts to close The Stonewall and harass its patrons adds a touch of irony to the gay struggle.

One evening following the police raid and the riot is precipitated, I came across Paul Goodman among the crowd lining the street outside the club. I expressed my surprise at seeing him there since I knew that he seldom visited gay bars, preferring instead mixed working-class places. His reply, "Why not? This is where tonight's revolution is taking place," startled me and alerted me to the true significance of what was occurring around me. I looked again at the crowd milling about, a mixture of "just curious" types with a few obvious gays, and wondered where the battlements were.

The arrival of the Tactical Police Force gave me my answer. They piled out of their vans cursing and shoving the until-then passive crowd. I, as well as others, quickly realized that we were all "up against the wall," even those of us who taught college and led polite Peace Marches. Not only a revolution, but also a sense of community, was

Grateful acknowledgement is given to the following Gestalt therapists who assisted in the writing of this chapter: Michael Altman, Marion Howard, Karen Humphrey, John Kane and Gloria Wilson.

219

spawned on the streets that evening. No longer were we to separate ourselves with labels like "butch" or "queen"; we were all of us *"gay"*.

Some three years later this sense of community had grown to the point that gays had bonded together to provide their own psychological services, a walk-in peer counseling service at a newly founded center called Identity House.* We also provided a referral service to therapists who were screened for their attitude towards sexuality.

Historically, Gestalt therapy has attracted a large number of gays. It is our contention that this phenomenon occurred because it respected the integrity of the individual's sexual identity. "In therapy, the so-called 'regressions' are aware loyalties and it is pointless to deny or denigrate what the patient has really felt as his own; . . . The classical instance is the impossibility of 'changing' homosexuals who have once gotten important sexual satisfaction, especially since they have creatively overcome many social obstacles in order to get it" (Perls et al., 1951, p. 424).

The Gestalt concept that perhaps it is not necessarily the individual's task to adjust to society is clearly at odds with the conventional medical model. We Gestalt therapists, in fact, hold that at times it is society's task to adjust to the individual. Furthermore, we assume that there is an ongoing process of self-regulation in the healthy individual's interaction with the environment. Healthy behavior is defined in terms of the *quality* of the contact, which includes, naturally, the context within which it occurs. It does *not* depend on the form which that behavior takes. *"The achievement of a strong Gestalt is itself the cure, for the figure of contact is not a sign of, but is itself the creative* integration of experience" (Perls et al., 1951, p. 232) .

Thus, for example, it seems that from a Gestalt perspective *any* consensual sexual act is a reaching out and therefore may be considered healthy in a sexually repressed society. More important, every publicly acknowledged sexual act disturbs the status quo and is, therefore, a potentially revolutionary action.** A restrictive society is necessarily rigid;

---

* Today Identity House serves the following functions in addition to peer counseling: weekly rap groups for men and for women; monthly co-educational rap groups; referral services to therapists screened for attitude toward gays; weekly supervisory groups for peer counselors; educational workshops; and social events, such as dances.

** This helps explain the hysteria of Anita Bryant in the late 1970s as well as the vehement responses and heavy penalties for draft card burning in the '60s. In Ms. Bryant's fundamentalist world, the concept of a loving sexuality based on an ever-renewing free choice does *threaten her style of family structure.* Without the introjected precepts of "morality" and "duty," the patterns of submissiveness to authority would disintegrate. People would be free, and free beings are likely to reject or change restrictive situations.

unsanctioned protest has to cause the established structure to either crack down or be cracked. "The aggressive drives are not essentially distinct from the erotic drives . . . when the [y] . . . are anti-social, it is that the society is opposed to life and change (and love); then it will either be destroyed by life or it will involve life in a common ruin, make human life destroy society and itself" (Perls et al., 1951, p. 351).

Back in 1946, Paul Goodman, in writing of his visionary concepts for political change, agreed with Wilhelm Reich's thoughts. "We must allow and encourage the sexual satisfaction of the young, both adolescents and small children, in order to free them from anxious submissiveness. . . . This is essential in order to prevent the pattern of coercion and authority from reemerging, no matter what the political change has been" (Goodman, 1946, p. 36). Our world has changed so much in the past three decades that it is difficult to appreciate how revolutionary this was when it was written (to be sure, small children still are excluded from the fruits of the "sexual revolution"). It was equally radical at the time to live together without getting married, to have "open" relationships, to maintain a public bisexual or homosexual life-style (to introduce someone as a lover, rather than a roommate), to consider the advisability of sexual relations with clients. These issues, so taken for granted today, were at the cutting edge of an emerging culture generated by Freud's findings on the nature of man's and woman's pansexuality.

The Gestalt concept of excitement and growth occurring *at the contact-boundary* between the organism and its environment continues to encourage healthy individuals to forage in disestablishment pastures. This is why Gestalt therapists were drawn to Identity House. It also explains why Identity House people were drawn to Gestalt therapy.

In the context of a volunteer service organization proffering peer counseling to the Gay Movement (a community in active revolt against the status quo), the interactions necessarily entailed elements of Gestalt experimentation. All of the elements of good contact—spontaneous concentration, novelty and excitement—were present, plus a basic concept of emotional growth as a necessary component for living life outside of the closets of our minds.

The concept of Identity House being a Gestalt experiment was presented at a membership meeting of The New York Institute for Gestalt Therapy in December 1975. Six members, past and present, of the steering committee of Identity House told the Institute membership about their experiences and what it had meant to their growth as people. The quotations below are excerpts from a transcript of that presentation.

Karen: When I was initially contacted by people from Identity House, I didn't know what they wanted—if I was coming in as a peer, or as a therapist. I was immediately put into the category of therapist— not only that but I was supervising a group of counselors—at a point at which I was very hesitant about whether I dared to really consider myself a therapist, whether I could be that ambitious, that out-front. And there I was trying to teach other people. Lo and behold, I discovered that they really *needed* what I knew *and* that I knew something. It was a fantastic affirmation for me, professionally.

This concept, testing oneself in the doing, forms the crux of any Gestalt experiment. "The answer to the question 'Can you do it?' can be only, 'It's interesting.' A sense of adequacy and power grows as the particular problem is met and generates its own structures and new possibilities are found in it, and things surprisingly fall into place" (Perls et al., 1951, p. 415). That Identity House provided an arena for personal and professional growth had to be the end result of contacting a new environ- ment, de-structuring old ways of doing things, assimilating new ways, and integrating all of this into a self-support system.

Gloria: In the beginning it was almost an addiction. I was so excited and so involved, so fascinated by the whole process of being with my own people. I'm a lesbian—I was very angry when Marian, my separatist friend over there, started being involved and relating with men, but now I feel good about that.

I was shy and timid and frightened and little; I feel strong and big and great now. First it was counseling, then it was short-term counseling, then social work school and Pat's practicum; I've learned ever so much, and grown a lot. And I've weaned myself away a little bit; I'm not addicted now, but still very much involved and much caring, and much loving and much growing for me.

An integral part of our unwritten philosophy at Identity House is that we exist for our internal community as well as for the larger outside one. Therefore, people who came on staff (either as therapists or peer counselors), who appeared to have "gotten it all together," i.e. who had no problems on the outside, tended to leave before long. They already had what we had to offer them. On the other hand, those who appeared least together during screening often moved into leadership roles, in effect returning the strengths and gifts that they received from it. This growth was certainly not easy, but then, as Fritz Perls loved to say, "Jah, there's no growth without frustration."

John: I don't think we're at all giving a flavor of what goes on at Identity House. I think what we have said is *true,* but there's a lot of other stuff, too. It's a constant struggle, going through the anger—after *that* you get this kind of love feeling. I've been in therapy groups before I came to Identity House, and the relationships that I've been able to develop with people at Identity House come closest in terms of the exploration to what goes on in Gestalt groups. And that's really good for me because I was thinking for a long while, "Great, I can go to a therapy group, a Gestalt group, and do all my stuff there and have all kinds of wonderful exchanges and love and hate and everything," but it was so terribly secluded from the rest of my life. And what I've found is that all of this can go on in *real* life, and that's exciting. It's the totality, not just the loving and good feeling; it's the intensity of the relationships.

In retrospect, by fighting for the right for each person in the community to establish her/his own identity, we at Identity House often discovered "our own thing," which in turn led us to discover who we really were, and that is certainly a prime goal of therapy. Often these new identities were different, even opposite, from those we brought with us. That was to be expected. What was not expected was how pervasive the changes were in some individuals. Dogmatists became compromisers, while in others caution replaced rashness.

Marian: Being at Identity House has affected me . . . I *could* have become Mommy but I had to change that, I had to change me. That's one big area.

Another is going through changes—growing—in doing counseling. I was very nice and sweet at the beginning and now I'm becoming stronger. I think I'm still nice, but I get angrier—somehow it works better. People benefit; they get a more genuine me. What I've also gotten out of it is that I *like* doing counseling, and the feeling now of wanting to do therapy.

In the area of relationships, I always loved to be loved, but now I'm beginning to feel that it's OK if I'm not loved; it's OK if I'm not liked—by women. I don't have to always be center, and that's been very hard.

As to men, I was one of the separatists. I was one of the ones who fought very hard. I didn't want anything mixed going on in this place, no heterosexuality—until I became involved with a man from Identity House and that changed things for me. I'm a lesbian now, but I am attracted to men and I would be involved with a man. It's harder for me to get close to a man than to a woman; I don't like most men, but I would be involved with a man whom I like and a man whom I'm attracted to, although my life is one of a lesbian.

The close working relationship of lesbians and gay men has led to a lot of bisexual behavior. After all, a person cannot be one thing without also being its opposite. "Once a person discovers his retroflecting action and regains control of it, the blocked impulse will be recovered automatically. No longer held in, it will simply come out" (Perls et al., 1951, p. 148). While serving bisexuals was not a goal in forming Identity House, they were included in our prospectus as a portion of the community we hoped to reach. This would indicate that it was not all that surprising that bisexuality should occur among us.

Patrick: I think that what we're doing in the community is similar to what we're doing with ourselves. That's one of the reasons I have no compunctions about describing Identity House as a Gestalt experiment. When we formulated ourselves, we really didn't know where we were going to go. We still don't. We know where we are now, and that may give us a base to move somewhere else, but I would hate to predict where *that* will be. We're still flexible. We still fight.

Marian: I suspect that was one of your fears, that we wouldn't.

Patrick: Well, yes. To think of a volunteer organization of 86 people, servicing, on various levels, three, four thousand people in the past three years and there's not been any untoward situation—at the same time we're working with a crazy community—that is, we don't know who's going to come in, and there's been no scandal. A lot of clinics would be hard put to equal our record.

Voice: So it's a Gestalt experiment because you're willing to stay in contact with potentiality rather than predict what's going to happen. How is this reflected in your structure? How do you build that in?

Patrick: Well, partly we're anarchic in setup. The newest member has a vote equal to our Executive Director, who is a peer. Our steering committee has nine peers and five therapists on it.

Karen: The steering committee meetings are a uniquely Gestalt experience, in that what is foreground is always attended to. The business at hand may have to wait, while whatever is going on in the present among everybody there is allowed to emerge, and contact made, etc.

In terms of organizational expansion I think of a finished Gestalt; contact is completed before the next contact is made. Therefore, the background is what we've already accomplished, and that in many ways dictates where we go next.

Mike: Part of the point is that we are willing to put in six hours at a meeting, struggle with whatever is going on. Contact comes about because we are constantly dealing with each other, not within roles, but as people, so that there is a continual struggling with how I feel, how you feel, and working with that.

Karen: I think that our experience is not *so* unique. It wouldn't be something that everyone here has not shared at one point or another with another kind of group. What is unique about Identity House is trying to combine it administratively, to function on this level and still . . .

Mike: Struggle between running the place and being who we are with each other.

Karen: It's something that I had no previous experience in, and I don't think that in our culture or in our structures of things there's been room for all this. It has been very hard to adhere to a Gestalt way of going about things *and* to accomplish something.

Patrick: And the tone that has been set by our steering committee has percolated through the entire organization. If our people don't like what's happening, they'll stop the clock until something gets settled, whether that's at a meeting of our total membership—that might be 60 people—or whether it's at a supervisory meeting—the shit *doesn't* get swept under the rug.

Voice: No introjects allowed.

Patrick: I really do believe that. I was talking before about the structure of Identity House being Gestalt, and I'm not speaking necessarily about Gestalt therapy, I'm talking in the broader sense of Paul Goodman's community of interest, consensus—things being on a human scale—that is *basic* to our philosophy.

Voice: You were talking about this as a Gestalt experiment, and as a Gestalt experience for you. How much of this, and in what way, reaches and touches the person coming in the door? Is it a Gestalt experience for them in the sense you're using it? How does it flow for them?

Karen: Probably because of the demands of the structure, really structureless structure, I would say, there is a demand that we be *present* in working at Identity House—that we be willing to at least attempt to make *contact.* With Identity House, you can't just go in and ride out your involvement; people are either *here* and they're very much *present* or they drop out. That intensive immediacy of presence is what we bring to the counseling situation . . .

Patrick: And when that contact is made, something different and new happens. Interestingly enough, many of our peers coming on staff today originally came to be counseled, moving from there to the rap groups, to the discussion groups, and eventually signing up as counselors. A number of our therapists were former peer counselors while they were in training in social work schools or at therapy institutes. We are, in effect, spawning our own membership.

Mike: What we've been talking about is self-help, not *just* within ourselves, but in terms of the gay community. Somebody who's alone and doesn't have any contact can come here and get to meet other people like himself, people who were where he was but have moved on. There's a kind of sharing and giving back and forth—with skill thrown in, with training so it's not *just* my life experience, but using my life experience in a particular way to help the person. Training becomes integrated with sharing . . .

John: It seems to me that while each of us here has a role in Identity House, as a peer counselor, or therapist or member, that *most* of us have been through a lot of the experiences that people coming in have had. In that sense we're all peers, and that's the basis for our relationship.

Identity House, as a therapeutic community, provides some additional benefits not ordinarily available in conventional psychotherapy. The sense of community which peer counselors share at Identity House has a therapeutic effect on the peers (counselors) themselves. Another factor for some is the experience of participating in a joint effort with their therapists. This community activity alleviates the alienation that most of us have experienced in our lives. "Since Gestalt theory clearly states that people create their identities through group loyalties, part of the educational process is to help clients recognize their social/political bonds with others" (Sparks, 1978, p. 98).

Our experience with community therapy brings to mind the early findings concerning therapy in groups stemming out of World War II. Faced with large numbers of patients and short of professionals qualified in psychotherapy, the Veterans Administration Hospitals began to place disturbed G.I.s into group therapy so that they would receive *some* treatment. Surprisingly, the group experience provided an impetus to the therapeutic process above and beyond the increment that might have occurred in the same number of hours of individual therapy. It is our contention that therapeutic community processes take this group dynamic a step forward. This is so because every interaction is potentially the subject for an impromptu "therapy" session with follow-up at the next supervisory group or a membership meeting.

For example, if a person does not perform a particular task for which (as is true for all tasks) he/she has volunteered, this infraction might be ignored or vigorously challenged at the time, depending on its context. A series of such events, however, would surely lead to a private talk with someone else affected by the event, or with one of the appropriate officers, or to a public discussion at her/his supervision group or with a group of Identity House friends—whichever seemed most appropriate. More important, the person is more likely to be chided for taking on too much than for not performing the promised task. One's need for approval or one's inability to ask for help might be explored with as much energy and interest as the original transgression. And this exploration might very well be extended into the person's individual or group therapy session. Indeed, some of the challengers are likely to be the transgressor's fellow group-therapy members or his/her therapist—or client.

Not all Identity House members make use of these processes to the same degree; we are, after all, a volunteer association of people giving time and energy. A person is free to use as much or as little of what Identity House offers as he/she chooses. However, since we are in the "growth business," it is difficult to remain central and active in the organization without some of this type of involvement. Indeed, for many of us, it's what we're all about.

The man who can live in concernful contact with his society, neither being swallowed up by it nor withdrawing from it completely, is the well-integrated man . . . The goal of psychotherapy is to create just such men. The idea of democratic community, on the other hand, is to create a society with the same characteristics, a community in which, as its needs are determined, each member participates for the benefit of all. Such a society is in concernful contact with its members (Perls, 1976, p. 26).

16

Application of Gestalt Therapy Principles to Organizational Consultation

JOAN S. ALEVRAS and BARRY J. WEPMAN

Theoretical research specific to the organizational processes of a work system is a relatively recent phenomenon. At the turn of the century, Frederick Taylor and his colleagues developed a theory for American business and industry called "Scientific Management" (Weissenberg, 1971). Their theories supported the then current belief that the key to effective management of an organization was impersonal, cool efficiency arrived at by central managerial control, planning and decision-making. However, research from the 1920s and '30s revealed that workers could be motivated best if management demonstrated that it cared about its employees (Weissenberg, 1971).

Since the 1960s, another trend in organizational behavior theories has been emerging: a "human relations" concept. This concept stresses increased worker participation by including employees at all levels of organizational decision-making.

Just as a therapist with an individual focuses on the client's potentials for growth, so can an organizational developmental consultant use these potentials for growth as a helpful frame of reference when involved with a work system. A consultant, like a therapist, is engaged in assisting a poorly functioning system to increase its ability to achieve specified goals.

Thus there are parallels between a Gestalt therapist's functioning with an individual and a Gestalt-oriented consultant's work with an or-

We gratefully acknowledge the contributions of our colleague Jeffrey Atlas, Director and Vice President of Block-Petrella Associates, whose guidance greatly aided us in writing this chapter.

229

ganization. These parallels will become clear as we present a comparison of a Gestalt therapist's orientation to the therapeutic process and a Gestalt consultant's view of the dynamics of organizational consultation. In addition, we will discuss ways in which a consultant may apply Gestalt concepts of individual behavior to organizational behavior.*

In individual therapy the process begins with a stated problem. Around this, the therapist organizes his/her perceptions of the client and begins to suggest experiments from which new awareness may emerge.

An organizational development consultant's client may be either an individual within a work group, various groups within an organization, or a whole organization within an external (social, political, natural resources, etc.) environment; yet the task is always essentially the same as with an individual: The consultant observes the client's behavior and decides on which behaviors the client can most advantageously focus. The realm of concern—i.e., the client's formation of perceptual information into conceptual wholes, the behavior(s) initiated in response to these *Gestalten* and the functioning of the client within the greater environment—is quite similar whether the client is an individual or an organization.

The disturbances and resistances of neurotic behavior are treated as raw material by Gestalt therapists (Polster & Polster, 1973, p. 71). A therapist attempts to design experiments to illustrate how these maladaptations manifest themselves in dysfunctional behavior, thereby providing a vehicle for the client to experience the extent of his or her reliance on projections, retroflections, introjections and confluence. The therapeutic setting provides a place of safety where a person can take risks in an effort to complete unfinished business and to deal with unquestioned developmental injunctions. The goal of this process is to arrive at a place of balance with one's needs and priorities in the environment, a state that is achieved by being fully present in the here-and-now. This allows the individual to make positive choices which extend from this congruent functioning.

Dysfunctional behavior in organizations has many parallels to neurotic behavior in individuals. As an example of "projection," one department sees others as destructively competitive in order to justify its rejecting or sabotaging proposals that come to it from outside. "Introjections"

---

* There are parallels to small group behavior also, but to explicate those is beyond the scope of this chapter.

TABLE 1

Major Parallels between Gestalt Therapy with Individuals and a
Gestalt Approach to Organizational Consultation

	Individual Therapy	Organizational Consultation
Realm of Concern	Individual within the environment	Individual within group; group(s) within organization
	Communication problems	Communication problems
	Individual not functioning up to own or societal expectations	Organization not meeting (management, material resources, profits) requirements to maintain functioning
	Individual's patterns no longer serving him/her	Organization's structure, methods, no longer serving company goals
	Presenting problem, complaints usually surface symptoms of internal tensions	Presenting problems, needs and complaints usually surface symptoms of tension within company
	Individual complains of outside forces causing his/her problem	Department or organization complains of outside factors causing problems
View of Client	Organism with systems— intellectual, emotional, physical—which are experienced as in conflict	Organization with subsystems—such as production, sales, research— which have conflicts within and between
Data Collection	Personal contact, e.g., interview, observation, questionnaires, tests	Personal contact, e.g., interview, observation or structured instruments: questionnaire
Dysfunctional Behavior	Projection, confluence, introjection, etc.	Projection, confluence, introjection, etc.
Client's Expectations	Support, justification and being cured	Support, justification and being cured

TABLE 1 *(continued)*

	Individual Therapy	Organizational Consultation
Therapist/ Consultant's Concept of Client's Needs and Tasks	To integrate intra-personal polarities with environmental realities	To integrate interpersonal departmental needs, goals with environmental realities
	To expand awareness of own functioning	To expand awareness of group's functioning
	To bring into focus intrapersonal conflicts and how they contribute to the dysfunctioning of the individual	To bring focus interpersonal conflicts and how they contribute to the dysfunctioning of the system
	Expand awareness of options and choices	and choices Expand awareness of options

emerge as rigid procedures and standards. These standards are "swallowed" by individuals rather than being evaluated in light of their results.

"Confluence" emerges as a corporate image: a prescription that imposes a firm, narrow range of behaviors on employees. Thus, one is evaluated on willingness to conform, sometimes even to the exclusion of the quality of one's work. And once a structure is firmly and formally set, it becomes increasingly difficult for employees to respond fluidly to changing demands from both internal and external sources. Consultants handle these manifestations of confluence and conformity in ways similar to those of therapists—by pointing out the discrepancy between what should be and what is, between what is pretended and what is actual. Furthermore, consultants illustrate these discrepancies with exercises and experiments, thereby creating a climate in which the behaviors which facilitate the real goals of work and those which interfere can emerge.

SAFETY ISSUES

A problem encountered by any therapist operating in a system where the contract is maintained or subsidized by a party other than the client (parents, school, insurer, industry) is the problem of primary loyalty.

This issue must be addressed and resolved before a client can accept the therapist as a change agent operating in the client's best interest. This issue is equally relevant whether the client is an individual or an organization: The organizational development consultant's first task is to identify exactly who the client is.

Loyalty and protection are also safety issues. One factor which promotes safety is the consultant's external status. Because O.D. consultants are strangers to the groups with whom they work, their loyalties, biases, and proclivities are not seen as necessarily reflecting the "company line."

Another way consultants structure a safe environment in which clients can dare to explore their distress is to hold the consulting sessions at a location remote from "home territory." Meeting away from "company turf" often helps to reduce the sense of territoriality as well as to isolate the participants from routine business interruptions. A further benefit is that confidentiality may be more easily maintained when a group is isolated. (It is important that what happens within the group be kept confidential, although decisions and action steps usually need to be disclosed when they relate to the organization as a whole.)

INTERNAL CONFLICTS

As with an individual client, if a part of the organization is operating at a level that restricts or diminishes general organizational functioning, the whole system may be in jeopardy. The presenting problems are often symptoms of underlying conflicts which a consultant can help to surface. For example, a work group may see outside forces as causes of internal problems. The task of the consultant here is to help make it possible for the client to recognize how the interactions and the structure of the group or company may be interfering with its own process. Sometimes, however, outside forces are, indeed, responsible for causing problems in an organization, so the consultant must explore each situation without bias.*

VIEW OF CLIENT

A Gestalt therapist views an individual client as an organism in disharmony within and without, i.e., in interaction with the environment. The therapist's task is to expand the client's awareness of how he/she

---

* It is common that an outside force such as a labor union or government agency, such as the Environmental Protection Agency or Equal Employment Opportunity Commission, does impose regulatory standards on a work environment which significantly affect one or many aspects of an organization.

creates this disharmony within by blocking his/her energy; also the therapist helps the client identify actual conflict with his/her environment.

Similarly, an organization may be creating disharmony, blocking the flow of energy within, that is, among its subsystems. These subsystems, such as top management, middle management, and production areas, often have different goals, needs and priorities which generate intersystem conflicts. The consultant needs to focus attention on the subsystems and on the ways in which their operations contribute to the functioning of the whole, being aware that an overpowering subsystem can create disharmony within the whole as surely as a weak, limping one can.

DATA COLLECTION

Gestalt therapists use the therapeutic setting to gather information about the client. How they do this varies greatly. However, direct contact with the individual and observation are the prime sources of information about a client. Observation involves listening to the content while noticing the client's "music"—tone of voice, gestures, facial expression. While gathering information about an organizational client may be accomplished in various ways (telephone interviews, personal meetings, reports, questionnaires, etc.), the most valuable data source an O.D. consultant has is direct observation of the client system and subsystems within the work environment. Implicitly agreed-upon patterns of behavior may be in direct conflict with the formally established patterns of communication channels. For example, the hierarchial structure of a company may prescribe communication between departments by formal contact between department heads. The consultant, however, may observe that an informal arrangement exists between the head of research and a vice-president of marketing to drive to work together. This situation offers many opportunities for informal transactions. Consultants help to identify such conflicting behaviors and assist the client in coming to an agreement about how to proceed in the face of such knowledge.

CLIENT'S EXPECTATIONS

Clients often begin a therapeutic relationship with the expectation that they will be cured by the therapist. The client thus invests in the therapist the magical power to affect change. On the other hand, the client clearly has a need to involve a disinterested person or expert in his/her life situation. Usually he/she acts on this need after much resistance and the exhaustion of other environmental resources, and see as his/her task submission to the therapist's magic.

An organizational development consultant, too, is often approached by a client system for magical curative powers to deal with situational work problems. Whether the consultant is approached by the primary client or hired by a level of management that perceives itself as uninvolved in the work problem, the thinking can be magical. The client views the consultant as an agent who may, by the mere fact of presence or involvement, identify and neutralize the factors, events, or transactions that are causing the presenting problem. Once again, the client assumes a passive stance while waiting for miracles.

This point can serve as a focus for struggle early in the process of reintegration: Who is responsible for the hoped-for change? The clients angrily express that if they could initiate change, the consultant would be unnecessary. It is an early task of the consultant to turn this demand back onto the client, to enable the client to perceive his/her own power and responsibility for change. At this point the client needs the support of the consultant. The art of providing support consists of giving not less and not more than absolutely necessary. The effect of putting responsibility for change back onto the client remains even after the departure of the consultant. In this way, as the consultant keeps focusing attention on the interaction within the client group, he/she works most directly to bring about change. Participation in these activities away from home eventually helps to create a safe climate in which people have permission to communicate more directly with each other even back on the job.

Consultants' Conceptualization of Clients' Needs and Tasks

While clients may often see therapists or consultants as magicians and themselves as helpless in the distorted way described above, effective change agents conceptualize their own role and clients' needs quite differently. Their tasks involve, for example, helping clients to expand their awareness, to see a wider range of options, to bring into focus conflicts and polarities.

Gestalt therapists aid a person's integration of intrapersonal polarities so that the client can better respond to environmental realities. Consultants also work toward integrating pieces (interpersonal, departmental needs, goals, etc.) of the whole so a collaborative relationship with the environment is possible.*

One means of integration is "team building," an organizational development intervention used to bring a work team to an increased level of efficiency. This strategy is used to bring to the surface the conflicts among and within work groups, to help them resolve the conflicts, and to develop a sense of cooperative team effort. The consultant designs exercises or experiments to make available to the group information that previously existed below the level of awareness and was, therefore, unavailable. The exercises are structured to provide an opportunity for people to talk about their feelings about each other and their tasks in new ways. When these feelings, are brought into the open, the contact-boundaries between people become more sharply defined, and differences, similarities and conflicts become clearer. From this position group members can make decisions based on less distorted data. These decisions are then more appropriate to situational demands and are therefore likely to be more successful for individuals and the group.

Consultants frequently focus on process as well as content during conflict resolutions. The consultant designs communication experiments for the participants in which they give feedback to each other on how their behavior influences the movement and the outcome of their team activity. In this way participants can learn how their specific team works together, what behaviors enhance that process, and what activities interfere with problem-solving. The ability to communicate openly, even in conflict situations, is a skill that remains long after the consultant has left.

TERMINATION

The termination process in consulting can take various forms. One of the major goals is to get a commitment from the team to follow through with the steps which have evolved during the process. This is accomplished by involving as many people as possible in the agreement. At this point the consultant eases out, perhaps by being available for periodic visits or by coming in again only as another distress situation emerges. However, even when the appropriate group decision is *not* to implement any action plans, agreement and cooperation are still essential for just continuing with the routine tasks of the organization.

---

* The word "environment" is used here to represent that which exists beyond the immediate boundaries of the group being consulted with.

There is one essential difference here between consultation and psychotherapy: While the individual therapist's goal is to enable a person to permanently function well on his or her own, with self-support and environmental support, an organizational development consultant can rarely achieve this with organizations. By and large, an organization needs continued maintenance work, and so a consultant must be satisfied with temporary improvement.

CONCLUSION

Gestalt therapists work toward helping clients to take full responsibility for themselves. The goal is for the client to be more aware of his/her capacity for self-support, as well as to use directly environmental supports, enabling him or her to meet the needs of the situation—his/her own needs, the needs of the other person(s), and the requirements of the task or situation as it is experienced in the present. The organizational development consultant achieves a similar goal; first, by assessing the blocks that inhibit the free flow of information; second, by seeing how subsystems within an organization are responsible for perceptual distortions which result in inappropriate responses; and third, by developing processes of communication that provide a break from habitual patterns and allow the roots of dysfunction to become more visible within the system. Thereby the O.D. consultant has promoted a more fluid movement of energy within the organization and an increase in its ability to meet its own goals.

Ideas and techniques from Gestalt therapy can be applied usefully in the consultation process. The consultant utilizes direct observation, focuses on the here-and-now, and designs experiments to help clients expand their vision of those work situations into which they had felt locked, and to discover previously unavailable options.

Postscript

It is clear from the contributions to this book that Gestalt group approaches have grown well beyond their early stages, moving from leader orientation toward group orientation: While one-to-one work—with or without the "hot seat"—is still used frequently by most group leaders, it is no longer the primary vehicle for change and growth. Our contributors are increasingly aware of group process and of the need to balance focus on the individual with focus on the group-as-a-whole.

As Gestalt therapists, we were not surprised to find that the styles of leadership among our contributors vary widely, for we expected to see a development paralleling that in the field of individual therapy where, as Laura Perls states (1976), "there are as many styles as there are therapists and clients who discover themselves and each other and together invent their relationship." However, it is not only style that varies. What also varies is the degree to which different contributors are integrating in their practice group dynamic concepts with Gestalt therapy principles.

We therefore consider this volume as a beginning: We are fully aware that the theory and practice presented are by no means complete, and that they do not reflect a unified conceptualization of Gestalt group process. Nevertheless, they are indicative of a trend in the field. We hope this book will serve as a base for continuing development of those conceptualizations which focus on promoting awareness, through group process, of organismic needs as well as of the means whereby those needs can be met.

Bibliography

ASTRACHAN, B. M. Towards a social systems model of therapeutic groups. *Social Psychiat.*, 1979, 5:110-119.

BACH, G. R. The marathon group: Intensive practise of intimate interaction. *Psychological Reports*, 1966, 18:955-1002.

BARTH, J. *The End of the Road.* New York: Bantam Books, 1969.

BERGANTINO, L. Gestalt therapy. *J. Humanistic Psychol.*, 1977, 17:51-61.

BEHRENSON, P. *Finding One's Way With Clay.* New York: Simon & Schuster, 1972.

BERNE, E. *Principles of Group Treatment.* New York: Oxford University Press, 1966.

BION, W. R. *Experience in Groups and Other Papers.* New York: Basic Books, 1959.

BION, W. R. *Experiences in Groups.* New York: Basic Books, 1961.

BUBER, M. *I and Thou.* New York: Scribners, 1970.

COHN, R. C. The theme-centered interactional method: Group therapists as group educators. *Journal of Group Psychoanal. and Group Proc.*, 1969-70, 2:19-36.

COHN, R. C. *Von der Psychoanalyse Zur Themenzentrierten Interaktion.* Stuttgart: Ernst Klett, 1975.

DERMAN, B. The Gestalt thematic approach. In: E. W. L. Smith (Ed.), *The Growing Edge of Gestalt Therapy.* New York: Brunner/Mazel, 1976.

DOSTOEVSKY, F. *The Brothers Karamazov.* New York: Random House, 1937.

FEDER, B. A survey of Gestalt group therapy. Unpublished manuscript, 1974.

FEDER, B. Responsibility and the Gestalt therapist. *The Gestalt Journal*, 1978, 1:83-87.

FRANKFORT, H. Freedom of the will and the concept of a person. *Journal of Philosophy*, 1971, 7-20.

GOODMAN, P. *Five Years.* New York: Brussell and Brussell, 1966.

GREENWALD, J. A. The art of emotional nourishment: Nourishing and toxic encounter group. In: C. Hatcher and P. Himelstein (Eds.), *The Handbook of Gestalt Therapy.* New York: Jason Aaronson, 1976, 505-521.

HESS-MICHAEL, J. American artist. *American Artist Magazine*, January, 1969, 33:22-31.

JOURARD, S. *The Transparent Self.* New York: Van Nostrand, 1964.

JUNG, C. G. Psychological types. *Collected Works of C. G. Jung.* Vol. VI, Bollinger Series 20. Princeton, New Jersey: Princeton University Press, 1971.

KEMPLER, W. *Principles of Gestalt Family Therapy.* Salt Lake City: Deseret Press, 1974.

KOEHLER, W. Co-founder with Wertheimer of Gestalt Psychology.

KRISHNAMURTI, J. *Life Ahead.* Wheaton, Illinois: The Theosophical Publishing House, 1967.

LEVITSKY, A. and PERLS, F. S. The rules and games of gestalt therapy. In: J. Fagan and I. L. Shepherd (Eds.), *Gestalt Therapy Now.* Palo Alto: Science and Behavior Books, 1970.

MEAD, G. American sociologist.

MILLS, J. *On Liberty.* New York: Everyman's Library, 1910.

MINTZ, E. E. *Marathon Groups: Reality and Symbol.* New York: Appleton-Century, 1971.

MINTZ, E. E. Gestalt therapy and psychoanalysis. *Psychoanalytical Review,* 1973, 60: 407-411.

MINTZ, E. E. On the dramatization of psychoanalytical interpretations. In: L. Wolberg and R. Aaronson (Eds.), *Group Therapy.* New York: Stratton Intercontinental, 1974.

MORSE, H. M. *Current Biography Yearbook,* 1958, 381-382.

MOWRER, O. H. Learning theory and neurotic paradox. *Amer. J. of Orthopsychiat.,* 1948, 18:571-610.

MULLAN, H. and ROSENBAUM, M. *Group Psychotherapy.* New York: Free Press of Glencoe, 1962.

NARANJO, C. I and Thou—Here and Now. In: H. Otto and J. Mann (Eds.), *Ways of Growth.* New York: Grossman, 1968.

NEVIS, S. *Lectures on Group Process.* Cleveland, Ohio: Gestalt Institute of Cleveland, 1977.

PERLS, F. *Ego, Hunger and Aggression.* New York: Random House, 1969. (Vintage paper edition, 1969.)

PERLS, F. *Gestalt Therapy Verbatim.* Moab, Utah: Real People Press, 1969.

PERLS, F. Group vs. Individual Therapy. *Etc. A Review of General Semantics,* 1967, 24: 306-312.

PERLS, F. *The Gestalt Approach and Eye Witness to Therapy.* Palo Alto: Science & Behavior Books, 1973.

PERLS, F. *The Gestalt Approach and Eye Witness to Therapy.* New York: Bantam Books, 1976.

PERLS, F., HEFFERLINE, R., and GOODMAN, P. *Gestalt Therapy.* New York: Dell, 1951.

PERLS, F., HEFFERLINE, R., and GOODMAN, P. *Gestalt Therapy.* New York: Dell, 1957.

PERLS, F., HEFFERLINE, R., and GOODMAN, P. *Gestalt Therapy.* New York: Bantam Books, 1977.

PERLS, L. Comments on new directions. In: E. W. L. Smith (Ed.), *The Growing Edge of Gestalt Therapy.* New York: Brunner/Mazel, 1976.

PFEIFFER, J. W. and JONES, J. E. *A Handbook of Structured Experiments for Human Relations Training.* La Jolla, Ca.: University Associates, 1975.

POLSTER, E. and POLSTER, M. *Gestalt Therapy Integrated.* New York: Brunner/Mazel, 1973.

REDL, F. and WINEMAN, D. *Children Who Hate.* New York: Collier Books, 1962.

REICH, W. German psychoanalyst who parted with Freud, emphasizing the bodily parallels to the mind.

ROGERS, C. *Client-Centered Therapy.* Boston: Houghton-Mifflin Co., 1951.

RONALL, R. and WILSON, B. Theme-Centered Interactional (TCI) groups. In: R. Herrink (Ed.), *Psychotherapy Handbook.* New York: Jason Aaronson, in press.

ROSENBLATT, D. *Opening Doors: What Happens in Gestalt Therapy.* New York: Harper & Row, 1975.

SARTRE, J. *The Philosophy of Jean Paul Sartre.* Edited by R. Cumming. New York: Vintage Books, 1965.

SCHUMACHER, E. *A Guide for the Perplexed.* London: Jonathan Cape, Ltd., 1977.

SCHUTZ, W. *The Interpersonal Underworld.* (Original title, FIRO: *A Three-Dimensional Theory of Behavior*). Palo Alto: Science & Behavior Books, 1966.

SIMKIN, J. S. *Mini-Lectures in Gestalt Therapy.* Albany, Ca.: Wordpress, 1974.

SINGER, D., et al. Boundary management in psychological work in groups. *J. of Applied Behavior Sci.,* 1975, 2:137-176.

STEVENS, J. *Awareness.* New York: Bantam, 1971.

WEISSENBERG, P. *Introduction to Organizational Behavior.* Scranton: Intext Educational Publishers, 1971.

WERTHEIMER, M. Co-founder with Koehler of Gestalt psychology.

WIITAKER, D. S. and LIEBERMAN, M. A. *Psychotherapy Through Group Process.* New York: Atherton Press, 1964.

YALOM, I. *The Theory and Practice of Group Psychotherapy.* New York: Basic Books, 1970.

YALOM, I. *The Theory and Practice of Group Psychotherapy.* New York: Basic Books, 1975.

ZINKER, F. Phase theory analysis of a small group. Unpublished manuscript, 1975.

ZINKER, J. *Creative Process in Gestalt Therapy.* New York: Brunner/Mazel, 1977.

About the Authors

JOAN R. SAARINEN ALEVRAS, M.A., is the Director of the Resource Center, Inc., Nutley, N.J., a non-profit educational corporation. As an organizational development consultant, she designs and implements training programs using a Gestalt approach for various governmental agencies and business corporations, including the U.S. Civil Service Commission and Exxon Corporation, as well as in academia and the arts. She has been a faculty member of Kean College, Montclair State College, and Fairleigh Dickinson University. She is Co-Director of Resources, Inc., a firm specializing in Affirmative Action and Career Development training. She is Chairperson of the Organizational Development Committee for the Gestalt Association of New Jersey. She is one of the organizers of a group of external consultants, the Consultants Consortium. As a therapist, she maintains a private practice in Gestalt therapy.

SUSAN CAMPBELL, Ph.D., has been practicing individual, group, couple and family therapy for the past 12 years. She also trains graduate students in these fields, formerly at the University of Massachusetts and currently at the Humanistic Psychology Institute in San Francisco. While at the University of Massachusetts' School of Education's Counselor Education program, she initiated graduate level courses in Gestalt therapy, family counseling, Gestalt applications in Education, and Gestalt applications in Personal and Organizational Development. She received her Gestalt training at the New York Gestalt Center and the San Diego Gestalt Center. She has recently completed an article on Gestalt couple counseling and a book entitled *The Couple's Journey: Intimacy as a Path to Wholeness* (Impact Publishers, San Luis Obispo, CA, in press).

BUD FEDER has been a practising psychologist for 20 years and a Gestalt therapist for eight. His current professional interests include: developing Gestalt group process, with special concern for group safety level;

training Gestalt therapists in New Jersey, individually and in groups; leading training weekends in England; and integrating Gestalt therapy with other wholistic health disciplines. He organized the Gestalt Association of New Jersey, and is on the faculty of the New York Institute for Gestalt Therapy.

JOHN DAVID FLYNN is Assistant Professor of Philosophy at Livingston College of Rutgers University in New Jersey. He has served on a recent graduate faculty committee to organize an M.A. program in philosophy for high school teachers. He has presented papers and led workshops on the problem of teaching philosophy and the humanities—at Livingston College, the University of California at Santa Cruz and at other colleges. In 1973, he was selected to participate in a three-week institute on interdisciplinary teaching and research sponsored by the National Endowment for the Humanities, held at Williams College. There he presented a paper on teaching critical thinking in philosophy.

In addition to teaching philosophy, he is an individual and group counselor at the Livingston College Counseling Center. He is an associate member of the New York Institute for Gestalt Therapy and an organizing member of the Gestalt Association of New Jersey. He has also published articles in the fields of existentialism and the philosophy of clinical psychology.

PATRICK KELLEY is a Fellow of the New York Institute for Gestalt Therapy. He is one of the founders of Identity House and worked for several years as its Clinical Director. Earlier in his career, he worked with the New York City Youth Board and with various community organizations and social work programs. He has taught Human Relations at New York University, is currently involved in training and supervising therapists, and has a small private practice.

ELAINE KEPNER, Ph.D., as one of the founders of the Gestalt Institute of Cleveland and of its professional training program, is now committed to training the next generation of Gestalt practitioners. Her present work is based on the conviction that Gestalt provides some unique tools for a transformation of consciousness in women, men, couples, families, groups and organizations. Coming to this point involved many years of teaching psychology at Case Western Reserve University, San Francisco University, and the California School of Professional Psychology and directing educational and community development programs. She is currently living in New York City, but maintains her faculty appointment with the Gestalt Institute of Cleveland, and teaches Gestalt therapy in this country and abroad. Her interest in systems and individuals has led to the development of a new NTL lab: Individual Development and Systems.

RICHARD KITZLER is a Fellow and past Vice-President of the New York Institute for Gestalt Therapy. He has been in private practice in New York City for many years. His current main interest is in the training and supervision of Gestalt therapists.

GINGER LAPID has a Ph.D. in Confluent Education from the University of California at Santa Barbara where she also taught in the Teacher Education Program. An ex-cheerleader, she is now a sex-role stereotyping consultant for schools and organizations throughout California. She is also a Gestalt awareness trainer, an organizational consultant and teaches Public Service Management for the University of Redlands.

RONA LAVES received her M.A. in clinical psychology from Fairleigh Dickinson University and her Ph.D. from New York University in community psychology. She is a member of The New York Institute for Gestalt Therapy and the Gestalt Association of New Jersey. She trained in Gestalt group therapy with Bud Feder. Other major academic pursuits involve research in the area of community psychology, including crisis intervention, effects of stress on coping, and social support networks as they affect coping. She now teaches at Montclair State College, N.J., and is in private practice.

NORMAN LIBERBMAN . . . Last-born into a textile family, 1921, Paterson, New Jersey—the Silk City. As only boy-child, was already "student of psychology" in family that was growing by marriage and dramatic interaction. Roles as protagonist constitute a lifelong development from athlete to poet, soldier to therapist, businessman to religious mystic . . . Cohn-discipline to Gestalt-group-leader. Education acquired in five states and four countries. Inspiration and example come, above all, from the Machovers, the Morenos and Ruth Cohn whose workshop Institute for Living-Learning and generous teaching during two decades have helped me "to get it all together." Most of all I owe to my two beautiful sons, my father and mother who gave me the heritage of

Chassidism, and the contagious wisdom of the women with whom I learned to love and to share.

DELDON McNEELY TYLER received her doctorate in clinical psychology from Louisiana State University. Until recently she practised pyschotherapy in New Orleans. Into her psychotherapeutic work, which combines Gestalt techniques and Jungian concepts, she enjoys incorporating life-long hobbies of music and dance. This had led to the development of her own form of workshops in movement therapy. She is currently on leave-of-absence from studies in the Interregional Society of Jungian Analysts, in order to accompany her husband, Charles Tyler, on a job assignment in Russia, along with their children Romaney, Jonathan, and Yseulte.

ELIZABETH E. MINTZ sees herself as someone who has been privileged to study and experience several major therapeutic theories and techniques, including classical psychoanalysis and encounter, and who is now able to draw upon this total training as it seems appropriate. In groups, however, she uses the Gestalt approach primarily. She teaches her methods each year in Holland and in Germany, and also in clinics and institutes throughout this country. Currently she has become interested in the transpersonal aspects of psychotherapy. She is author of the book *Marathon Groups: Reality and Symbol* and of numerous professional articles.

ELAINE RAPP, stone carver, registered art therapist, Glockenspiel player, Full Member—New York Institute for Gestalt Therapy, former Horn and Hardart Children's Hour performer, Assistant Professor—Pratt Institute, mother of a Himalayan cat, Director of Art Therapy—New York Institute for Gestalt Therapy, homeowner, Field Faculty—Goddard College Graduate Program, lover, mother, mother-in-law, current and expectant grandmother, Faculty—Center for Expressive Analysis, constant dieter—Faculty—Humanistic Psychology Center, traveler, workshop leader, dedicated New Yorker, Gestalt therapist in private practice, beachcomber, teacher, supervisor, trainer.

RUTH RONALL, M.S., Psychotherapist in private practice. Born in Vienna, left Austria in 1938. Lived in Egypt, Israel, England, the United States and Japan. Finally settled with family in New York City. Faculty, The New York Institute for Gestalt Therapy; faculty, Alfred Adler Institute and Workshop Institute for Living-Learning. Besides maintaining her practice in New York, travels in the United States, Canada and Europe to lead Gestalt training, personal growth and Theme-Centered Interactional workshops. Currently interested in further exploration of group process in Gestalt groups and in experimentation with Theme-Centered Gestalt workshops, in support of a lifelong passion for bringing together people of diverse background and ideas from diverse sources.

BARRY WEPMAN was born in Pittsfield, Mass. and grew up in the Boston area where he first learned about and explored Gestalt therapy. He received his Ph.D. in pyschology from The University of Houston in 1973, and since then has taught at New York University and The College of Medicine and Dentistry of New Jersey where he is currently a faculty member. In addition he maintains a private practice in psychotherapy in West Orange, New Jersey, and runs stress reduction and communications skills programs for health care providers in both professional office and family setting.

JOSEPH C. ZINKER, Ph.D., a clinical psychologist, is a Gestalt therapist in private practice, as well as a consultant and teacher. He is Chairperson of the Three-Year Post Graduate Training Program in the Gestalt Institute of Cleveland. He has explored the relevance of art, drama, and directed conflict to personal growth in the workshop situation, and has developed innovations in areas of experiment and dreamwork as theater. His book, *Creative Process in Gestalt Therapy* was selected by *Psychology Today* as one of the best psychotherapy books for 1977.

Index

Acting-out:
  and family dynamics, 80
  in groups, 58
Active imagination, 107
Adler, Alfred, 183
Affiliation needs, 16
Alevras, Joan S., xi, 229ff., 245
Altman, Michael, 219n.
American Psychological Association, 8, 41
Anarchism in groups, 25
Anima, group, 61
Animus, group, 61
Anti-Semitism, 185
Anxiety:
  in art workshops, 90-91
  and group process, 42, 58, 75
  in marathons, 121
  and personality, 118
Arica Training Institute, San Francisco, 6
Armature wire, therapeutic uses of, 99-100
Art therapy, Gestalt groups for, 86ff.
  anxiety in, 90-91
  materials for, 91-92, 103-104
    armature wire, 99-100
    crayons, 100-102
    stone, 92-98
    watercolors, 98-99
  sculptures, 88-89, 95, 103
  setting for, 86-87
  situations in, 87-88
  workshops, 89ff.
Astrachan, B. M., 13, 241n.
Atlas, Jeffrey, 229n.
Autonomogenic process, 134, 143, 149-50

Autonomy. See also Education for autonomy
  and community, 183
  and education, 155-58
  and free will, 138-40
  needs for, 16
Awareness-excitement-contact cycle, 58-60,
  75-76

Bach, G. R., 119n., 241n.
Barth, John, 140, 241n.
Behrenson, Paulus, 86, 241n.
Bergantino, L., 119, 241n.
Berne, E., 13, 241n.
Bioenergetics, 121
Bion, W. R., 13, 27, 241n.
Bisexuality, 224
Body-mind warm-up in movement ther-
  apy, 110-12
Boundaries of groups, 6-7, 158
Brinley, John, 120n.
Bryant, Anita, 220n.
Buber, Martin, 78, 241n.

Campbell, Susan M., x, 78ff., 245
Catharsis, overemphasis on, 43
Childhood experiences and Gestalt groups,
  124
Closure group stage, 22-23
Cohn, Ruth C., 183, 184, 188, 190, 241n.
College teaching, 143-52, 155ff. See also
  Education for autonomy
  and competing Gestalts, 162
  conclusion on, 166

251

contact-boundary in, 158
noncontact awareness, 166
novelty-excitement in, 162-65
process/self-support in, 158-61
and resistance, 161-62
skillful frustration in, 165-66
Communication:
  and creativity, 102
  in families, 81
Community:
  in art therapy, 96-97
  and autonomy, 183
Confluence as corporate image, 232
Conscious integration in movement therapy, 114-15
Counterdependency, 118
Crayons, therapeutic use of, 100-102
Creativity:
  and communication, 102
  and emotions, 92
  in movement, 112-14

Dancing, ritual, 105, 115
Dependency:
  and education, 135-36
  and group process, 7, 51
Derman, B., 43, 241n.
Developmental process in Gestalt groups, 55ff.
  comments on, 75-77
  development stages and experiment, 62-75
  goals, values, role definitions, 59-62
  group cycle, 56-59
Dialogue-process:
  in families, 81-82
  polarities in, 27
Donne, John, 179
Dora, case, 31n.
Dostoevsky, F., 135
Dreams:
  in art therapy, 89
  dancing out of, 112
  Gestalts in, 101-102, 107
  and group process, 5, 27
  homosexuals in, 173
Drug treatment, 108
Dynamic balancing, 187, 198

Education for autonomy, 133ff. *See also* Autonomy; College teaching
  in college teaching, 143-52

experiments, 150-52
  text interpretation, 146-50
  conclusion on, 152-54
  and free will, 138-40
  nature of, 141-43
  and socialization, 135
  and social progress, 136
Ego:
  in group volunteers, 27
  -ideal, 30
  regression in service of, 38-39
Ego, Hunger and Aggression (F. Perls), 9
Encounter exercises, 119, 121
End of the Road (Barth), 140
Enmeshment in family systems, 79
Environmental Protection Agency, 234n.
Equal Employment Opportunity Commission, 233n.
Esalen workshops, 119, 130
Experiential learning, 9

Family metaphor and cohesiveness, 69-75
Family sculpting technique, 82-83, 194n.
Family therapy, Gestalt, 78ff.
Fantasy:
  in art therapy, 103
  in classroom teaching, 145-48, 153
  and education, 158
  Gestalt approach to, 107
  in movement therapy, 111, 112-14
  of pregnancy/childbirth, 114
  in writing, 147-48
Farau, Alfred, 183
Feder, Bud, ix-xi, 41ff., 42n., 167ff., 170, 187, 191, 241n., 245-46
Feedback:
  in education, 160, 165
  in group training, 169
  in marathons, 121
  organizational, 236
  in workers, 189
Fertility dance, African tribal, 115
Fight/flight dynamic, 32
First-order/second-order volitions, 137-40
Fishbowl technique, 216
Flynn, John David, xi, 133ff., 155n., 246
Frankfort, Harry, 137, 138, 138n., 140, 241n.
Frankl, Victor, 163-64
Free will and autonomy, 138-39, 138n.
Freud, S., 30, 31n., 38, 106, 163, 165
From, Isador, 9, 11

Gay, as label, 220. *See also* Homosexuals
"Gemeinschaftsgefuehl," 183
Gerstenberg, Wolfgang, 194n.
Gestalt Approach and Eye Witness to Therapy (F. Perls), 89
Gestalt Association of New Jersey, 168
Gestalten, fixed, 66-67
Gestalt Institute of Cleveland, x, 6, 10, 10n., 11, 55n., 57, 60
Gestalt-thematic approach, 43
Gestalt Therapy (F. Perls et al.), 9
Gestalt workshops, experiences in, 179ff.
    art materials for, 208-209
    community promoted, 181
    conclusion on, 210-11
    endings in, 205-206
    language in, 206-208
    leaders for, 186-93
    place in, 198-200
    planning for, 183-86
    theme in, 197-98
    time in, 200-205
Goldstein, Kurt, 8
Goodman, Paul, 9, 11, 25, 26, 30, 31, 107n., 156, 198, 202, 219, 221, 241n., 242n.
Grand Inquisitor, 135
Greenwald, J. A., 43, 44, 46, 241n.
Group leader, as term, ixn. *See also* Leaders
Group member, as term, ix
Group process, Gestalt, 5ff. *See also* Gestalt workshops, experiences in
    anxiety in, 42, 58, 75
    boundaries in, 6-7, 17-18
    dependency in, 7, 51
    described, 13ff.
    and dreams, 5, 27
    emergent synthesis on, 10-13
    leader in, 13, 27-29, 30-36
    research for, 8-10
    stages in, 16-23
    techniques and essence of, 5-6
    theoretical perspective on, 29-30
    and therapy techniques, 25-27
"Group vs. Individual Therapy" (F. Perls), 41

Hampshire, 142
Hefferline, R., 9, 25, 26, 30, 31, 107n., 156, 198, 202, 242n.
Hillel, Rabbi, 24
Hirsch, Leonard, 10n.
Holocaust, Jewish, 185

Homosexuals, 219ff.
    in dreams, 173
    object choice, 30
    panic, 75
Hot seat techniques, ix, 27, 43n., 121
Howard, Marion, 219n.
Humphrey, Karen, 219n.
Hyper-mentation, 33

Identification and father, 30
Identified patient (IP) and family, 81-82, 83n.
Identity and dependence group stage, 16-19
Identity House, 220ff.
Impasse and authenticity, 117
Implosive therapy, 40
Individuality and social progress, 136. *See also* Autonomy
Individually-oriented group model, 10, 11
Individual therapy and group process, 8-9, 14, 26-27
Individuation in groups, 69
Influence and counterdependence group stage, 19-21
Intimacy:
    and exclusion, 196
    and interdependence group stage, 21-23
Introjection:
    in art therapy, 87
    and education, 156
    and father, 30
    of mother, 124
    organizational, 230, 232
    role-playing, 125-30
Island communities, 180
I-thou relationships, 78, 181
I-We-It definition, 40

Jesus, 135
Jones, J. E., 144, 164, 242n.
Jourard, S., 188, 241n.
Jung, C., 106, 106n., 107, 107n.

Krane, John, 219n.
Kant, 151
Kelley, Patrick, xi, 219ff., 246
Kempler, Walter, 12, 241n.
Kepner, Elaine, x, 5ff., 246-47
Kitzler, Richard, 10, 25ff., 247
"Klausureffekt," 180
Koffka, 7

Köhler, W., 7, 39, 40, 241n.
Krishnamurti, J., 90, 241n.

Lapid, Ginger, xi, 212ff., 247
Laves, Rona Gross, xi, 155ff., 247
Leaders:
    in art therapy, 94-95
    depression in, 51
    and experiment, 65-66
    and Gestalt workshops, 186-93
    in group process, 13, 27-29, 30-36
    in group training, 170
    information sharing by, 61
    and safety needs, 50
Lesbians, 224. *See also* Homosexuals
Levisky, A., 190, 241n.
Lewin, Kurt, 7, 8, 25, 40
Liberman, Norman, x, 37ff., 247
Lieberman, M. A., 13, 243n.
"Life Space Experiment," 203
Lukensmeier, Carolyn Hirsch, 10n.

Marathons, Gestalt therapy, 116ff.
    anxiety in, 121
    defined, 119n.
    development of, 121-30
    surprise in, 120
    values of, 119
Mead, G. H., 40
Mill, John Stuart, 136, 241n.
Mintz, Elizabeth E., xi, 116ff., 119, 119n.,
    120n., 123, 242n., 248
Morse, Marston, 102, 242n.
Movement therapy, Gestalt groups for,
    105ff.
    conditions for, 107-108
    for integrated, 109-15
    for poorly integrated, 108-109
Mowrer, O. H., 40, 242n.
Mullan, H., 29, 242n.
Multi-larity, family, 81

Naranjo, C., 78, 242n.
Narcissistic homosexual object choice, 30
National Training Laboratories, 6, 43n.
Nevis, Edwin, 10n.
Nevis, Sonia, 55n., 70n.
New York Institute for Gestalt Therapy, 9,
    27, 42-43, 167, 221
Nietzsche, Friedrich, 105
Norms in groups, 19-20

Oedipal group, 29
On Liberty (Mill), 136
Or-energy, 40
Organismic formulation, 37ff.
Organizational consultation, Gestalt prin-
    ciples in, 229ff.
    client expectations, 234-35
    client view of, 233-34
    consultation on, 237
    consultant conceptualizations, 235-36
    data collection in, 234
    focus in, 229-30
    and individual therapy, compared, 230-
        32
    internal conflicts, 233
    introjection in, 230, 232
    projection in, 230
    safety issues, 232-33
    termination of, 236-37

Pairing dynamic, 32
Para-Freudians, 30
Participant as term, ixn.
Passivity in learning, 156
Perls, Fritz, ix, 7, 8, 9, 11, 12n., 25, 26, 27,
    27n., 30, 31, 39, 40, 41, 42, 43n., 45,
    81, 89, 107n., 116n., 119, 121, 129,
    130, 156, 169n., 182, 187, 190, 198,
    202, 213, 220, 221, 222, 223, 224, 228,
    241n., 242n.
Perls, Laura, ix, 7, 9, 11, 41, 42, 43, 45, 167,
    169n., 181, 207, 238, 242n.
Personal growth group model, 10
Personality traits and impasse, 116n., 117,
    118
Person-environment configuration, 8
Peterson, Peter, 180n.
Pfeiffer, J. W., 144, 164, 242n.
Phobia, 119
    of snakes, 124
Plastelene clay, therapeutic use of, 91-92
Plato, 135
Playing-out in education, 158
Polster, E., 155, 158, 160, 230, 242n.
Polster, Miriam, 57, 155, 158, 160, 230,
    242n.
Prisoners Dilemma, 164
Projection:
    in art therapy, 88-89, 95, 103
    and education, 158
    in family system, 79

organizational, 230
in sculpting process, 83-84
Pseudo-analysis, 33
Pseudo-intimacy, 21
Psychoanalysis:
developmental therapy of, 30
on groups, 29
and prediction, 120
snakes in, 123
Psychodrama, 27, 82, 121, 124, 164-65
"Psychological Types" (Jung), 106n.

Rapp, Elaine, xi, 86ff., 248
Reaction formation, 116n.
Redl, F., 203, 242n.
Regression:
and homosexuality, 220
in service of the ego, 38-39
Rehearsing in education, 158
Reich, W., 40, 106, 110, 221
Repression, 116n.
in education, 155
in groups, 31
Republic, The (Plato), 135
Resistance:
in group training, 174
in teaching, 161-62
Rogers, Carl, 46, 160, 164, 242n.
Role-playing. *See also* Sex roles
and authenticity, 117, 119
in education, 151-52, 165
in groups, 20-21, 27
and introjections, 125-30
in marathons, 124ff.
and sexuality, 129
Ronall, Ruth E., ix-xi, 48, 179ff., 183, 190,
198, 242n., 248-49
Rosenbaum, M., 29, 242n.
Rosenblatt, D., 43, 44, 242n.

Safety/danger in Gestalt groups, x, 40ff.,
174
frustration, uses of, 45
group climate as figure, 44-45
history and technique, 42-43
later considerations, 50-52
recent contributions on, 43-44
therapeutic safety, creation of, 46-50
Sandplay, 106
Sartre, J., 146, 151, 242n.
Satir, Virginia, 194n., 196

Scapegoating, 21, 78, 79, 197
Schumacher, E. F., 23, 242n.
Schutz, W., 16, 242n.
Scientific Management, 229
Sculptures:
family, 82-83, 194n.
process in, 88-89, 95, 103
in workshops, 209
Selective authenticity, 188
Self:
inner construct of, 55-56
polarities in, 107, 107n.
Self-actualization, 40, 59, 85
Self-differentiation in family systems, 79
Sensitivity training, 25
Sex roles in Gestalt workshops, 212ff. *See
also* Role-playing
contact-withdrawal patterns, 217-18
figure-ground growth, 213-14
polarity in, 214-17
Sexuality. *See also* Sex roles
in groups, 51
revolution in, 221
Sibling rivalry, 31
Simkin, James, 41, 43, 89, 242n.
Singer, David, 10, 11, 15, 242n.
"Slaves" (Michelangelo), 104
Snakes:
phobias of, 124
symbolism of, 123, 125-29
Socialization:
and education, 135
sex-role, 212
Sociogram, group dynamic, 194n.
Sparks, 227
Sponsors of workshops, 184, 193-97
Stereotypes:
of individuals in groups, 69
sex-role, 212, 213
Stevens, J., 163, 166, 243n.
Stones, therapeutic use of, 92-98
Stonewall, 219
Student-centered education, 160
Style, definition of, 34
Superego, group, 27
Symbolism:
in artwork, 104
of snakes, 123, 125-29

Tavistock group model, 13, 27
Taylor, Frederick, 229

Teal, 219
Theme-Centered Interaction (T.C.I.), 183, 183n.
Tragedy, Aristotelian idea of, 40
Training groups, Gestalt, 167ff.
  benefits in, 168
  model for, 169-71
  purpose of, 168-69
  sample session, 171-75
Transactional analysis, 13, 121, 174
Transference in groups, 27
Trust in group process, 42-43, 69
Tyler, Deldon McNeely, xi, 105ff., 248

Veterans Administration Hospitals, 227

Wallen, Richard, 10n.
Warner, Bill, 57
Watercolors in art therapy, 98-99
Weissenberg, P., 229, 243n.

Weisz, Paul, 9, 11
Weltanschauung of group, 39
Wepman, Barry J., xi, 229ff., 245
Wertheimer, M., 7, 39, 40, 243n.
Whitaker, D. S., 13, 243n.
Whitehead, Alfred North, 34
Wilson, B., 183, 190, 198, 242n.
Wilson, Gloria, 219n.
Wineman, D., 203, 242n.
Wopman, Barry, 249
Workshop Institute for Living-Learning (W.I.L.L.), 183n.

Yalom, I., 12n., 13, 25, 62, 75, 76, 243n.
Yoga, 110-11, 153
Yom Kippur War, 185

Zero-sum games, 164
Zinker, Joseph C., x, 43, 44, 55ff., 59, 67n., 190, 243n., 249